Eliza Lowe and the Founding of Woodard Schools for Girls

S. Anne's Chapel (exterior).
Photograph courtesy of Niki Gandy, September 2020.

Eliza Lowe and the Founding of Woodard Schools for Girls

Penny Thompson

The Lutterworth Press

For Circle R

The Lutterworth Press

P.O. Box 60
Cambridge
CB1 2NT
United Kingdom

www.lutterworth.com
publishing@lutterworth.com

Hardback ISBN: 978 0 7188 9565 5
Paperback ISBN: 978 0 7188 9566 2
PDF ISBN: 978 0 7188 4825 5
ePub ISBN: 978 0 7188 4826 2

British Library Cataloguing in Publication Data
A record is available from the British Library

First published by The Lutterworth Press, 2021
Copyright © Penny Thompson, 2021

Front cover image:
S. Anne's Chapel, Abbots Bromley School.
Painted by Rev. Á.R. Ladell, chaplain of the school,
1933-60, and dated 1951. Photograph courtesy of Stacy
Mates, daughter-in-law of Barbara LaRose, a former pupil
of the school, to whom I am grateful for permission to
reproduce the painting here.

All rights reserved. No part of this edition may be reproduced,
stored electronically or in any retrieval system, or transmitted
in any form or by any means, electronic, mechanical,
photocopying, recording, or otherwise, without
prior written permission from the Publisher
(permissions@lutterworth.com).

Contents

List of illustrations	vii
Acknowledgements	ix
Foreword	xi
Introduction	1
PART ONE: PUTTING THE STORY IN CONTEXT	7
Chapter 1. The Woodard Schools and Their Founder	9
Chapter 2. Girls' Education in the Nineteenth Century	25
PART TWO: THE STORY OF ELIZA LOWE	47
Chapter 3. Early Life of Eliza Lowe	49
Chapter 4. Eliza's School in Bootle and Seaforth	59
Chapter 5. The Langton Connection	78
Chapter 6. The Lucy Landor Reminiscences	93
Chapter 7. Mayfield – Eliza Lowe's School in Southgate	110
Chapter 8. Alice Rathbone and Eva Müller	124
Chapter 9. Mayfield after Eliza and S. Winifred's	141
Chapter 10. Eliza's Letters	152
Chapter 11. Eliza Lowe and the founding of S. Anne's	163
PART THREE: THE RELEVANCE TODAY	179
Chapter 12. Of More than Passing Interest?	181
Bibliography	190
Credits and Permissions	192
Index	194

List of Illustrations

Frontispiece: S. Anne's Chapel (exterior)		ii
Fig. 1	Memorial plaque to Eliza Lowe, 1803-72	2
Fig. 1a	Memorial plaque in context	5
Fig. 1b	Memorial plaque to Mary Manley Lowe	5
Fig. 1c	Memorial plaque to Charlotte Lowe	5
Fig. 2	Lancing College Chapel	15
Fig. 3	Liverpool Institute High School for Girls, Blackburne House, Liverpool	26
Fig. 4	Honours board	26
Fig. 5	Brighthelmston School	33
Fig. 6	Auction of the house in Whitchurch	50
Fig. 7	Former monastic infirmary and St Modwen's Church from the 1790s	53
Fig. 8	'The Abbey' where Samuel Lowe and his family lived	54
Fig. 9	Samuel Lowe's signature	54
Fig. 10	Map of Everton, 1851	56
Fig. 11	Everton Terrace view	56
Fig. 12	Everton Village, c. 1820, W.G. Herdman	57
Fig. 13	Everton Village, c. 1843, W.G. Herdman	57
Fig. 14	The North Shore, W.G. Herdman	58
Fig. 15	Advert for Edmondson school in Bootle	61
Fig. 16	Location of the two schools in Bootle	62
Fig. 17	Bathing machines	63
Fig. 18	Seaforth House	63
Fig. 19	Map showing location of Eliza's school	66
Fig. 20	Map showing Charles Lowe's properties	67
Fig. 21	'The Shakspeare Monument'	72
Fig. 22	Riverslie House	76
Fig. 23	The site of Eliza's school in 2020	77

Fig. 24	Blythe Hall	78
Fig. 25	The Langton house in Bootle	79
Fig. 26	Miss Harriet Lowe	80
Fig. 27	Barrow House	84
Fig. 28	Hopefield House, Manchester	85
Fig. 29	Sutton Oaks	89
Fig. 30	Gertrude Langton's house	92
Fig. 31	Cecilia Landor	99
Fig. 32	Miss Fazakerley and her schooner	101
Fig. 33	Business advertisement	109
Fig. 34	Map showing location of Skinner Langton's property in Southgate	111
Fig. 35	Mayfield House, Southgate	112
Fig. 36	Map showing location of Mayfield House	112
Fig. 37	Mayfield Hall, Tutbury	113
Fig. 38	Eliza Lowe's income tax receipt for 1867	113
Fig. 39	Memorial to Eliza, Mary Manley and Charlotte Lowe in Christ Church Southgate	115
Fig. 40	Credenhill Court	119
Fig. 41	Thornton Lodge	120
Fig. 42	Cicely Tunstill	121
Fig. 43	Dolly Tunstill	121
Fig. 44	The McConnel factory in Manchester	122
Fig. 45	Essay title page	126
Fig. 46	Alice Rathbone	129
Fig. 47	Electioneering in Inverness	134
Fig. 48	Letter from Eva McLaren	137
Fig. 49	Eva's signature	137
Fig. 50	Walter McLaren – Bodnant Garden, Conwy	138
Fig. 51	Eliza's grave	141
Fig. 52	Eliza Lowe's burial certificate	142
Fig. 53	Emily Landor Lowe	147
Fig. 54	Garfield Terrace	148
Fig. 55	The Crofts, Abbots Bromley	165
Fig. 56	An early postcard of S. Anne's	167
Fig. 57	S. Anne's Chapel (interior)	173

Acknowledgements

Many people have helped me with the writing of this book. Alice in my local library explained the mysteries of Ancestry.com so that I could view the census records; the excitement of finding Eliza Lowe on the 1841 record will stay with me for a long time. The staff of the Sydney Jones Library at Liverpool University were generous with their time. As a former student I was given free access and whatever help I asked for. I am also grateful to Manchester Central Library, the London School of Economics and the British Library. Staffordshire County Record Office and John Clark at Enfield Local Studies Library and Archive provided useful information and assistance.

I discovered that local history groups were not only rich sources of information but unfailingly willing to answer my queries and assist where possible. In particular I would like to thank Elaine Summers of the Abbots Bromley Nostalgia Team who did considerable work for me in the early stages of my research. I would also like thank Marion Kettle of the Landor Local Historical Society in Rugeley, Ian Brown and Peter Laybourne of the Milngavie and Bearsden Historical Society, Chris Horner of the Southgate Green Association, Jean Ingham of the Pendle and Burnley branch of the Lancashire Family History and Heraldry Society and Graham Moodie of the Mayfield Heritage Group.

Reverend Dr Chrichton Limbert sent me photographs of the plaque to Eliza and her sisters in Christ Church Southgate. Allan Johnston, an expert on the local history of Seaforth and north Liverpool gave me sight of his private papers. Chris Kay supplied the photograph of sailing on Merseyside. Sarah Akhtar gave me advice and put me in touch with Barbara LaRose who supplied a photograph of a painting of S. Anne's Chapel. Both are old girls of 'AB'. Jan Owen and Judy Bemrose helped me with information about their old school in Birkdale, Brighthelmston. Lynn Murthwaite kindly read and commented on early drafts. Her encouragement was most welcome. My husband Andrew has supported me faithfully in countless ways and I thank him for his wisdom and practical skills on the computer. He has also passed a critical eye over the work though I cannot blame him for its inadequacies.

Members of the Guild of S. Mary and S. Anne, the old girls' association of my school, henceforth called 'the Guild', have always been supportive and I have valued their interest. Alison Kingshott spent many hours copy-editing my work, a mammoth job for which I cannot thank her enough. June Cairns Smith, Guild Manager, and Pat Clare, Guild Archivist, provided access to the Guild archives and June gave unstinting help on several occasions. June arranged for Niki Gandy to come to the chapel to take photographs for me. Niki taught art and photography at Abbots Bromley School for eleven years until the school closed and I am very grateful to her for her expert photographs. All the photographs taken in the chapel in the Introduction are her work. Susan Willmington, my friend from school, kindly read the book and contributed a recommendation. I am grateful to Canon Brendan Clover, Provost of the Woodard Society and Warden of the Guild for writing a foreword and for his support all along. My sincere thanks to the Woodard Community of Schools for generously providing financial support for publication. I would like to give particular thanks to the team at The Lutterworth Press for their detailed and careful attention both to editing and taking the book to production.

An entry in Wikipedia for Edward Clarke Lowe started me off on this project in early 2019. It stated that Lowe was educated by his sister who ran a school in Bootle and then Seaforth on Merseyside. Living close to Seaforth this sparked my interest. I was able to make contact with Tim Tomlinson who contributed the entry. Tim is a descendant of the Lowes and provided me with details about the lives of Lowe family members which considerably enriched my story. He supplied six letters written by Eliza herself and I have devoted a whole chapter to these. Tim, too, has been unfailingly helpful and patient. My thanks also to his cousin, Rachel Gatfield who owns the copyright to the material and kindly searched out and posted some documents to me.

Finally, I would like to thank my friend Steve Evans who has acted as a research assistant. Not only has he carried out valuable research, including, in particular, the story of Eliza's brother Charles, he has read and commented on every chapter. Without his assistance my story would have been very much the poorer.

The danger in giving thanks to people is that one forgets someone or perhaps several people. I apologise if this is the case. It probably is. I would also like to apologise in advance for inaccuracies that I fear will become evident. Writing a book like this brings to mind the phrase 'where angels fear to tread'.

Foreword

Canon Brendan Clover, Provost of the Woodard Schools

Canon Edward Lowe was the first Provost of the Midland region of Woodard Schools and was in post from the founding of the first school in the region, St Chad's School, at Denstone in 1868. The Woodard educational movement was on a march north.

For the past few years I have held the same office and I took particular pleasure – when the school at Abbots Bromley was open – to recount how the Founder, Nathaniel Woodard, was a 'utilitarian and being so could see little point in the education of the female gender, given their limited access to the corridors of power in Victorian society'. My *coup de grâce* was to tell the pupils that it was the Provost who persuaded the founder to go ahead with S. Mary and S. Anne's School in Abbots Bromley, thereby covering myself with reflected glory. Pride, after all, does come before a fall!

It has taken this wonderful book for me to realise the error of my ways and my deception of countless pupils over past years! For the author tells us that Nathaniel was never convinced that the education of the female gender was a worthwhile and godly pursuit and therefore my revered predecessor did not win the argument: it is simply (though it isn't simple, of course) that he and the Founder managed to 'disagree well', to respect the integrity of each other's arguments and not to allow them to destroy their friendship and mutual respect. They moved on. The rest they say is history and history is a succession of events. (Discuss?)

So already I have learnt something new from Penny Thompson and I am grateful for it. I must stop talking about matters that are not true. The devil, they say, is in the detail.

I am convinced that this book will vouchsafe to you many insights and delights – and perhaps take you to places you have not inhabited before. It is well worth the read.

When I talk to young people about Nathaniel Woodard, I ask them whether they know the name of the most significant Victorian engineer.

They tend to. And then I make the suggestion that our Founder was as significant in the educational world of Victorian England as Brunel was in civil engineering. And I believe it to be true: for the Founder's vision was about the transformation of society through the gift of Christian education. The fact that the education of women became aligned to it only accentuates the prophetic element of the Woodard movement. We might think twice about Nathaniel's attitude nowadays, but we can give thanks for the Lowe family and for all that flowed from them. Now, thanks to this book, we know a lot more about it.

Introduction

This is the story of Eliza Lowe and the school that she ran with her sisters. It is, in parallel, the story of her influence upon the founding of the School of S. Mary and S. Anne, Abbots Bromley of which I was a pupil between 1959 and 1966. Over the years the name of the school changed. First, it was S. Anne's, then, S. Mary and S. Anne, later, Abbots Bromley School for Girls and, finally, Abbots Bromley School. In this book the name appears as is appropriate for the historical context.

A further note about nomenclature is necessary. It has become the norm in publications to use St rather than S. For example in the most recent book about Woodard by David Gibbs, published in 2011, St is used throughout. Copy-editors do not like inconsistencies. However the use of S. in relation to the school of S. Mary and S. Anne has persisted from its inception and old girls are rather particular about it. So I have retained this tradition throughout in relation to Woodard schools except when quoting others who use St.

Eliza Lowe was a remarkable woman, the second eldest of fourteen children who took on responsibility for her siblings after the death of her parents. Her youngest brother was Edward Clarke Lowe, born in 1823 when Eliza was 20 years old and already started upon her long teaching career. She saw to it that her brother was educated, going on to graduate from Oxford and to be ordained into the Church of England.

Edward Lowe became a close colleague of Nathaniel Woodard, who built public boarding schools for boys of the middle classes in Sussex and later in the Midlands. Lowe was headmaster of one of these schools for many years and Woodard's closest colleague. In 1874 Edward Lowe opened S. Anne's School in Abbots Bromley with eight girls and a vision to create six more girls' schools associated with Woodard. He did this on his own as Nathaniel Woodard was not in favour of public-school education for girls. The question arises therefore as to what led Lowe to differ from Woodard and found schools for girls.

To the glory of God;
in reverent and grateful remembrance
of Eliza Lowe,
at Seaforth in Lancashire,
and afterwards at Mayfield in Southgate
in the County of Middlesex,
for fifty years,
until on Aug. 9 1872 she rested from her labours,
the wise and loving teacher and friend of youth,
the Choir of this Chapel
is erected
as a fruit of her training
and a tribute to her worth
by many who cherish her memory,
in the hope
that the Worship of this Holy Place
may perpetuate in others
the piety she taught themselves to pray.

Blessed are the dead which die in the Lord, even so saith the Spirit,
for they rest from their labours, and their works do follow them.

Introduction

*Fig. 1 (opposite) Memorial plaque to Eliza Lowe, 1803-72.
Photograph by Niki Gandy.*

To the glory of God;
in reverent and grateful remembrance
of Eliza Lowe,
at Seaforth in Lancashire,
and afterwards at Mayfield in Southgate
in the County of Middlesex,
for fifty years,
until on Aug. 9 1872 she rested from her labours,
the wise and loving teacher and friend of youth,
the Choir of this Chapel
is erected
as a fruit of her training
and a tribute to her worth
by many who cherish her memory,
in the hope
that the Worship of this Holy Place
may perpetuate in others
the piety she taught themselves to prize.

Blessed are the dead which die in the Lord even so saith the Spirit,
for they rest from their labours, and their works do follow them.

As stated in the Acknowledgements, I came across, quite by chance, an entry in Wikipedia for Edward Clarke Lowe which stated that he was born in Everton, Liverpool and educated by his sister who ran a school in Bootle and then Seaforth, suburbs of Liverpool, close to where I live. I began to wonder whether it was the fact that he owed his early education to his sister that influenced him to want to extend the Woodard tradition to girls.

What could I find out about Eliza Lowe and her school and would it reveal any clues as to why Lowe determined to found boarding schools for girls? To my surprise, and helped by a lot of people, I was able to track her life, her school and some of her pupils. Enough to write a book – and to suggest a strong link with Abbots Bromley School.

Shortly after I began my research the closure of the school was announced, in March 2019. This was a bitter blow to many, including me, and I wondered whether it was worth proceeding. I decided that it was perhaps more important now than ever that the history of Eliza be told. I had time to investigate the Guild archives and take important photographs in the chapel before the school closed in July that year. I carried on and this book is the result.

The book is divided into three parts. Part One explores the background to my story. Chapter 1 introduces the Woodard Community and is followed by a chapter on the education of girls in nineteenth century Britain. Both chapters are important in putting the story of Eliza in context and demonstrating the pioneering nature of Edward Lowe's vision. Part Two introduces Eliza Lowe. Chapters 3 to 9 tell her story and that of some of her pupils up till her death in 1872. Chapter 10 considers letters written by Eliza and Chapter 11 looks at the events surrounding the creation of S. Anne's and how the inspiration of Eliza lay behind Lowe's endeavour. Part Three is a reflection on the relevance of my story today.

Eliza's story can only be told in fragments, yet these fragments bear witness to a remarkable lady. Apart from the six letters that have survived I have found no photographs, no books, only one early curriculum outline and few direct references to her work. However, the evidence I have found is compelling.

My eight-year-old grandson Charlie was very interested in the fact that his grandmother was writing a book. I told him that it was non-fiction. Then I began to wonder. I had told him I was writing a story and stories are fiction. All I can say is that I have tried hard to stick to the facts but there is interpretation here too and I have become enamoured of Eliza which introduces a further element of subjectivity.

The first and most important clue to her life is a plaque mounted prominently in the chancel of the chapel of Abbots Bromley School, a plaque which is by far the largest. The plaque is of high quality. It must have seemed an expensive item at a time when her brother was working hard to raise the funds to pay for the chapel and other school buildings. Nevertheless, the plaque to Eliza clearly mattered to Edward Lowe and it had to be impressive.

The plaque is situated on the north side at eye level jutting out from the wall of the sanctuary with a dramatic brass canopy above it. The canopy supports seven candle holders forming what resembles a crown. As can be seen from the photograph below, it forms the border or edge of the Sanctuary and is very close to the altar. Immediately opposite is an identical canopy above a cupboard and piscina for the use of the priest, the cupboard serving as an aumbry where the Blessed Sacrament may be reserved. The altar had to be the centre of attention and focus for those present but Edward Lowe could hardly have chosen a more prominent position for the plaque.

Fig. 1a (opposite) Memorial plaque in context. Photograph by Niki Gandy.
Fig. 1b (opposite) Memorial plaque to Mary Manley Lowe. Photograph by Niki Gandy.
Fig. 1c (opposite) Memorial plaque to Charlotte Lowe. Photograph by Niki Gandy.

✠ To the Glory of God
In affectionate remembrance of Mary Mapley Lowe
through life the devoted sharer of her sisters' work
in death the partner of her rest
the REREDOS of this altar is placed by her
surviving brothers and sisters A.D. Mdccclxxix.

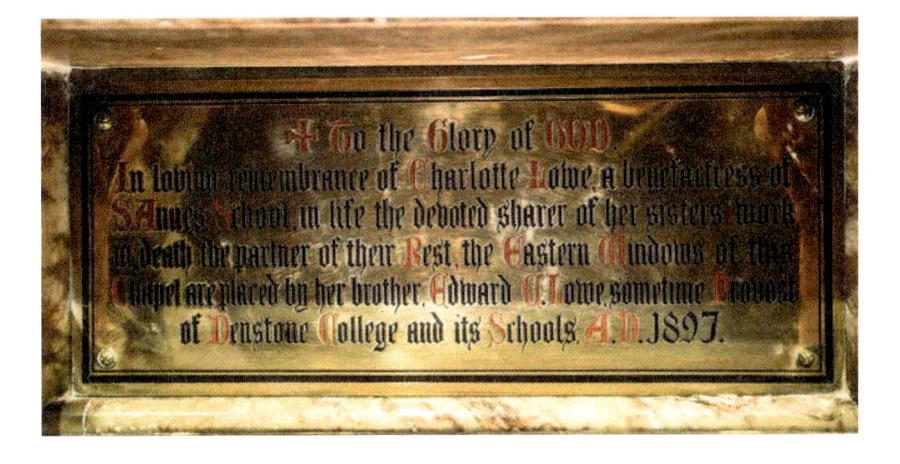

✠ To the Glory of GOD
In loving remembrance of Charlotte Lowe, a benefactress of
S. Anne's School, in life the devoted sharer of her sisters' work
in death the partner of their Rest, the Eastern Windows of this
Chapel are placed by her brother, Edward C. Lowe, sometime Provost
of Denstone College and its Schools. A.D. 1897.

Underneath the plaque to Eliza may be seen a smaller plaque. This plaque is a memorial to Mary Manley Lowe, Eliza's sister who died in 1874. As the plaque states Mary Manley worked with Eliza in her school throughout her life. The fine reredos was given in her memory by her surviving brothers and sisters.

Opposite, in a similar position under the piscina, is another plaque, this time to the youngest sister Charlotte who died in 1897. She too had worked all her life in Eliza's school. The Eastern windows of the Chapel in her memory were the gift of Edward Lowe.

In Lancing Chapel, a far grander affair, there are chantry chapels erected on either side of the altar, one to the memory of Nathaniel Woodard and one to his son Billy, who had managed the project for many years. The scale is different but the intention is the same. Honour the founders. It is surely significant that Edward Lowe chose to put these memorials to Eliza, Mary Manley and Charlotte in the sanctuary, either side of the altar.

So here in the beautiful chapel are clues to the lives of Eliza and her sisters and hints of their importance in the founding of the school in Abbots Bromley, a Woodard school, which was to give a Christian education to girls (and latterly boys) for nearly 150 years. In 1998 an illustrated booklet giving the history of the chapel was published.[1] It is a fine publication which describes each area of the chapel, and lists many of the memorials and donors of furnishings etc. However, there is no mention of the memorial to Eliza Lowe, nor of those to her sisters. Yet, according to Eliza's memorial plaque, the Choir of the Chapel, the first section to be built, was erected in her memory and as a 'fruit of her training'. This book is her previously un-told story. Surely a story worth telling.

---

1. Anna Wells and Muriel Roch, *S. Anne's Chapel, The School of S. Mary and S. Anne, Abbots Bromley, Staffordshire,* July 1998.

Part One

Putting the Story in Context

Chapter 1

The Woodard Schools and Their Founder

Woodard Today

Woodard schools have a long and honourable history. At the time of writing (2021) these schools educated 30,000 pupils in the independent, academy and state-maintained sectors. They make up the Woodard Community of Schools, a registered charity with 40 schools associated with it in one of several ways. The largest group, fifteen schools, is made up of independent schools which, although having their own governing boards, are owned by Woodard. The second largest group, fourteen schools, is made up of maintained schools which have chosen to affiliate to Woodard because they share its ethos and aims. They are neither owned nor governed by Woodard but share in programmes for students and teachers. Two independent schools operate similarly and there are six schools which are part of the Woodard Academies Trust. There are two overseas schools. St Thomas School in Sri Lanka is an affiliated school and there is also Langalanga Secondary School in Kenya. This school was set up to commemorate the bicentenary of the founder's birth in 2011 for which the Woodard Community raised £250,000.[1] This rather complex mix of schools may be unique.

Woodard today is trying to create a supportive environment for its schools and does this in several ways. A quarterly newsletter is published with school news and events, carrying information about best practice and events for governors, teachers and pupils. Hub schools have been named with particular expertise which can be shared across the schools. Expertise includes encouraging aspiration to higher education, developing independent thinking and help with teaching and learning. In recent years Woodard has sponsored educational publications. *Establishing a new school and getting it right from the start* appeared in 2015. *Schools for Human Flourishing* in 2016 and *Establishing an international school* in 2017. All these are available as free downloads.

1. Information from www.woodard.co.uk, accessed 28 August 2020.

The corporation's logo is *Faith, Unity and Vision*. While these words are not explored in detail on the website, the Woodard ethos is, both in its sections on a Woodard Education and Hallmarks of a Woodard School. Clicking on the logo makes it clear that Woodard is a Church of England foundation and strives to follow in the footsteps of its founder, a nineteenth-century cleric, Canon Nathaniel Woodard.

Nathaniel Woodard

It is evident that one man, Canon Nathaniel Woodard, born in 1811, is responsible for what we see today, although as we shall see this was not the case for the girls' schools. On the face of it, his life bears little relationship to that of citizens living in the 21st century, over 200 years later, nor does that of Eliza Lowe. Yet, the website briefly described above exhibits a clear connection and Chapter 12 considers the ongoing influence and importance of the Woodard community today.

Nathaniel Woodard, the ninth of twelve children, was born on St Benedict's Day, 21 March 1811, in Essex.[2] His father was a country gentleman whose income was scarcely enough to support his large family, despite (or because of) living at Basildon Hall. The Hall had a farm and land attached but the income was not enough for school fees and Woodard's first lessons were from his mother. The family attended the local Anglican church, prayed at home and read the Bible. The young boy was devout and made a covenant with God at the age of 19. He was attracted to church music, and music would later become an important part of life in his schools. However, for ordination a university degree was necessary. This required funds and a certain academic standard. Two aunts supplied the funds and tutors in Norfolk and Bishop's Stortford provided the education. The curate of the latter parish, George Leicester, was a distinguished academic who tutored him in return for Woodard teaching his young sons. He also taught in the village school set up there by Leicester. Leicester may have influenced his religious philosophy, too, being a firm believer in the dictates of the Prayer Book of 1662, dictates which would undergird the religious life of all Woodard's schools.

He entered Magdalen Hall, Oxford in 1834 at a time when the Oxford Movement, spearheaded by John Henry Newman, John Keble, Hurrell Froude and Edward Pusey was gaining strength. The Oxford Movement is also known as the Tractarian Movement because of the large number of

---

2. The most recent book, by David Gibbs, uncovered new evidence. It was commissioned by the Woodard Community to commemorate the 200th anniversary of Woodard's birth.

tracts that they published.[3] Little is known about Woodard's time at Oxford, but he emerged a keen Tractarian. His six years at Oxford coincided with the full flowering of the movement, and while Newman and others went to Rome, Woodard never deviated from Anglican Tractarian principles learned in the 1830s. I consider links with Newman later in this chapter. It took him six years to graduate with only a pass degree. Marriage in 1836 and the birth of three children by 1840 are thought to have constrained time for study.

Shortly after leaving Oxford, Woodard was ordained deacon by the Bishop of London and given charge of Bethnal Green parish, an overcrowded, poor area of East London. Woodard threw himself into parish work, was dismayed at the godlessness of all kinds, founded a school and completed the church building, just as Newman had done at Littlemore outside Oxford. Two years later he ran into trouble after delivering a sermon on the practice of confession and was later that year relieved of his post. The bishop found him another, but, after five years in the East End, thanks to friends, he moved to a parish on the Sussex coast, Shoreham-by-Sea, where the vicar was a Tractarian.

First School

It was not long after his appointment as curate to the parish of St Mary in Shoreham that he opened a day school for boys in his own vicarage. The curriculum included land-surveying, navigation and bookkeeping. Latin and French were extras. Living in a port town he met sea captains and sailors as well as a variety of tradesmen associated with them. His curriculum reflected local needs and had a practical bent. A year later he founded a boarding school next door, known as Shoreham Grammar School. Both schools were declared part of the Society of S. Mary and S. Nicolas.[4] It was not unusual for Anglican clerics to found schools in their parish, usually strictly a local affair. Woodard had, at this early date, something much grander in mind. In the year that he founded the grammar school he issued his manifesto, *A Plea for the Middle Classes*. However, it was not just the middle classes that he had in mind:

> It is my earnest wish and the object and intention of all the Benefactors, that for all future time the sons of any of Her then Majesty's subjects should be taught, together with sound grammar learning, the fear and honour of Almighty God, the Father, Son and

---
3. Known as *Tracts for the Times*.
4. St Nicolas was the parish where his vicar lived, just outside the town.

the Holy Ghost, according to the doctrines of the Catholic Faith as is now set forth in the Book of the Offices and Administration of the Sacraments of the Church of England.[5]

The Church of England as the Educator of the Nation

The idea that the Church of England should take on responsibility for teaching the nation's children (though his efforts were for boys) and make Anglican faith central to the endeavour seems extraordinary today. Few in our current situation would question the idea that the State should pay for and, to an extent, direct and inspect the teaching. Decades of secularism and the retreat (or dismissal) of religious faith from the public square have rendered the idea of education for all based on one denominational formulary, even if that of the nation's established Church, way off the mark of what a proper education should look like. As Brian Heeney argues in his thorough account of Woodard's life-work, it could never have succeeded even in his time because Dissenters and Radicals of various hues would never have accepted it.[6] Nevertheless, education had to be based on some philosophy, however attenuated, and this remains true today.

Woodard believed in the historic responsibility of the Church for educating the nation's children and he sensed that the Church had failed, particularly in relation to the middle classes. There was a time when canon law ordered that no man could keep a school without a licence from the Church. Matters started to change with the repercussions of the Reformation. However, it was not until 1779 that Dissenters could teach in their own schools and Roman Catholics in 1791. This meant that well into the nineteenth century the Church of England was a main provider and many of Woodard's friends simply could not contemplate the idea of the State taking over what had always been the Church's responsibility and privilege. Edward Lowe, Woodard's closest colleague, believed that education was of first importance in the ministry of the Church, that duty being 'mainly concerned in seeing that all, from the highest to the lowest, are educated and trained in the revealed truths of our holy religion'.[7] Woodard put it more strongly: 'we consider it would be a very serious evil to hand over our schools to any government'.[8] A lifetime supporter of Woodard was

---

5. Quoted in David Gibbs, *In Search of Nathaniel Woodard: Victorian Founder of Schools* (Chichester: Phillimore & Co., 2011), p. 18ff.
6. Brian Heeney, *Mission to the Middle Classes: The Woodard Schools, 1848-1891* (London: SPCK, 1969). See chapter 4 passim.
7. Ibid., p. 91.
8. Ibid.

Chapter 1. The Woodard Schools and Their Founder

Lord Salisbury, who served three terms as Prime Minister. He harboured a deep distrust of government intervention into education. He described as 'repulsive' the idea 'that the State should undertake the responsibility of seeing that all, or any one, of the classes which form the nation are well educated'.[9] He believed that the Government generally achieved little and that often the opposite of its intentions actually happened. However, he trusted Woodard.

Creeping Secularism

The failure of the Church, as Woodard saw it, cleared the way for secularism. He was deeply concerned about creeping secularism both in British society and in education. All his life he resisted the conscience clause and the diluted form of religious education imposed on schools receiving state funding and, later, in the board schools set up after the Elementary Education Act 1870, known as The Forster Act after the name of the minister responsible. The former allowed pupils to be excused from religious teaching and observance, the latter forbade any denominational formulary to direct the teaching.[10]

In his public *Letter to Lord Salisbury* he highlighted what he saw as the evils of the 1869 Endowed Schools Act which threatened the religious freedom of the endowed grammar schools. Commissioners were authorised to redirect financial endowments, reorder their constitutions and governing bodies, take away the right of the Church to license masters and require a conscience clause. The Act was also strongly resisted by the famous headmaster at Uppingham, Edward Thring, and led to the setting up of the Headmasters' Conference. Lord Salisbury had himself taken the opportunity in his maiden speech in Parliament to speak against secular education and there were many others who took this line. Many more did not, and it was becoming clear that the Churches did not have the resources to teach the increasing numbers of children being born. Woodard, for whom one important principle was not to take on the world, concentrated on building up his own schools and did not resist the incursion of the State into education although he could write sharply about the consequences. He wrote of the 'secular spirit now deluging the country' and foresaw that this would be to the 'radical detriment of the Catholic Church in England'. It would also, in his opinion, be to the detriment of the country whose Christian principles were once 'the glory of England'.[11]

---

9. http://www.libertarian.co.uk/lapubs/libhe/libhe020.htm, accessed 2 December 2020.
10. Such as the Anglican Catechism or the Westminster Confession.
11. Heeney, *Mission to the Middle Classes*, p. 94.

The Scheme

Thus, a poor curate, who had been dismissed from his first post and awarded only a pass degree, took on the mantle of providing schools for a nation. He believed that, if he could rouse Church people to the task, much could be done. He was not the only Anglo-Catholic to go about setting up schools but no one else had quite the same ambition. Moreover, they tended to be less rigorous about their Anglo-Catholicism.

He did not do it on his own but he was always the driving force to whom others were drawn. The number and prestige of his supporters was remarkable. Before the day school in Shoreham had opened, he had written to the future prime minister, William Ewart Gladstone, and soon after this he was able to report to a supporter at Magdalen College that he had secured between £150 and £200. Gladstone remained a lifelong supporter and addressed public meetings to raise money. Lord Salisbury, who was Prime Minister for an even longer period than Gladstone, was also a staunch and lifelong ally. Gladstone promoted both Woodard and Lowe to Canon of Manchester and Canon of Ely, respectively.

Woodard's strength of personality and religious ardour was no doubt part of it. However, the vision of being part of a national movement, as opposed to setting up the odd school here and there must have played a part. Woodard's scheme envisaged the nation being divided into five, the first was the South, then the Midlands, the North, the West and the East (though the latter never came to fruition). Each area was to be governed by a Provost who would be supported by a group of Fellows, thus forming a college or religious community. All the schools that he himself founded were called colleges, quite deliberately. Not only the Fellows were part of this community. His very first day school was described by Woodard as a Christian brotherhood and boys at the schools were expected to contribute small amounts to a common fund upon which they would later in life always have a claim.[12] On the Woodard website one reads: 'Woodard is a unique expression of Church of England schools in the nation. The Founder's vision of the family of schools as a Society is guarded by its Provosts and its Corporate Fellows and the group is characterised by mutual support, help and encouragement.'[13]

At the centre of this Christian society was the chapel to be built at Lancing. A library was planned and the building had to be both large and magnificent, as it was to act rather as a cathedral does for a diocese. It took a long time to get it started and even longer time to get it finished. In fact,

---
12. Although certain specific crimes would lead to withdrawal of support.
13. Accessed 7 January 2020.

Chapter 1. The Woodard Schools and Their Founder

Fig. 2 Lancing College Chapel.

it was only in 2019 that a fund-raising committee felt confident that their latest design would do the job. Announcing plans in 2019 to complete the chapel, the secretary of the Friends of Lancing College wrote:

> 'To preserve to the Country a system of solid Christian education, when the ideal of the nation is purely secular, is a work which the highest angels might envy', wrote the Founder in a begging letter to Martin Gibbs, one of his most lavish supporters. 'That is why I think so much of the Chapel. Till that is finished we have no home; no centre to our work; no spiritual starting point. When we have that, we may rejoice before the Lord in hope and look out at the world with an anxious concern for its good, but with assurance that we must be of service to it.' I trust He will not be disappointed by our efforts![14]

A modern-day descendant of Gibbs, David Gibbs, quoted Woodard:

> The great chapel, as it will be hereafter, is I know open to the criticism of those who only look at it as a chapel for a school of three or four hundred boys; but to those who regard it in its true

---
14. *Voice*, Winter 2019 edition of the Woodard magazine.

character as the central chapel of a great society consecrated to a noble effort for the defence and support of Christian Truth, it will not appear to violate the rules of modesty and prudence, but rather to represent the faith in the essential strength of the Church in those who promote it.[15]

Towards the end of his life, when hopes of being the nation's educator must have seemed a distant dream, the 74-year-old Woodard carried out a symbolic act which can only be described as defiant. He had the east end of Lancing Chapel built up to full height and insisted on setting the top stone himself, saying: 'Now should a niggardly generation arise and decide that it is too costly to build to the height I desire, then they will have to pull down my work.'[16]

Woodard was used to getting his own way. Kenneth Kirk, whose book about Woodard Schools was published in 1937, wrote, quoting Woodard: 'Everybody thinks that it is no use opposing me . . . even the Earl of Chichester, a Whig and an inveterate Low Churchman, told me that I must succeed.'[17]

Religion as the Basis of the Schools

For Woodard, religion and learning were all a piece. Woodard could contemplate no division of sacred and secular and believed that, once religion was divorced from education, education would have no time for religion. In a letter of 1866 Woodard wrote that he and his colleagues were 'in favour of religion being made the foundation and starting-point, not only of [religious] education properly so-named, but indeed of every ordinary instruction'.[18] The effect of a conscience clause was to destroy the unity of knowledge and open up the field to any number of false pretenders as to the aim of education. This was put eloquently by Newman around the same time. I take this up shortly. So when, in 1883 Convocation, the governing body of the established Church proposed to set up the Church Schools Company to provide church schools with a conscience clause, Woodard opposed the scheme as heretical.[19] It invited 'people to exercise a

---

15. Gibbs, *In Search of Nathaniel Woodard*, p. 32ff.
16. Quoted in *Voice*, Winter 2019.
17. Kenneth E. Kirk, *The Story of the Woodard Schools* (London: Hodder & Stoughton, 1937), p. 33.
18. Heeney, *Mission to the Middle Classes*, p. 97.
19. A conscience clause allowed parents to withdraw their children from religious instruction and worship. It still exists today in state-maintained schools. It allowed church schools to teach according to their own formularies.

right which they do not possess, of choosing their own religion'.[20] Edward Lowe, always more temperate than Woodard, was sent to speak against it in Convocation.

Meanwhile, Lowe had also written about the unity of education. In 1852 he made a speech in which he insisted that a religious school did not simply mean filling children's heads with texts and taking them to services all the time. At his school (Hurstpierpoint) a religious school was one in which 'the power and love of God entered into the performance of all the various duties and businesses of life'.[21] In a sermon in 1856 he maintained that education was about the 'completion of the whole man; the setting it in entire conformity to the Divine Image'.

The liturgical life of the school was entirely uncompromising. Boys were expected to be confirmed unless the school thought a candidate unsuitable. Prayer Book formularies such as the creed and the catechism were the backbone of the teaching. Each school appointed a chaplain whose authority was independent from the headmaster and whose task it was to attend to (and direct) the spiritual life of the pupils. Exception was taken only to the practice of confession, which, as a result, was carefully hedged about with conditions but never disallowed. At Hurst (short for Hurstpierpoint) under Lowe, there were eleven divinity classes which were 'arranged with reference to the Confirmation which the Bishop held annually for the school'.[22] Instruction given was based on the Bible and the Prayer Book and an English Primer compiled for the school. In addition, there was daily chapel, attendance at communion on Sundays and saints' days. Dissenters could send their sons but they would not be excused from religious observance and teaching. Lowe reported that S. John's College, Ellesmere, was much favoured by Welsh non-conformists.

Woodard laid great emphasis on the beauty and elegance of both his chapels and his buildings. The Oxford Movement laid emphasis on such matters and Gothic was the preferred style. Certainly, his schools were all built to a high architectural standard. His architect was R.C. Carpenter and, later, his son. Educational facilities were of less importance. The chapel was to glorify God and only the best would do. Writing about the chapel at Lancing he argued that it was constructed so that boys 'may rejoice that the system in which they have been educated and taught to worship

---

20. Heeney, *Mission to the Middle Classes*, p. 98.
21. Heeney, *Mission to the Middle Classes*, p. 96.
22. Edward C. Lowe, *S. Nicolas College and Its Schools: A Record of Thirty Years' Work in the Effort to Endow the Church of England with a System of Self-Supporting Public Boarding Schools for the Upper, Middle and Lower Middle Classes*, Leopold Classic Library (first published 1878), p. 26.

the God and Saviour of the world has shown itself equal to the highest effort of reverence and acknowledgement of His mercy and His sovereign power'.[23] Music, too, was carefully considered and Gregorian plainsong required in services. Woodard frequently referred to his chapels as 'part of our educational scheme'.[24]

The Academic Curriculum

This poses the question of the curriculum of his schools. Schools were not all the same. There were three types or grades of school. Higher schools, such as Lancing, prepared boys for university, middle schools prepared boys for the professions and business and lower schools prepared boys for skilled occupations, such as farming and carpentry. Considerable thought and a degree of innovation went into fitting the education to the needs of the pupils. For the first-grade schools the curriculum emulated that followed by the public schools, such as Winchester. Lancing was said to offer an education of a 'Church of England Public School, chiefly preparatory to the Universities'.[25] Hurstpierpoint offered two quite distinct courses at upper school level, one 'a thorough Commercial Education for those who are going into Trade or Commerce' and one for 'persons intended for our English Universities, or any of the learned professions, a Classical and Mathematical Education'.[26] The former included science, bookkeeping and land-surveying. At S. Chad's Denstone there was a special department for pupils preparing to become engineers, architects or surveyors. It was stated that this department was intended to meet the needs of youths 'for whom the ordinary course of a Grammar School is not suitable'. Lowe added that the department 'does not recognise any system of cramming'.[27] S. George's Military and Engineering School was intended as a preparation for candidates for army commissions, the East India Company Military Seminary or those wanting to pursue a civil engineering path. It opened in 1851, close to the beginning of Woodard's project. It included surveying, levelling, hill drawing, fortification and landscape drawing – and even Hindustani was planned. Similar innovation was shown at Ardingly, a lower school, where boys could receive instruction from the stonemasons, carpenters and bricklayers employed at the school.[28] A broad curriculum, indeed.

---

23. Heeney, *Mission to the Middle Classes*, p. 72.
24. Ibid.
25. Lowe, *S. Nicolas College and Its Schools*, p. 49.
26. Ibid., p. 50.
27. Ibid., p. 59.
28. Heeney, *Mission to the Middle Classes*, p. 106.

Training Teachers

Teachers for the practical subjects mentioned above were at hand but it was not a straightforward matter to get teachers to cover all the subjects required. Teacher training colleges were virtually non-existent, so Woodard created his own. In 1854 a Training School for Commercial Schoolmasters was opened at Hurst with accommodation for 30 students. A period of three years was needed to qualify for a certificate as Associate of S. Nicolas College. This seems to have worked well but jobs at schools where salaries were higher meant that retention was difficult. As well as being able to teach at middle and lower schools[29] of the Society of S. Mary and S. Nicolas, a certificate allowed a man to open a school of his own which could become an affiliated school of the Society, thus overcoming to an extent the problem of losing teachers. Heeney estimates that the scheme had produced 73 qualified teachers at the time of Woodard's death.[30]

It is also worth noting that Woodard and Lowe wanted to help their poorer students to live cheaply at university and considered several ways of doing this. Lowe was in favour of grants to attend existing colleges. Woodard wanted to set up a cheap college of his own at both Oxford and Cambridge. He attempted to buy a site of an old monastery but his bid was not accepted. Later he wrote to Lord Salisbury and hinted that Newman had offered him a site in Oxford but nothing came of that either.[31]

Woodard and John Henry Newman

Writers about Woodard have generally referred to his great contemporary, John Henry Newman, since 2019 elevated to sainthood by the Pope. Newman has already been mentioned several times in this chapter and it is interesting to speculate how far Woodard (and Lowe) were influenced by him. Woodard (as stated earlier) was a student in Oxford between 1834 and 1840 at the same time as Newman and 1833 is generally cited as the beginning of the Oxford Movement. During the years Woodard was at Oxford, therefore, the movement was at its height and Newman at the forefront of Anglican thinking and preaching. Woodard must have heard

---

29. Woodard's upper schools were ideally staffed by clergy.
30. Lowe gave details of the course of study for these teachers. It included one Gospel in Greek, three books of Virgil, Euclid and two special subjects. See *S. Nicolas College and Its Schools*, p. 16. Not for the faint-hearted.
31. Heeney, *Mission to the Middle Classes*, p. 123.

Newman preach and perhaps even visited Newman's church in Littlemore, dedicated to St Mary and St Nicholas.[32] Heeney states that Woodard left Oxford a 'convinced disciple of Keble, Pusey and Newman'.[33] It is also certain that Woodard would have sought support from his High Church friends. Heeney found letters from Pusey, Marriott and others in the archives at Lancing. Apart from the note that Newman had offered him land, there is no evidence that Woodard corresponded with Newman. However, Newman may have had some sympathy with him. I come to this shortly.

After his time in Dublin where he set up the Catholic University, Newman opened a school in the Birmingham Oratory at the request of parents who wanted a Catholic education for their boys. Schools for middle-class Roman Catholics, like Anglicans and Dissenters, were in short supply. Newman took personal control of the school and, although he was never headmaster, he did some teaching and was the one to intervene when there were problems. In this way he acted very much as Woodard did, although Woodard, of course, ran a much larger scheme. In mid-nineteenth century England the Roman Catholic Church was in a minority and Newman would not have been able to call on a wealthy constituency in the way that Woodard was able to. They shared a passion for education and for much the same reasons.

'From first to last education . . . has been my line', wrote Newman in 1863.[34] He had had to give up his teaching career at Oriel following a dispute over the role of a college tutor. He wanted a more personal teaching relationship with students than was favoured at the time. Later on, aged 63, he filled in for an absent teacher at his Oratory School. He enjoyed it so much that he declared: 'if I could believe it to be God's will [I] would turn away my thoughts from ever writing anything, and should see, in my superintendence of these boys, the nearest return to my Oxford life'.[35] He had seized the chance to help found the Catholic University in Dublin and later was similarly attracted to founding a school. Like Woodard he was also proud that his school had led to educational improvement on a large scale through the Catholic community. The website for the Oratory School today states that Newman founded it as a public school along

---

32. Interesting that Woodard chose to call his society S. Mary and S. Nicolas; although it is generally thought that the choice of name is related to the two churches in Shoreham.
33. Heeney, *Mission to the Middle Classes*, p.54.
34. Quoted in Ian Ker, *The Achievement of John Henry Newman* (Notre Dame, IN: University of Notre Dame, 1990), p. 2.
35. Ibid., p. 3.

Winchester lines but with Catholic teaching and practice. The mention of Winchester parallels exactly Woodard's words in his *Plea*. The original curriculum of the Oratory School included classics, history, science, maths and geography, borne out by some notes written by Newman himself.[36] So it would seem that the curriculum of both founders followed similar lines at least in relation to Woodard's upper schools.

Newman could not conceive of education without a religious foundation. For Newman religious truth was not a portion but a condition of general knowledge, the guarantee that there could be knowledge at all. Newman argued forcefully that, if religion were not to be the basis of education, some other idea would take its place.[37] Heeney quotes a lovely passage where Newman expresses the idea that the Creator is so implicated with our universe that it is impossible to truly or fully contemplate it without contemplating God Himself.[38] For Newman a liberal education was one in which the mind was trained to think, to weigh evidence, to sift arguments and to come to a judgement. Woodard may not have been the great religious thinker and writer that Newman was, not many are, but they shared a common vision and it is not fanciful to think that Woodard, in his views on education, was influenced by Newman.

Newman had some pointed things to say about how Catholics treated non-Roman Catholics. This was particularly so in relation to high churchmen with whom he had every sympathy when they were persecuted for ritualism since it reminded him of the time when he suffered as an Anglican. This may not have been a reference to the trouble Woodard had over the practice of confession and accusations of ritualism, but it shows that he would have had sympathy for him (and been therefore inclined to offer him land). He wrote: 'One of the most affecting and discouraging elements in the action of Catholicism just now in English society, is the scorn with which some of us treat proceedings and works amongst Protestants which it is but Christian charity to ascribe to the influence of divine grace'.[39]

One final link between the two men, entirely insignificant, is that both graduated with only a pass degree. This did not stop Newman going on to become one of the intellectual greats or Woodard from developing a grand scheme of Christian education that still exerts influence today.

---

36. Ibid., p. 7.
37. For a study of Newman's views on education see www.newmansociety.org/newman-on-education, accessed Feb 10, 2021.
38. Heeney, *Mission to the Middle Classes*, p.96.
39. Quoted in Ian Ker, *John Henry Newman: A Biography* (Oxford: Clarendon Press, 1988), p. 569.

Woodard and Schools for Girls

It will not have escaped notice that Woodard did not include girls when he aimed to educate the nation's children. Neither, of course, did Newman. Throughout his life Woodard was entirely resistant to the idea of extending his scheme of public school education to girls. The next chapter shows that such an omission was in keeping with mainstream opinion of the day. As early as 1849, right at the beginning of his work, he wrote a letter to Eliza Lowe in which he made clear his view on educating girls: 'It is a matter for consideration whether large schools are good for girls. A public school is the very thing for a boy because the world and public life is his destiny. But can this rule be applied to girls? . . . A large religious Sisterhood with small filiations about the country to teach girls of all ranks is the only thing that I can see likely to succeed on a large scale.'[40] No one was to persuade him otherwise.

However, he did agree to take over S. Michael's School for girls in 1855, possibly because of ties of friendship. The founder of S. Michael's was a great friend of his, Miss Mary Anne Rooper, who ran the school in Hove. On her death he was persuaded to help her successor, Lady Caroline Elliot, to establish it at Bognor, near to his schools. The school was referred to as 'allied' to the Society of S. Mary and S. Nicolas and, as he had written to Eliza Lowe, he wanted the school to be run like a convent rather than as a public school.

It was to be Lowe, not Woodard, who pioneered education for girls and founded the girls' schools in the Midland Division and these schools were similarly 'allied' to the Society until well after Woodard's death. In 1875, a year after S. Anne's was founded, Woodard wrote to Lowe, not congratulating him but, rather, worrying that entering the world of girls' education would detract from the work of educating boys.[41] He need not have worried as Lowe proved equal to the task of providing for both.

A letter written in 1880 shows that he had not changed his views, if anything they had hardened:

> Public schools for girls are of very doubtful merit. Religious houses or convents are more in harmony with my ideas. . . . The High School system, and knowledge without the grace of female gentleness and devotion, is another cloud in the gathering storm which is awaiting society. So far as we have gone with girls' schools it is all very well, but the question is shall we commit ourselves to a

---

40. Heeney, *Mission to the Middle Classes*, p. 107. This letter is further discussed in Chapter 11.
41. See Marcia A. Rice, *The Story of S. Mary's, Abbots Bromley* (Shrewsbury: Wilding & Son, 1947), p. 18ff.

general scheme? The banners of St Michael and St Anne might be at our gathering at Taunton, to show that we will do what we can, but so slippery are women that we must watch our own progress before we promise more.[42]

In 1884, in what Heeney called an outburst, he wrote:

These fancy schools set up for girls are more fitted for show than solid and practical use. After all, we know what women are for, and to draw them from these purposes and put them into conflict with men in universities, the Forum, and the public streets can only have an un-Christian ending.[43]

It is difficult not to be shocked at sentiments such as the 'slipperiness' of women and 'what women are for' expressed in the last two letters. He did not write in similar vein to Eliza Lowe and so we may assume that he would not have expressed himself in public in this way. However, as I show in the next chapter, his views on the role of women were entirely conventional in the nineteenth century and on into the twentieth. 'What women are for' is likely to be interpreted in a narrow sense today but in Woodard's time there was a developed and complex understanding of their role in life, a role which had great importance to society and will be examined in the next chapter. It is possible that Woodard thought himself veering towards the progressive in supporting S. Michael's and allowing S. Anne's to bring their banner to large gatherings.

Woodard did preach at one commemoration service at S. Anne's. This was on S. Anne's Day in 1884 (26 July being the date of the festival) and is the only record of him visiting the school. The letter quoted above was written on 9 October 1884. It was in reply to one from Lowe four days earlier in which Lowe conceded Woodard's right to restrict the Society's operations. On 10 October, just one day later, Lowe replied: 'I do not agree with you.' It may be that Woodard's visit to S. Anne's sparked off this exchange. In which case it appears that a visit to the school had not moved Woodard to change his opinions, rather the opposite. Being present as honoured guest at the prizegiving would have been an eye-opener. He would have heard of university certificates from St Andrews and Cambridge being awarded and of past pupils finding their way in the world of work as teachers, nurses and music students.[44]

---

42. Gibbs, *In Search of Nathaniel Woodard*, p. 41.
43. Heeney, *Mission to the Middle Classes*, p. 108.
44. The *Staffordshire Advertiser* regularly reported details of the Commemoration

The tone of the letter suggests that Woodard knew he was losing the argument over girls' education. Of course, Woodard did not believe that girls should have no education at all and it is likely that in this passage he was decrying educating girls for exams leading to university education. If so, then Lowe's reply is revealing. Lowe's reply shows that he had ambitions for girls in his schools to be educated for university just as they were in all the in Woodard's schools for boys. Heeney confirms that Lowe believed in university education for women, which, as the next chapter will show, was beginning to become a reality.

A central question of this book is why it was that Lowe determined to open the Society of S. Mary and S. Nicolas to girls despite Woodard's antagonism. It is therefore of great interest that Eliza Lowe appears right at the start of the Woodard project, raising the topic and presumably recommending that girls be educated in Woodard's scheme. Moreover, Edward and Eliza Lowe have been entirely vindicated. Today, despite the bitter loss of its girls' boarding schools, every Woodard boarding school admits girls alongside boys.

---

service at S. Anne's School, e.g. 29 July 1882.

Chapter 2

Girls' Education in the Nineteenth Century

> If we would really teach man, our duty is of necessity first to teach woman. It is on the household hearth that the pyramid of empire rests: it is from the domestic board come the aspirations, and hopes, and resolves, which redeem and sustain nations.
> *Thomas Wyse MP, 29th January 1844*[1]

These words were spoken by Wyse at a meeting in Liverpool, held to promote the creation of a girls' school to exist alongside, but separately from, the Liverpool Institute for Boys which had opened in 1838. Wyse, who had been chairman of the Parliamentary Education Committee, also spoke at the opening of the boys' school.

In his speech in 1844 Wyse dwelt on the importance of women's influence and commented: 'the middle class of all others has the worst provision for the education of its daughters'. The prospectus for the girls' school stated: 'the course of instruction would embrace English, reading, spelling, grammar, etc., arithmetic, drawing, vocal music, natural philosophy, natural history and chemistry, needlework in all its departments, and calisthenics'.[2] French and dancing would be extras. It was suggested that a fee of four guineas[3] per annum per pupil would be sufficient for the school to become self-supporting. In fact, the charges were £5 for the senior school and two guineas for the infant school, the latter open to boys as well. This compares to fees in 1844 at the boys' school of twelve guineas in the senior school and six guineas in the preparatory school. The great and the good gathered in Liverpool in 1844 believed that girls deserved an education and one not too dissimilar from that of boys. There is a sense that, now that boys had a fine school, it was time to do something for their sisters.

---

1. Quoted in Herbert J. Tiffen, *A History of Liverpool Institute Schools 1825-1935* (The Liverpool Institute Old Boys' Association, 1935), p. 103.
2. Tiffen, *A History of Liverpool Institute Schools 1825-1935*, p. 104.
3. A guinea was equivalent to £1 and 1 shilling.

George Holt, a wealthy cotton broker and banker, bought the building specifically for the use of the new school to be called Liverpool Institute High School for Girls. It was originally a private house built by John Blackburne, one time mayor of Liverpool, and the school was later called Blackburne House. The school closed in 1986 but the Grade 11 listed building is still used today to promote the education of women.

Fig. 3 Liverpool Institute High School for Girls, Blackburne House, Liverpool.

Fig 4. Honours board.

By the 1870s university examinations were becoming open to women. It is interesting that in 1874 Latin was introduced to the school in Liverpool and by 1876 French and German were standard subjects. The honours board (see opposite) shows that at least from 1894 girls were entered for examinations and talented girls won scholarships to university. The board is preserved today in the reception area of Blackburne House. Note that until 1904 pupils were recorded as going on to study at University College (Liverpool) but by 1907 the college had been awarded university status.

It can be seen that one pupil won a scholarship but was recorded as ineligible to take it up. Other boards in Blackburne

House show that several pupils won scholarships for which they were deemed ineligible. Often the deed awarding scholarships stated that they were for men. The governors of the girls' school clearly wanted to record success in a prestigious exam regardless.

Here, in essence, one can see much of what this chapter will set out to demonstrate about the place of women in Victorian England and the education that was considered suitable for them: although women's vocation lay in the home, women exerted a profound influence for good in society and so they had to be educated.

It was felt necessary to assure the great and the good of Liverpool that this education could be given more cheaply, in fact at less than 50 per cent of the cost for boys. This imbalance did not trouble those gathered there in 1844 and, as we shall see, it did not trouble Edward Lowe and his colleagues who, from 1872, worked to establish girls' schools in the Woodard tradition. Education of girls was felt to be 'a good thing' but secondary in importance to that of boys, despite the high-sounding words which begin this chapter. At the same time change was afoot and the nineteenth century would witness greater opportunities being opened to women, opportunities that Edward Lowe was keen to offer girls in his schools.

SEPARATE SPHERES

Wyse expressed the view that a woman's sphere was the home. He did not argue the case or put forward rational arguments. Rather it was presented as uncontroversial. This shows how strong such belief (and practice) was. Carol Dyhouse writes of the 'dignity and separateness of the man's world'.[4] Men took part in public life; women, although allowed in public, unmarried ladies suitably chaperoned, were not expected to speak in public meetings. Men elected men to Parliament and advised the Queen. Men went to university and became clerics, lawyers and businessmen. Men built railways, worked in mines, designed and built bridges, sold artworks and wrote music. One could go on. For most of the nineteenth century upper middle-class girls were kept busy at home paying visits and leaving visiting cards, learning the social etiquette that required dancing lessons and how to behave at dances. There would be visits to sick relatives and a certain amount of charitable visiting and fund-raising. It often included writing and performing plays, as was the case for Alice Rathbone (whom we shall meet later) who performed in plays before close friends and relatives at her home in Liverpool.

---

4. Carol Dyhouse, *Girls Growing Up in Late Victorian and Edwardian England* (London: Routledge & Kegan Paul, 1981), p. 8.

Even in the home the separateness could be seen. A father's study was sacrosanct and not to be entered without permission.[5] After dinner the ladies would retire so that the gentlemen could get on with manly things like discussing politics or business, or the next grouse shoot. Most reforms to education (as in Liverpool) were initiated by men who kept control thereafter. Dyhouse shows that, although this separateness was beginning to break down by the end of the nineteenth century it was still felt, and sometimes very strongly, by those whose lives were challenging it. She writes that the 'sense of insignificance was . . . confirmed by the experience of going to college'.[6] Yet, society was already depending on working-class women and a small number of their middle-class sisters, to say nothing of the Queen. The fact that working-class women had to work, often from the age of 14 until they married, augured the eventual breaking down of this separation.

There were exceptions but it was a brave woman who ventured into a man's sphere. Or a desperate one. Women (and children) did in fact work in coal mines till a law was passed in the 1840s to prevent it. One opportunity for middle-class women, generally those who were single and could therefore own property,[7] was to set up a school in their home and very many schools of this sort were set up in the nineteenth century. However, here the ideal of womanhood persisted. Self-denial, forbearance and fidelity were the hallmarks of these teachers.[8] Dyhouse argues that this was an extremely consistent pattern amongst nineteenth- and early twentieth-century teachers and heads of colleges, who dedicated their lives to their charges with self-sacrifice and devotion. Pupils were called 'daughters' or 'children' and were mothered as such by the women who ran them. So, the lady proprietor of a school lived out the role of a devoted mother without having to get married. Not infrequently their careers were regarded as a religious vocation or duty.

The Redemptive Companion of Man

Another important role for woman was acting as helpmeet for man. June Purvis argues that it was widely held that woman was made for man: the 'confidante and companion of manhood'.[9] Her role and very identity was

---

5. Men might have their own personal toilet in the home. See p. 120.
6. Ibid., p. 65.
7. Before 1882 any income or property belonging to a woman passed to her husband on marriage.
8. Dyhouse, *Girls Growing Up in Late Victorian and Edwardian England*, p. 32.
9. June Purvis, *A History of Women's Education in England* (Milton Keynes: Open University Press, 1991), p. 3.

therefore determined relative to manhood, a view that she says received strong verbal support throughout the nineteenth century. The word 'helpmeet' reflects the Genesis creation story where Eve is given to Adam, flesh of his flesh, so that she can be a worthy and equal companion. Purvis quotes John Ruskin who wrote that education for women was important so that they could understand and assist the work of men. Yet the words of Ruskin again augur change. If women could both understand and aid men in their work, then they could also do work that men were doing.

The words of Wyse quoted at the beginning of this chapter reveal remarkable things about how the role of woman was perceived at the time. The pyramid of Empire rested on woman and her influence extended to redeeming and sustaining nations. The language of redemption recalls that of Christian faith and the role of Christ. Women were there to create a sanctuary where man could recover from the brutality and compromises of business and be 'civilised'. Home was the sphere where gentleness and peace reigned, a holy refuge from a hostile world, and woman, with her refined nature and purity, could restore both man's peace and stability. More than this, women were regarded as 'the natural guardians of national culture'.[10]

Men could rely on their wives for this cultural refinement when their days were taken up with business. Accomplishments like music, art and dancing were required to be pursued by girls as part of their education.

According to Joan Burstyn women were 'men's superior consciences'.[11] As such they were the standard-bearers of morality. It was widely believed that men's intellectual capacity and business acumen far outdid that of women, but that this was matched by woman's superior morality and her powers of intuition. Through their unique intuition and the social arts that they had perfected, women were able to manipulate men for benign (or not so benign) purposes. Thus, the ideal of femininity was important. Women were to be 'ladylike', submissive, curb their spirits and self-sacrificing. This even extended to the role of sisters towards their brothers whom girls should wait on for their comfort.

One might argue that this was all a means of control, intended to justify keeping women out of public life and, indeed, any area of life where men were thought to hold sway. However, there was a genuine fear that, once women strayed from the domestic sphere, dire social consequences would follow.

---

10. Joyce S. Pederson, *The Reform of Girls' Secondary and Higher Education in Victorian England: A Study of Elites and Educational Change* (New York: Garland, 1987), p. 125.
11. Joan N. Burstyn, *Victorian Education and the Ideal of Womanhood* (London: Croom Helm, 1980), p. 31.

Education of Girls

What sort of education was available for girls in Victorian England? A lot depended on the income of the family.

Before 1870, when the Forster Act provided funds for the setting up of board schools across England and Wales, working-class girls, if they had an education at all, would have been sent to dames' schools, charity schools or the schools which were provided by the (Anglican) National Society and the (non-denominational) British and Foreign Bible Society. The Quakers were active in education too. In working-class families, it was likely that mothers also worked and were not able to teach their daughters – even if they had the ability to do so. Furthermore, children who worked (and the minimum working age was nine) would have little time available for education and attendance was often sporadic. Marriage certificates of working-class women in the nineteenth century often have the bride and female witnesses making their mark 'X' rather than signing their name. So, although education was available, the children of working-class families did not always receive it.

Before the mid-1850s there simply were no public schools like Repton, Eton, Winchester and so on for the girls of wealthy upper-class families. Education for the daughters of the well off was often provided by governesses or visiting tutors and sometimes the mother would take charge. It could be a joint effort. In a later chapter we shall hear of the father of one wealthy family who took his whole family off on a grand European tour to improve their education and experience the culture and languages of the great cities.

As Wyse pointed out, it was girls from middle-class families who had the least opportunity for education. Such families were often too proud to send their children to the free schools since it would label them as economic failures, yet could not afford private tutors and they were often suspicious of the many private schools that sprang up to fill the gap.

The example of the Brontë family, living in Haworth, Yorkshire, gives an indication of how a middle-class family might educate their daughters. The Brontë girls experienced both good and bad private schools as well as learning at home. Patrick Brontë, the father of one son and five daughters, was vicar of the parish but it was not a wealthy living. The girls were taught at home but also went to day schools, had private lessons and went to inexpensive private boarding schools. Anne, for example, had lessons from the church organist at Keighley Church and from John Bradley of Keighley. Keighley was a local artist engaged by Patrick Brontë who exhibited widely in the area and helped to run the Mechanics' Institute in Keighley.

Patrick Brontë's extensive library offered a wide range of reading material and the literary careers of Charlotte, Emily and Anne were nurtured there as

Chapter 2. Girls' Education in the Nineteenth Century

much, if not more than, as at their schools. One private school in Cowan's Bridge, Lancaster was a disaster, and Patrick took his daughters away when they fell seriously ill. Indeed, Maria and Elizabeth died of tuberculosis shortly after being removed from the school. However, Charlotte spent three happy years at Miss Wooler's school in Roe Head where she was treated well and made two lifelong friends. She taught there to help pay for her sisters at the school. In 1842, trying to broaden their education and with financial help from their aunt, Charlotte and Emily went to school in Brussels for six months. Their intention was to start a school on their return with an emphasis on the correct learning of foreign languages. In Brussels they learned French, German, maths, Belgian history, geography, piano, writing to a high standard and they read works of both a general and philosophical nature. They were pupil-teachers, Charlotte teaching English and Emily piano. All three Brontë sisters went on to become governesses from time to time and, of course, to write. The former career was conventional, the latter not so.

This pattern of some learning at home and some at school was the same in the case of Emily Davies, born in 1830, later to become a very successful protagonist for access to universities for women. She was largely taught at home by her mother who ran a private school. Like the Brontës, she was the daughter of a clergyman. When she was nine, she did spend a few months at a day school with her sister but, perhaps due to the fact that the family moved around a lot, was thereafter taught at home, presumably along with pupils in her mother's school. However, alongside her education, she was expected to look after sick relatives and neighbours when necessary and resented the fact that her brothers all attended Repton, a public school, and then went on to university. The boys were not expected to attend to domestic duties.

These private girls' schools were generally modelled on life in the family home. Frequently they were kept small so that the family atmosphere was maintained. Relations between teachers and pupils were marked by ties of affection, dependence and personal obligation. Schools could be literally an extension of family life. Alice Ottley helped her mother in a school following the death of her father. An income was needed to educate her younger brothers and sisters and so a few girls were taken in to be educated along with them. The aim of their school in Hampstead was to foster femininity in a religious atmosphere. Dyhouse quotes a pupil as saying: 'the girls were emphatically made to feel they were part of the home, and being few in number, were brought into close[r] personal touch with Alice . . . she was their elder sister and never-failing friend'.[12]

A school on the Isle of Wight run by the Sewell sisters included as pupils nieces of the proprietress, resulting in the teachers being called aunts

---

12. Dyhouse, *Girls Growing Up in Late Victorian and Edwardian England*, p. 49.

even after the nieces had left. Hannah Pipe opened a small school in the late 1840s in Manchester. She taught the girls and her widowed mother looked after household matters. She was known as the 'school mother' and the pupils her 'school daughters'. Her school had an excellent library and lessons from distinguished teachers. Many girls went on to higher education and one became a teacher of history at Newnham College in Cambridge. Yet Pipe herself did not believe in exams, competitiveness and achievement for its own sake. Dyhouse writes: 'she saw herself as fostering intellectual "accomplishment": not achievements to be measured against those of men'.[13]

The proprietresses of the private schools set up schools in their (generally, large) houses without any need for registration, exam certificates, training or evidence of capability to teach or look after girls. Rather like the mothers of the children that they emulated. As the century went on this was to change, although small private schools for girls continued to operate until well into the twentieth century – as was the case with Brighthelmston School, which shall be discussed next.

Hannah Wallis and Brighthelmston School

Hannah Wallis was a Quaker and a close friend of Priscilla Bright, who is commemorated on the Millicent Fawcett memorial in Parliament Square to those who figured prominently in the women's suffrage movement. Between 1822 and c. 1830 Wallis' mother ran a school in Liverpool, which was attended by Priscilla Bright and her sister, also from a Quaker background. Hannah married and lived in Brighton. When her husband died, she took up teaching, like her mother before her. Girls' boarding schools had proliferated in Brighton so she decided to move up to Southport in Lancashire, a coastal town just north of Liverpool not unlike Brighton and becoming fashionable as businessmen (and tourists) sought cleaner air. The 1861 census records her living in Bold St, Southport with pupils and her own three children. By 1871 she had moved to Albert Road Birkdale with her daughters and niece named as teachers. She had sixteen pupils living with her, some from eminent Quaker families. German, French and music teachers were employed. She had ties with Miss Clough of Newnham College, Cambridge and her girls were soon entered into the Cambridge local exams. Pupils also attended 'Lectures for Ladies' organised by Wallis herself in Southport. By 1881 she was established in a large house two miles outside Southport in Waterloo Road, Birkdale. The house was built to her own specifications, a note of which she had placed in a local paper. In 1881 the school had eight teachers and 48 pupils and a curriculum which included botany, geology, philology and Latin.

---
13. Ibid., p. 48.

Chapter 2. Girls' Education in the Nineteenth Century

Fig. 5 Brighthelmston School.

She named the school Brighthelmston School, after the original name for Brighton where she had lived with her husband.[14] The image above is found on a postcard which, on the rear, shows that a halfpenny stamp was required for inland postage and a penny stamp for foreign postage. This was the postage rate applicable between 1891 and 1921. On the postcard it is stated that it was printed in Berlin. This probably means that it was pre-war, so this dates the postcard to between 1891 and 1914 and the photograph could have been earlier. Close inspection shows about 40 pupils. Note that the girls are engaged in cricket, holding rather large cricket bats. The girls of S. Anne's also played cricket (see p. 174). It is interesting that cricket was chosen for the photograph rather than a more ladylike activity like croquet although propriety is maintained by the wearing of boaters and skirts. The message would have been clear; this is a school which educates girls along similar lines to boys.

Wallis retired in 1891 handing over to a daughter as the next principal. In a presentation to her by past pupils a tribute noted her 'large-hearted Christian motherliness'. It would seem that Wallis combined the private school characteristics of acting as mother to her pupils at the same time as pursuing ideas of academic excellence and opportunities for advancement of women. Notable is the fact that she encouraged her pupils to take the

---

14. I am grateful to Judy Bemrose, an old girl of Brighthelmston School, who provided much of the information about the school. For further information see *The Friend* magazine in the Quaker Library in London.

exams for Oxford and Cambridge. Old girls remember the 'back boards' in the assembly hall which recorded the names of all the girls who passed these examinations.[15] The school closed in July 1993.

Training for Women Teachers

In 1848 Frederick Denison Maurice and a small group of tutors at King's College, London established Queen's College in Harley Street. This was an attempt to improve the standard and competence of those who would take up employment as governesses. Funded by the Governesses' Benevolent Institution, the first group of students to attend this new training school for teachers included Dorothea Beale and Frances Mary Buss. Maurice, who was Professor of Theology at King's College, London, became principal and the main lecturer at Queen's College. Both Miss Beale and Miss Buss went on to become headteachers of schools that aspired to a high standard of education for their pupils, the former at Cheltenham Ladies' College which opened in 1854, where she became head in 1858, and the latter at the North London Collegiate School in London, which was founded by Miss Buss in 1850 and where she was headmistress from its opening until her death in 1894. June Purvis suggests that the first curriculum at Cheltenham was similar to that in the private boarding schools: scripture, liturgy, history, geography, grammar, arithmetic, French, music, drawing and needlework with German, Italian and dancing as extras, not dissimilar to that of the Liverpool girls' school founded in 1844. Miss Beale still expected her pupils to be good wives and mothers: 'Every pupil should know . . . enough of public affairs to be able to discuss them with her menfolk.'[16]

Moreover, both these schools, and others founded later in the century, expected their pupils to be 'genteel' and not to challenge the traditional role of womanhood. The reforms in women's education in the middle of the nineteenth century created two new female roles, that of the celibate careerist (generally a teacher) and that of the cultured, well-educated wife who was an intellectual partner to her husband.[17]

Emily Davies and Exams

Meanwhile, Emily Davies, living in London, had found her vocation and was appointed secretary (from October 1862) to a committee set up to secure the admission of women to university examinations. In October

---
15. Similar to the Honours Board on p. 26.
16. Purvis, *A History of Women's Education in England*, p. 87.
17. Ibid., p. 78.

1863 the committee, chaired by Henry Alford, Dean of Canterbury, and supported by prominent women educationists, such as Frances Mary Buss and Elizabeth Bostock, persuaded the Cambridge local examination syndicate to open its examinations to girls on an experimental basis. Given only six weeks' notice, Emily Davies found 83 girls to present themselves (25 from Miss Buss' North London Collegiate School). While not all were proficient (especially in arithmetic), many passed and none was hysterical or seized by brain fever as some gainsayers said would happen and no scandal ensued. In October 1864, at the instigation of Davies, nearly a thousand teachers and more than a hundred 'ladies of rank and influence' requested that the Cambridge examinations be permanently opened; the proposal was accepted in the following year.

Davies then successfully lobbied the schools' inquiry commission (the Taunton commission), appointed by the government in December 1864, to include girls as well as boys in its investigations of middle-class education. She gave oral evidence to the commission on 30 November 1865, the first of nine female witnesses. Her appearance was significant: it was the first time women had given evidence in person to a royal commission as expert witnesses, and she and Miss Buss, who gave evidence on the same day, were nervous, but impressed the commissioners with their 'perfect womanliness'. The report of the commission, signed in December 1867, was a landmark in the campaign for an academic secondary education for middle-class girls.

THE TAUNTON COMMISSION

The Commission is also important because there is a dearth of evidence for these private schools. One scholar has written: 'Accounts of real-life ladies who kept fashionable private schools in the early 19th Century are hard to come by. A handful of biographies and autobiographies of such schoolmistresses exist, and they figure now and then in studies of eminent women who happened to attend their schools.'[18]

The Commission reported that the wealthy upper middle classes typically educated their daughters at home. It was also common for the burgeoning professional and merchant class to teach girls at home. James Bryce, Assistant Commissioner to the inquiry, thought the pattern he found in Lancashire was typical of the whole country. Girls would be taught at home by governesses until they were about ten. This would be followed by two or three years at a local (fee-paying) day school. At the age of twelve or thirteen

---

18. Joyce S. Pedersen, 'Schoolmistresses and Headmistresses: Elites and Education in Nineteenth Century England', *Journal of British Studies*, Vol. 15, no. 1 (Autumn 1975), p. 135.

girls would be sent to a select boarding school until the age of seventeen and then perhaps a year at 'finishing' school. The most fashionable boarding schools were in the south of England, in London, Brighton, Clifton and Bath. Bryce estimated that there were 500 such boarding schools in Lancashire alone, of whom very few took more than 50 pupils. Most had fewer than 30 pupils. Mostly, the schools were in large private houses and were described as 'homely'. Indeed, sometimes the Commissioners were chided for inspecting establishments which were 'homes' rather than 'schools'. This makes sense when one remembers that homes were the places largely where well-to-do girls had been, and continued to be, educated.

It was noted that great emphasis was placed on caring for the individual girl, efforts rather than achievements were praised and character was foremost. A girl was being prepared for life as a lady in the home and the social scene of middle-class society where she was not expected to have academic achievements, but where a smattering of general knowledge and accomplishments like piano playing, singing, drawing and needlework were prized. Hence private boarding schools in the early part of the nineteenth century did not have names, they were known by the name of the proprietress. Such establishments often ceased to exist once their owners either retired or died and few records were left. The Misses Wooler at Roe Head soon considered retirement when their father's death meant that they had independent means.[19] The schools, being generally very small and run like families, did not appear to have much problem with discipline. Girls formed close attachments, both to their teachers and their peers. Bryce remarked that at one school discipline was maintained by one proprietress saying, 'I don't love you.' That was enough to restore order.

The Commission was generally very critical of the standard of education in these schools. Many were said to be inefficient and uneconomic and the level of scholarship very low. The Commission wrote of shoddy intellectual content, academic incompetence and the closing of immature minds. This may have been because often schools were run by 'distressed gentlewomen' who needed an income but were neither academically suited to the task nor devoted to it. The ladies running these schools could be intimidated by the parents and were unable to exercise control over matters such as attendance, what pupils studied and who was accepted as a pupil. Pedersen quotes the words of one investigator who observed that:

> the first noticeable fact in ladies' boarding schools is the subjection of the teacher's will in every instance to the wishes of the parents, in many instances to the whims of the pupils . . . in their anxiety

---
19. Ibid., p. 140, n.18.

to exclude from schools patronized by themselves all girls of an inferior class, [parents] exercise a control over school mistresses which is often very oppressive and tyrannical.[20]

The curriculum was not necessarily lacking. As mentioned above there was a wide variety of subjects taught but there was little in the way of structured teaching and the fact that pupils often moved from one school to another and that pupils of different ages were often accepted into these schools did not aid coherent learning. For example the Commission's investigator for Warwick and Stafford found that it was common for one group of pupils at a school to arrive aged eight and leave at about twelve while, at the same school, other pupils would attend from the age of thirteen to sixteen or seventeen. It was also unlikely that one or two teachers could possess the necessary expertise to teach the large number of subjects required. Pedersen argues: 'teachers treated potentially serious subjects of scholarly inquiry in such a way as to make them seem merely ornamental'.[21] French was taught without attention to grammar, thus, in the Commissioners' view being of little value as an intellectual discipline, although it was noted that specialist teachers were often employed for music and foreign languages. The Commissioners' particular outrage was reserved for what was called 'the use of globes'. Pupils were given globes representing the solar system, which they learned to manipulate without the benefit of instruction in physics or astronomy: 'It was a curious adaptation of Newtonian physics to strictly ornamental ends.'[22] One might admire the teaching of French orally rather than grammatically of course, particularly, as was often the case, if taught by a native speaker – and the use of globes was at least an interesting start to astronomy which could spark a lifelong interest.

However, the Commission, too, was firmly held in the grip of feminine ideals of gentility and companionship. It was concerned that, while girls' minds should be sharpened, this should not be at the cost of the feminine graces or lead to them competing with men. Dyhouse explains the view of the Commission in this way: 'Women, after all, should be pleasing, supportive individuals. They might ideally help their husbands and share their interests, but no more than this'.[23] Perhaps the members of the Commission felt they must not alienate parents. The Commission argued:

---

20. Ibid., p. 146.
21. Ibid., p. 143.
22. Ibid., p. 144.
23. Ibid., p. 44.

Parents who have daughters will always look to their being provided for in marriage, will always believe that the gentler graces and winning qualities of character will be their best passports to marriage, and will always expect their husbands to take on themselves the intellectual toil and the active exertions needed for the support of the family.[24]

When it came to higher education, the reluctance of parents to further educate their daughters was considerable. Constance Maynard, who became principal of Westfield College in London in 1882, described the attitude of parents in this way: 'But, tell me, what is the use? If you could be a clergyman, now! – or a lawyer, or if it was training for missionaries it would be different. But that great effort, all that expense, all that absence from home, and whatever is gained by it?'[25]

The parents had a point. The expectation had to be that, as more women were educated to university level, more opportunities would open up for them.

The Bryce Report, 1895

At the end of the nineteenth century and into the twentieth this view of 'ladylike' schooling persisted. In 1894-95 a Royal Commission headed by James Bryce investigated secondary schooling in England. In some rural areas only private schools for girls existed at this level and it was estimated that there were between 10,000 and 15,000 of them across the country. An investigation into girls' schools in Devon found that schools of about twelve pupils were common and most popular with parents. While this report found widely different degrees of competence and efficiency, the dominant idea was: 'that it should be as far as possible claustral, that girls should be kept from any contamination with people who drop their H's or earn their salt. It is thought that careful seclusion is absolutely necessary for the development of that refinement which should characterise a lady'.[26] The writer of the report, Ella Armitage, stated that nearly half of the 70 schools were indifferent or worthless, seven were excellent and 35 fair.

It seems therefore that not all schools were intellectually worthless. Katharine Chorley spent four years at a school in Folkestone where the proprietress was a woman of some intellectual refinement. She taught mathematics and some Latin and history was well taught, both by herself

---

24. Ibid., p. 43.
25. Quoted in Burstyn, *Victorian Education and the Ideal of Womanhood*, pp. 59-60.
26. Quoted in Dyhouse, *Girls Growing Up in Late Victorian and Edwardian England*, p. 51.

and with the aid of Oxford University extension lectures. However, discussion of politics was not permitted and newspapers were not on offer. Careful supervision at the school kept pupils away from both the male sex and girls of a lower social status. Social snobbery, Dyhouse concludes, 'formed part of the "hidden curriculum"'.[27] The stated aim was to turn out 'high-minded and cultured home-makers'.[28] The parents would want nothing less and nothing more.

Women Writers on Education for Girls

Emily Shirreff

Emily Shirreff was a friend of Hannah Wallis, whose school was described earlier. Emily was born in 1814 and her sister, Maria Grey (née Shirreff), born two years later. Both Emily and her sister were Quakers and strong supporters of the education of women. They took a particular interest in improving women for educational work and, in 1858, Shirreff published *Intellectual Education and Its Influence on the Character and Happiness of Women*.[29] In 1869 Shirreff was for a short time honorary mistress of Girton College and she also served for many years on the council of that institution and of the Girls' Public Day School Company. She took a leading part in establishing and developing the Maria Grey Training College for teachers, founded by her sister. Shirreff was a firm believer in Froebel's system (which encouraged a child to be led by his own interests under the guidance of the teacher) and she wrote a short memoir of him and several books on kindergarten methods.

Intellectual Education gives a detailed account of what she thought should be taught to girls and what principles should guide practice. One imagines that her book and ideas became the inspiration behind the teaching at her sister's training college.

Hers was a deeply religious vision, although she attempted to steer clear of controversy in religious matters. So, unlike Woodard and being a Quaker, she did not insist on collects and catechisms. However, since her book was addressed to mothers, she would have assumed that such matters would have been included at their discretion. Like Woodard she believed that education could not be separated from a religious view of life. God had given women the power of intellect and it was their duty and privilege to cultivate it. The character of women was a great concern to her and almost as much of her book is taken up with how to train character as how to

---

27. Ibid., p. 55.
28. Ibid., p. 42.
29. Emily Shirreff, *Intellectual Education and Its Influence on the Character and Happiness of Women* (London: J.W. Parker, 1858); I can only sketch out some of her ideas here.

train the mind. Qualities such as perseverance, patience, ability to admit mistakes, concern for the sick and the less fortunate, self-control, honesty, moral courage and cheerfulness were listed and she carefully considered how each could be developed and how each impacted on the development of intellect. These qualities are all admirable but would not perhaps have figured highly in a boys' school at the time.

Intellectual Education is concerned with the education at home of girls between the ages of twelve and eighteen. Shirreff believed that teaching was synonymous with motherhood. Girls were best taught at home since this was where their future lay and, like Woodard, she believed that the rough and tumble of life together for boys in boarding schools was not suitable for girls. Intellectual education was vital because the life of girls was so circumscribed that, without the benefit of a thorough education, girls would become prey to boredom and all the perils that inactivity brought with it. She did not spell these perils out too clearly but she was not much in favour of balls, gossip, fancy accomplishments and novels. An inactive life brought distressing mental trials, particularly felt when girls did not marry young. So she wanted girls to be able to look forward to, not dread, the single life. In all other ways she accepted the contemporary view of what education for girls should be, although, as we shall see, she could highlight its drawbacks with sharp irony.

With regard to the teaching, perhaps the most extraordinary aspect of this is the expectation of what a girl might be expected to know at the age of twelve. She should read and spell English perfectly, write neatly and be able to compose a simple letter. She should know an outline of the Bible and the spread of Christianity, be well acquainted with the four Gospels, know something of the leading events of ancient and modern history and have read some lives of great men. She should be able to distinguish between which nations are subject and which powerful, geography as far as it pertains to her travels, have some poetry by heart, a basic knowledge of arithmetic including mental arithmetic and, most surprising of all, be able to speak and write the French and German languages with as much ease as her own. She should know the rudiments of music, plain needlework and simple household management. Yet Shirreff did not believe in overstraining young children!

From ages twelve to fourteen girls should rise at 6 a.m. and begin to learn Latin and Greek. Grammar of French and German could now be started. European history should be studied by reading fifteen pages a day of a suitable book and a chronological outline of what has happened in many different countries should be begun. Mental indolence should be challenged, and pupils helped to focus and appreciate the value of learning. They should be encouraged to discuss and express opinions, also to write simple compositions. Half an hour a day should be given to music practice.

Chapter 2. Girls' Education in the Nineteenth Century

From fourteen to sixteen the first three books of Euclid and quadratic equations should be attempted, along with zoology, animal physiology, Lyell's study of geology, the work of Professor Airey on astronomy, philology and comparison of the grammars of different languages, Addison, Johnson's *Lives of the Poets*, Joshua Reynolds on painting, a *cours de littérature Français* and the works of other great writers. Now was the time to introduce the 'commonplace book'. This was a record of both what the pupil was learning and her comments or questions upon it. One page would record what had been studied and the opposite page would record her thoughts. All this was so she could 'think out a subject'. Of great importance was the development of the power of judgement, to be able to weigh opinions and not just accept what she was reading. Self-governance for which strength of character was needed was the aim of it all. At the same time a girl was to be ready to respond to the needs of others in the household or out visiting. Attendance in the sick room was another duty, as was cheerfulness.

From sixteen to eighteen the emphasis on forming sound opinions continued. Six hours a day should now be devoted to study. The list of reading she was expected to undertake is staggering but the section is interesting also as it begins with a discussion of the role of doubt and probability in human life. A girl was to learn that doubt was an inevitable condition of earthly existence and that many judgements had to be based on probability rather than demonstration. Love of truth was what mattered, and she should learn not to be hasty in judging the opinions of others, since they were often held because a person 'could do no other'. An imaginative child would have read Pope's Homer and Dryden's Virgil for her own pleasure. Now she should be introduced to Butler, Paley and Bentham, works on logic and John Herschel's *Study of Natural Philosophy*. Scientists such as Lyell, Somerville and Humboldt should be on the syllabus, and evidences for Christianity and the history of the Bible. Ancient authors were on the list too: Plutarch, Plato's *Apology of Sophocles*, Crito and Phaedo, as well as Aeschylus' *Agamemnon* and Sophocles' *Antigone*. The list goes on: Thucydides, Herodotus, Tacitus, Livy. As light relief, Dante could be read in English, as could Niebuhr's *Roman History*. It was important to have some understanding of political economy and so they should be familiar with Adam Smith's *Wealth of Nations*. In history girls should learn about the achievements of the Reformation and the Jesuit fightback. Suddenly something of Shirreff's personal views emerges. She is clearly in favour of the former and not the latter which was said to have resulted in the intellectual darkness of both Italy and Spain. The American Civil War, the French Revolution, British India, all should be on the timetable. She had clearly read Newman's *Idea of a University*, published in 1852, which she quotes at some length. Not because she expected girls to read it, however! She liked his emphasis on developing the faculty of judgement.

At the end of this section of *Intellectual Education*, perhaps sensing its enormity, she suggested ways the scheme might be adapted for less able girls.

Shirreff often insisted in this work that she was not challenging the accepted order of things. She believed that women were divinely ordained to hold a subordinate position in relation to men and that men were her superior in physical strength, willpower and mental resilience. She stressed that she was not trying to alter the 'natural and inevitable subordination of women'.[30]

She did not like the tone of the women who insisted on women's rights. Equality might be an ideal but it was not a reality. She accepted that men were superior to women in both strength and mental stamina and had a natural authority over women. She saw it as a temptation to be resisted that women use their feminine guile and charm to manipulate men. She wrote: 'Men's faults and their virtues alike combine to throw them helplessly into the hands of any woman who is not scrupulous in using her power.'[31]

To define such demanding educational standards for girls and then to accept the inevitability of being second best and disqualified from public life on the basis of gender is remarkable.

She accepted that women were not going to be able to (and should not) work outside the home, nor learn a profession, take part in public life, vote, speak at public meetings on a level with men and so on. She wrote: 'What society wants from women is not labour, but refinement, elevation of mind, knowledge making its power felt through moral influences and sound opinions. It wants civilisers of men and education of the young.'[32]

To take up manual work would be to take away livelihoods from women who needed such work. To take up professional roles would be to take away jobs from men and lead to less remuneration for men who needed it. She was suspicious of Florence Nightingale and her band of middle-class unpaid nurses for similar reasons. Moreover, parents would not want their daughters to take their chances, unprotected, in public careers. Such careers demanded severe mental toil and close application, for which women were not equipped. Men would no longer be protectors of women and women would have to face contempt and frustration.

How far she was searching to find reasons here for a position that she felt compelled to take is an interesting question. There is plenty of evidence to suggest that she chafed against all this inferiority. She wanted

---
30. Ibid., p. 295.
31. Ibid., p. 109.
32. Ibid., p. 417ff.

girls to be trained to think of themselves as God's creatures, not as man's subordinate. As society was constituted, or, as she added, as human nature was constituted, she saw no relief. It was always important to remember that what a person is was more important that what a person does, but she wondered how men would cope if similarly repressed. At one point she almost gets angry: 'Unreasoning reverence for man as enjoying the higher position and right of command, the family deification of the right of the strongest, which is only too common.'[33]

She accepted it but the following passage, showing that she possessed a power of irony that reminds one of Newman, is revealing:

> A teacher may form a resolute character and yet must enforce diffidence in conduct and opinion: may inspire lofty aims but must beware of kindling ambition: may teach a bold spirit and a strong will but be content with submission: may insist on love of truth and scorn of the world's folly but also on deference to the world's opinion: may train a spiritual nature to its full powers for a career of dependence, of narrow aims and repressed actions.[34]

Twelve years later, in 1870, the *Contemporary Review* published a short article by Emily Shirreff, entitled 'College Education for Women'.[35] Her views had changed as she herself admitted. No longer was it necessary to argue that 'the mental condition of half the human race is of some national importance'. Society had changed and it was no longer appropriate to look upon domestic life as the one destiny of women. There was ferment and excitement everywhere and women were 'on the eve of gaining an altogether freer position'. Only a few escaped from idleness through intellectual endeavour and now two professions were open to them, medicine and teaching. Women were no longer debarred from high culture nor shut out from employment: 'Now at last she claims justice.' However, she had some concerns. She was clear that women who needed to work should be allowed to do so to support themselves and their dependents. However, she worried about how women could combine marriage with a career. What of the 'responsibility for the welfare of each new generation that God has placed in the hands and bound upon the hearts of women?' Furthermore, would contempt for domestic and family life be an unintended and unfortunate consequence? She insisted (as before) that there was a great power for good

---

33. Ibid., p. 389.
34. Ibid., p. 33.
35. Emily Shirreff, 'College Education for Women', *Contemporary Review*, Vol. 15 (1870).

that women could exert upon society through their domestic influence; and the preparation needed to exercise the callings hitherto exercised by men only dwarfed into insignificance compared with the preparation for that carried out by women in the domestic sphere.

Maria Edgeworth

Fifty years earlier, in 1798, Maria Edgeworth published a book with the more prosaic title, *Practical Education*. Written jointly with her father, this was a monumental work in two volumes. Maria Edgeworth was admired and well known in her day and, through her books, was respected abroad too. As well as having a passion for education, Edgeworth was a novelist and writer of short stories who gained the attention of Walter Scott, to name just one admirer. One of only four women to have been admitted to the Royal Irish Academy, she was clearly an intellectual of some distinction. In her writings she touched on matters of class, race and gender as well as education. John Locke and Jean-Jacques Rousseau were her inspirations.

She wrote that education should be fitted to the needs and interests of the child, a conviction borne out of the experience of being one of a very large family and taking charge of the education of 20 children, her siblings. It is interesting that she would be combining such hands-on practical experience with her strong intellectual abilities.

What is also interesting is that much of her book resonates with that of Emily Shirreff. She insisted that young children should not be overstrained, omitted any discussion of religion, wrote for mothers, insisted on the importance of character and behaviour as part and parcel of education, believed that education was vital to the happiness of society and wanted children to be independent thinkers who took responsibility for their actions. She, too, believed women were the equal of men both morally and intellectually, while at the same time praising domesticity and the female virtues. Accomplishments came under close scrutiny and the idea that they could aid husband-hunting was made to look ridiculous – as was rote learning for the sake of it. Edgeworth could do irony too:

> Her [woman's] imagination must not be raised above the taste for necessary occupations, or the numerous small, but not trifling pleasures of domestic life: her mind must be enlarged, yet the delicacy of her manners must be preserved: her knowledge must be various and her powers of reason unawed by authority; yet she must habitually feel that nice sense of propriety which is at once the guard and charm of every feminine virtue.[36]

36. Maria Edgeworth and Richard L. Edgeworth, *Practical Education*, 2 Vols (London:

In some ways Shirreff's work was the more practical, given that it prescribed a detailed curriculum, although Edgeworth's was not short of practical examples. One particular example was given in some detail: the use of globes (clearly the source of the practice in private schools described by the Taunton Commissioners). In this case, globes were intended to be used in geography lessons. This section was written by her father. He had in mind either silk globes, inflated by bellows or globes of between five and six feet in diameter made of lath and plaster. He suggested that they could be illuminated. Children would mark up the globe as they learned about cities, rivers and towns, working out where to put them using knowledge of latitude and longitude. This would certainly have created excitement.

Shirreff was clearly influenced by *Practical Education*. Perhaps the main difference is that Shirreff's book exhibits a profound religious sense, which is lacking in that of Edgeworth and which gives the former work, in my view, an extra dimension and sense of vocation.

Vera Brittain

Vera Brittain attended St Monica's, a private girls' school in Kingswood, Surrey, run by her aunt in the first years of the twentieth century. It was the practice of the school to allow the pupils to see carefully selected newspaper cuttings, under the influence of an inspired teacher who had a real intellectual bent. In 1911 this teacher introduced Vera to *Woman and Labour*, sometimes called the Bible of the women's movement. The author, Olive Schreiner, issued her manifesto: 'We take all labour to be our province.' A visiting teacher in her last term filled Vera with enthusiasm for Carlyle and Ruskin. There were no final term exams but Brittain wrote of her lessons: 'teaching in the real sense of the word – the creation in immature minds of the power to think, to visualise, to perceive analogies, they could hardly have been surpassed'.[37] Furthermore, from her exclusive private boarding school, a school that did not enter pupils for exams, her life was turned around from that of a leisured lady in Buxton to one, after the war, of studying at Somerville College, Oxford and fame as a writer. She wrote: 'Thus it was, in St Monica's garden ... that I first visualized in rapt childish ecstasy, a world in which women would no longer be the second-rate, unimportant creatures that they were now considered, but the equal and respected companions of men.'[38]

What seems to have happened is that, while private schools still carried on in much the same ways as they had done throughout the nineteenth century, the reforms that had been brought about since the 1850s were

---

J. Johnson, 1798), p. 550.
37. Vera Brittain, *Testament of Youth* (London: Victor Gollancz, 1933), p. 27.
38. Ibid., p. 29.

beginning to have an effect on the quality of women teachers. Girls' education was gradually transformed. Liverpool Institute for Girls was one example. Cheltenham Ladies College, the North London Collegiate and then the founding of the Girls' Public Day School Trust (GPDST) continued the development but perhaps it was the opening of higher education to women that made the real difference. Firstly with Queen's College (1848) and Bedford College (1849) in London. Later Girton (1969) and Newnham (1871) were the first colleges for women in Cambridge. In Oxford Somerville (1879) and Lady Margaret Hall (1879) were followed by St Hugh's (1886) and St Hilda's (1893). The University College which opened in Liverpool in 1881 admitted women from the beginning.

Conclusion

Throughout the greater part of the nineteenth century education for middle-class girls took place either in the home or in private schools and was of variable quality. In these private schools the emphasis was on providing a homely life and training which would fit girls to take up their position in society as a lady dependent on a husband or family. Cultural accomplishments such as music, drawing and dancing were an essential part of the curriculum. Girls came to school and left according to family circumstances with no necessity to attend and no exams to prepare for. The quality of teaching varied and at times was very poor. However, not all teaching in girls' schools was incompetent and intellectually febrile. The subjects studied were much the same as those studied in boys' schools. Expert teachers were often employed and exams are not necessarily the measure of a good education. Intellectual curiosity has never been solely a male preserve and, as we shall see, Eliza Lowe's private boarding school was not lacking in this respect. As always, it is the quality of the teaching that counts and this is best judged case by case. One should add that a studious girl will always find a way to learn. From about 1860 onwards things began to change. Training for governesses and teachers was formalised and exams hitherto open only to boys became available to girls. In the 1870s university education, though not qualifications, was opened to women. This marked the beginning of a profound change in attitude as to why a girl was educated. It was also, coincidentally, the point at which S. Anne's school in Abbots Bromley was opened as the forerunner of girls' education in the Woodard tradition.

This then was the milieu into which Eliza Lowe was born and ran her school. Part 2 investigates her life's work in education, beginning in the early part of the century and continuing till her death in 1872.

Part Two
The Story of Eliza Lowe

Chapter 3

Early Life of Eliza Lowe

Whitchurch

Eliza Lowe was born in 1803 in Whitchurch, Shropshire, the second child of Samuel Lowe and his wife Maria. Her father was a lawyer – or attorney, as he was referred to at the time. A record of 1799 in the *Chester Courant* shows that he was authorised to collect debts owing to one of his deceased clients:

> Whereas Richard Pate Manning, late of Whitchurch . . . surgeon, hath, by letter of attorney, authorized Samuel Lowe, of Whitchurch aforesaid, gentleman, to collect and receive all debts due to him.[1]

In the records of Whitchurch Museum there is a reference to Samuel Lowe being the 'Captain and Company Commander 1st Co. of the Whitchurch Volunteers'. This may have been part of the volunteer movement during the Napoleonic wars when many areas set up home guards in case of invasion. Members were often members of the elite in the area. It would appear that Samuel Lowe was a respected member of the community.

The family lived in St Mary's Street and there is a description of the house they lived in, from the details of an auction held on 14 August 1819 (see below). With nine bedrooms and generous accommodation on the ground floor, it was big enough for the family, which by 1819 had grown to ten surviving children. Interestingly, the notice of auction stated that the property was well adapted for use as a school. The property was sold with ownership of a family pew in prime position in the local church.[2]

A history of Hurstpierpoint College by Peter King maintains that Eliza ran a school in Whitchurch.[3] The advert in the next page would seem to

---

1. *Chester Courant*, 10 December 1799.
2. *Chester Chronicle*, 23 July 1819.
3. Peter King, *Hurstpierpoint College 1849-1995: The School by the Downs* (Bognor

> CAPITAL
> *Freehold House in Whitchurch.*
>
> TO BE SOLD BY AUCTION,
> *By Lokin and Son,*
>
> At the White Lion Inn, in Whitchurch Salop, on Saturday, the 14th day of August, 1819, at 3 o'clock in the afternoon, subject to conditions then to be produced.
>
> A VERY SUBSTANTIAL and COMMODIOUS HOUSE, with the Stable, Brewhouse, and other convenient buildings; Yard and Garden thereto belonging, situate in St. Mary's-street, in the town of Whitchurch, and late the residence of Mr. Lowe, Solicitor.
>
> The House is well adapted for a genteel family, or a school—It consists of a handsome entrance hall, and staircase, a dining room, 19½ by 17 feet, two good parlours, one 18 by 17 feet, and the other 16 by 15 feet, a spacious kitchen, a scullery, and pantry, on the ground floor, with three excellent cellars under; a drawing-room, 20 by 17 feet, and 5 good lodging rooms on the first floor, and 4 other lodging rooms in the attic story.
>
> There is a good pump on the premises, from which excellent water is conveyed into the scullery and brewhouse. There are also, an entire Pew, well situated in the middle aisle, and the whole (except one sitting) of another pew in the organ gallery, at Whitchurch Church, belonging to the property.
>
> Immediate possession may be had; and for a view of the premises, and further particulars, application may be made at the office of Messrs WRIGHT, BROOKS, and LEE, Solicitors, Whitchurch.

Fig. 6 Auction of the house in Whitchurch.

support the possibility of a school, although whether it was run by Eliza is less clear as she would have been only sixteen or seventeen years old when the house was sold. However, a later notice in the press reveals that Mrs Lowe ran a school with her daughter in Liverpool, so it is possible that Eliza was helping her mother at this earlier date.

BURTON-ON-TRENT

By August 1819 the family had moved to Burton-on-Trent, then in Derbyshire, where they had links. Samuel's sister Mary had married the Reverend John Clarke who, at this period, was headmaster of Rugeley Grammar School and vicar of the parish, some 20 miles from Burton. According to family records, Eliza was chiefly brought up by her aunt in Rugeley where she received a very good education.[4] The Clarkes had no children of their own. When Mary Clarke was widowed, she went to live with Eliza Lowe in Bootle and then in Mayfield, Middlesex (of which more later). It makes sense that she would go to live with a niece to whom she had given a home. In addition, when Edward Clarke Lowe was born in 1823, he was named after John Clarke.

At Rugeley Grammar School Eliza is not found in the list of pupils kept by John Clarke at the school between 1817 and 1822. However, her elder brother Charles was a pupil there in 1817 and her younger brother Samuel arrived at Christmas 1817, aged twelve, and was still there in 1822.[5] The school was for boys, of course. It is quite probable that Eliza and one or more of her sisters were educated there on an informal basis. This sort of arrangement was quite common. For instance, when Edward Lowe was headmaster of the Woodard school at Hurstpierpoint, his wife's much younger sister, Alice Mary Coleridge, was educated there.

Regis: Phillimore, 1997), p. 14.
4. *Lucy Landor Memorandum*, notes dictated by Lucy Landor to Walter Noble Landor, Tim Tomlinson, private papers.
5. *List of boys at Rugeley School, c. 1817-1822,* Staffordshire County Record Office, Ref No: D(W)1788/P10/B6.

Chapter 3. Early Life of Eliza Lowe

John Clarke is credited with restoring a classical education to Rugeley Grammar School and enlarging the buildings to allow for both improvement and expansion.[6] There is an amusing record of an invitation to a friend to come to dinner written by his wife Mary, followed by a longer one by Clarke to show that he too could write verse.

From Mrs Mary Clarke to Mrs Thomas Landor

My dearest Friend   This note I send
in hopes that you,   and your husband too,
will come to dine,   if the day be fine,
with us tomorrow;   nor cause the sorrow,
which the perusal   of a refusal,
will give to both,   upon my troth.
And so I pray,   you'll not say nay.
Adieu from me,   your true M.C.
   Rugeley Wed: evening
Make us your debtors, for Peter's Setters[7]
and in a crack,   we'll send them back.

From John Clarke to Thomas Landor

Dear Tom
I won't allow my rib,
Exultingly to cock her jib,
   As if none else could rhyme it:

So I'm resolved for once to see
And you shall judge twixt her & me –
   If I can't also chime it.

We've had today a sumptuous feast
– Quite unbecoming in a Priest –
   To treat Dame Hopkins' palate

Fish, flesh, & fowl, & sav'ry jelly
With soup that's made from Vermicelli
   And parmesan & sallad

---

6. Ernest Toye, *Rugeley: 150 Years of a Country Town* (Landor Local History Society, 2018), pp. 91 and 113.
7. Possibly this is a reference to a painting by the contemporary artist Johann Wenzel Peter titled *A Pointer and Two Setters*.

Pitchford & Letty Embrey came,
And many a beau, & many a dame,
   To eat our grand collation.

Our Colwich friends agree to stay,
To pass with us another day,
   Sans any hesitation.

Now, if your wife and you, quite snug,
Will come & taste the hash & jug,
   Making from Hare & Pheasant;

Remnants of creams, & custards too,
And other dainties not a few,
   T'will make it wondrous pleasant

I've often heard it said, at least,
The next day's better than the feast,
   And who shall dare dispute it.

If choicest dainties are set by,
And choicest friends, & gaity,
Succeed to pomp & pageantry
   No one will sure refute it.

Then come – our pleasures to increase;
Soon must my social comforts cease
   Nor think that I am humming

Tis not because my heart grows cold,
Tis not because I'm growing old,
   Black Monday is forthcoming!
      Yours truly J.C.

These amusing and cleverly crafted poems give an insight into life in the Clarke household, fun, good food and sociability but also powers of literary expression, a household in which Eliza grew up and, as will become clear later, emulated.

Samuel and Maria Lowe's thirteenth child, Charlotte, was born in 1819 and baptised in St Modwen's Church, Burton-on-Trent the same year. An obituary for Mary Manley Lowe, their third child, records Samuel as having lived at The Abbey, Burton.[8] The Abbey, close to St Modwen's Church, had originally been used as an infirmary on the edge of the extensive grounds of

---

8. *Wellington Journal*, 16 September 1876.

Chapter 3. Early Life of Eliza Lowe 53

the monastery, which escaped destruction under Thomas Cromwell. The picture below shows The Abbey and the church shortly before they moved there. It looks an idyllic scene.[9]

Fig. 7 Former monastic infirmary and St Modwen's Church from the 1790s.

The Abbey (in 2020, The Winery) was a separate, detached annex built in the time of William de Bromley who was Abbot of Burton from 1316 to 1329. As well as a great hall, it is known to have included an infirmary.[10] Remains of the medieval building are still incorporated in the present-day building but most of what exists now is a mock Tudor facing constructed at a later date. This is clearly visible in the modern-day photograph below. The building is still impressive. The large chimney can be seen on both images.

Liverpool

The family were still in Burton-on-Trent in July 1822[11] but before the end of 1823 the family had moved to Liverpool where Samuel continued as an attorney with offices in Exchange Street.[12] Exchange Street led into

9. www.british-history.ac.uk/vch/staffs/vol9/pp48-53, accessed 24 December 2020.
10. http://www.burton-on-trent.org.uk/burton-abbey-structual-history, accessed 9 April 2019.
11. The date is found in articles signed for son Samuel's solicitor training.
12. Gore's *Directory of Liverpool, 1825* lists him at 7 Exchange Street. The first ever printed directory of Liverpool was published in 1766 by John Gore (1738-1803). It contained an alphabetical list of the merchants, tradesmen and principal inhabitants of the town of Liverpool with their respective addresses. Initially quite irregular, it became biennial in 1803 until 1870, when it began to appear annually.

Fig. 8 The Abbey, where Samuel Lowe and his family lived.

Exchange Flags, a grand piazza in the centre of the town where merchants transacted business in the open air, absolutely the right address for an attorney. We can have no certainty about why Samuel Lowe moved his family and business as he did. However, one may speculate. Whitchurch was a small town on the Welsh border; Burton was not big either, but it was growing and had a major role to play in the build-up of industry and must have seemed more progressive. The move to Liverpool cemented the advance. Liverpool was shortly to be at the height of its success, with a rapidly increasing population and many opportunities for attorneys. Below is the signature of Samuel Lowe taken from articles signed with his son:

Fig. 9 Samuel Lowe's signature.

Everton

The first place in Liverpool where the family lived was the village of Everton on the outskirts of the city. It was here that the fourteenth child, Edward Clarke Lowe, was born in December 1823 and baptised in Holy Trinity Church, Wavertree on 16 January 1824.

Chapter 3. Early Life of Eliza Lowe

Everton was a fashionable, desirable area for the burgeoning professional and commercial classes. The family, despite having to provide for twelve children, must have been comfortably off. Liverpool at this time was a thriving commercial city where merchants earned vast sums and lawyers could expect plenty of work and, if they were good, handsome fees.

Liverpool Picturebook Online says of Everton: 'In more peaceful times the wealthier merchants of Liverpool chose it for their country mansions', and in 1824 it was described as follows: 'This village has become a very favourite residence of the gentry of Liverpool, and for the salubrity of its air and its vicinity to the sea, may not inaptly be called the Montpellier of the county.'

The family settled in 1 Everton Crescent. The Crescent was formed of sixteen houses, construction began in 1807 following the purchase of two fields along what was to become the main thoroughfare from Everton into Liverpool. Samuel Lowe would have had to travel only three kilometres from the Crescent to his office in Exchange Street. According to Robert Syers who wrote a history of the area, the houses were 'well calculated for the reception and uses of large, respectable families, most of the mansions affording . . . ample space and fitness to entertain expensive parties'.[13] Other much smaller buildings were later built behind the Crescent to its detriment, robbing it of the many advantages it had at the outset.

Around the corner from Everton Crescent, at 14 and 15 Everton Terrace, Miss Anne Sharp ran a private girls' school. Anne Sharp was a close confidante of Jane Austen whom she had met while working as a governess for Jane's brother Edward in the south of England. Claire Tomalin, in her biography of Jane Austen, says that Anne wrote plays for the children to perform. She was asked for advice by Austen and they kept up a correspondence after Anne left her employment in the south. One source says that by 1823 Sharp was running a boarding school in Everton.[14] According to the 1841 census she was still there with two teachers, three servants and eleven pupils, the latter mostly aged fourteen and fifteen. Syers' description of Everton suggests a lot of neighbourly activity and it is inconceivable that the Lowes did not know Anne Sharp. Anne Sharp, highly respected by Jane Austen, must have had remarkable gifts. She clearly ran a successful school. This begs the question as to whether she inspired Eliza Lowe.

---

13. Robert Syers, *The History of Everton* (Liverpool: G. & J. Robinson, 1830), p. 238. See digitised version on the Everton local history website: www.evertonhistory.com, https://archive.org/details/historyofeverton00syeruoft, accessed 11 Feb, 2021.
14. https://losttribeofeverton.com/histories/jane-austens-everton-link/, accessed 27 January 2021.

Fig. 10 Map of Everton, 1851.

Everton Terrace and Everton Crescent are long gone but the 1851 Ordnance Survey (OS) map of Liverpool shows that they were but a short walk apart. Everton Crescent is shown at the bottom of the map opposite, facing south, and Everton Terrace, facing west, is nearer the top of the map. This map, surveyed well after the Lowes left the area, shows that smaller properties had multiplied in the area. Note the long gardens of the Crescent, compared with the neighbouring houses. The properties on Everton Terrace look to be grander, with properties widely spaced and large gardens back and front.

Everton Terrace stood further up the hill from the Crescent and properties there would have had a stunning view over the Mersey to the Wirral, and out to sea. The photo below gives a feel of the elevation, taken close to where Everton Terrace was located. There is still a section of the road and walling in existence today.[15]

Fig. 11 Everton Terrace view.

The first picture below shows Everton c. 1820 and the second c. 1843, both were the work of W.G. Herdman who lived in Everton and painted many fine pictures of Liverpool in the nineteenth century. The buildings show very little difference but what looks like a pall of smoke rises in the background of the later painting. The family were shortly to move out of Everton and so avoided the unpleasant effects of industrialisation.

---
15. Photo taken in summer 2019 with author in the foreground.

Fig. 12 (top) Everton Village, c. 1820.
Fig. 13 (bottom) Everton Village, c. 1843.

Bootle

In the summer of 1824 the family moved three miles north to Linacre, the part of Bootle closest to the sea, close to the Mersey estuary and the port of Liverpool. In 1774 it was described this way:

Fig. 14 The North Shore.

Bootle cum Linacre lies near the sea on a very sandy soil and contains some well-built houses. A very copious spring of fine, soft, pure water rises near it, which about half a mile below turns a mill and soon after falls into the sea at Bootle Bay. Linacre, a pretty rural village, is a distinct township, but a member of the manor of Bootle. It lies adjacent to the sea, on the west.[16]

In 1812 the tourist's guide, *Stranger in Liverpool*, reported: 'The ride along the beach was, in the summer, remarkably pleasant and much frequented. The sands were hard and smooth, and the wind, especially if westerly, cool and refreshing.' In 1824 Baines' *Lancashire Directory* called Linacre: 'A pleasant marine village . . . much resorted to in the summer season as a sea bathing place.'

The lithograph above by W.G. Herdman shows a scene from 1790. Bathing machines are visible on the shoreline and ships can be seen entering and leaving the port of Liverpool. Bootle lay slightly to the north.

So, a desirable area in which to bring up the twelve surviving children of the family. However, there is evidence that Samuel Lowe had incurred debts.[17] A later chapter relates how family friends (the Langtons) moved to Bootle and rented property there because it was cheaper. The Lowes may have moved for similar reasons.

---

16. William Enfield, *An Essay towards the History of Leverpool* (London: Joseph Johnson, 1774).
17. Tim Tomlinson, private papers.

Chapter 4

Eliza's School in Bootle and Seaforth

The School in Bootle

On 8 June 1824 an advertisement appeared in the *Manchester Mercury*. The same notice appeared three days later in the *Liverpool Mercury*:

> ESTABLISHMENT of MRS. and MISS LOWE, of EVERTON CRESCENT, for the Education of Young Ladies, will, after the ensuing Midsummer Vacation, REOPEN Monday the ninth of August next, at Linacre Marsh, near Bootle, Liverpool, well known as one of the most healthy and pleasant situations on the Coast, and within four miles of Liverpool.
> TERMS:
> Boarders, 35 Guineas per annum. Entrance, two Guineas,
> Day Boarders 10 Guineas per annum. Entrance, one Guinea
> Day Pupils, a limited number, 10 Guineas per annum. Entrance, one Guinea. Italian, French, Music, Dancing, Drawing, and Arithmetic, on usual terms.

The Lowe establishment must have been in operation while they were living in Everton. Eliza, as the oldest daughter, would have been known as Miss Lowe. She was 21 in 1824 and listed along with her mother as running the school. Mothers generally educated the girls in middle-class families (see Chapter 2) so Mrs Lowe did what many others did and took on pupils to join her already existing class. Whether or not financial difficulties were the reason for running the school is unclear but Samuel was still alive and so the school was running concurrently with his work as an attorney.[1]

Following the custom of the time they did not use the word school but rather the more neutral 'establishment'. Nonetheless, it was engaged in education. The extra charge for certain subjects was the norm for the

---

1. Gore's *Directory of Liverpool, 1827* cites Samuel Lowe as an attorney, living in Linacre.

time and implied that outside teachers (masters) were employed for such matters. The move to Linacre may have attracted more pupils, with the opportunity of a larger property and the appeal of a seaside environment. The fact that the notice appeared in a Manchester newspaper may imply that they already had pupils from this commercially successful city and hoped for more. Linacre Marsh was directly on the coast. It offered sands and sea with opportunities for bathing and horse-riding. It was not yet built up and a 'pleasant marine village'. The fees were in line with other private schools of the time. Teachers and pupils would have had a short walk to the beach and it is certain that they did go swimming.

Two years after the move to Bootle another notice appeared in the newspaper:

> Mrs. and the Miss Lowes conduct an Establishment for a limited number of YOUNG LADIES, on a plan which unites the comforts of home with the means of acquiring a useful and accomplished education. Their house is pleasantly situated near the Sea.
> TERMS:
> Board and Instruction in English Grammar, History, Geography, Writing and Arithmetic, and plain and ornamental Needlework:
> To Young Ladies under 12 years of age 40 Guineas per annum; above that age, 45 Guineas per annum plus French, Italian, Music. Dancing, and Drawing, by the best Masters, on the usual terms. Laundress, 4 guineas. No charge made for entrance to the House. Reference may be made to: the Rev. J. Brookes, Everton; the Rev. W. Rawson, Seaforth; and P.W. Brancker, Esq., Liverpool.[2]

There were some interesting differences from two years earlier. Miss Lowe has become 'the Miss Lowes'. Eliza and her mother have been joined by one or more of the sisters. At this point Maria, the second sister, would have been 20 and Mary Manley, who was to remain with Eliza all her life, 18. The fees have jumped rather dramatically but the entrance fee has been dropped. Subjects covered as standard are listed and now include arithmetic. The most striking difference was that no day pupils are admitted. It would seem that the school is doing well and enough boarders are being recruited. The notice is also longer (and therefore more expensive). A fledgling philosophy is in evidence. There is a plan. Pupils may expect the 'comforts of home' while at the same time 'acquiring a useful and accomplished education'. This would seem to put the school on a par with most other private schools of the time. Naturally, of course, anything radically different would not have appealed to parents. An appropriate education for girls destined to

2. *Liverpool Mercury*, Friday, 29 December 1826.

life in the home included learning how to provide home comforts. An 'accomplished education', as shown in Chapter 2, indicated achieving a competency in subjects that would be expected in polite society, such as music, dancing and foreign languages, for which parents would pay extra.

The inclusion of Italian was unusual and may have been a specialism of the Lowes. A later chapter explores this aspect. A 'useful' education begs the question 'useful for what?' Emily Shirreff and Maria Edgeworth both had clear ideas of what constituted a useful education but a brief notice in a newspaper cannot be so specific. The references to the Reverends Rawson and Brookes doubtless reflect the family's Anglican church attendance in Everton and Seaforth (the next village north of Linacre). Brancker was a well-known Liverpool businessman who had been an alderman and must have been a friend of the family.

The fees and subjects covered clearly show that the school was aimed at girls from wealthy families. The advert of 1826 is the last I could find, indicating that Mrs Lowe and her daughters did not need to put a notice in the paper after this date. One of the wealthiest and most respected merchants in Liverpool, Thomas Horsfall, sent at least three girls to the school.[3] He was Mayor of Liverpool and an MP for several years and lived in Everton. He and his brothers were responsible for the building of several fine churches in the city.

Mrs and Miss Edmondson's Seminary

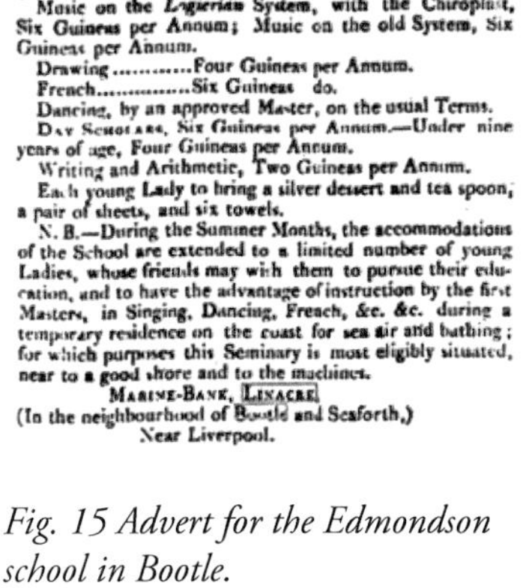
TERMS OF

Mrs. and Miss Edmondson's Seminary.

BOARD, and Instruction in English, Geography, History, Writing, and Arithmetic, Thirty-five Guineas per Annum; Entrance Two Guineas.

Music on the *Logierian* System, with the Chiroplast, Six Guineas per Annum; Music on the old System, Six Guineas per Annum.

Drawing ....Four Guineas per Annum.

French...............Six Guineas do.

Dancing, by an approved Master, on the usual Terms.

Day Scholars, Six Guineas per Annum.—Under nine years of age, Four Guineas per Annum.

Writing and Arithmetic, Two Guineas per Annum.

Each young Lady to bring a silver dessert and tea spoon, a pair of sheets, and six towels.

N. B.—During the Summer Months, the accommodations of the School are extended to a limited number of young Ladies, whose friends may wish them to pursue their education, and to have the advantage of instruction by the first Masters, in Singing, Dancing, French, &c. &c. during a temporary residence on the coast for sea air and bathing; for which purposes this Seminary is most eligibly situated, near to a good shore and to the machines.

Marine-Bank, Linacre,
(In the neighbourhood of Bootle and Seaforth,)
Near Liverpool.

Fig. 15 Advert for the Edmondson school in Bootle.

Nearby in the area was another private establishment for girls.[4]

The Edmondsons used the term 'Seminary'; rather more educationally specific than 'establishment'. The fees were similar and so were the subjects on offer (no Italian, however) and music was a speciality. The 'Logierian System' was a relatively new fashion, developed by the German Johann Bernhard Logier and widely used as a method of piano tuition. It involved a chiroplast (from the Greek word for hand), a wooden contraption which forced pupils to hold their hands in the correct position. Nevertheless, the Edmondsons hedged

3. *Lucy Landor Memorandum*, notes dictated by Lucy Landor to Walter Noble Landor, Tim Tomlinson, private papers.
4. *Staffordshire Advertiser*, 26 May 1821.

their bets by also offering the 'old System'. They also came up with a novel idea of inviting friends of pupils to sample the school in the summer holidays, perhaps with the idea that the friends would then want to be pupils throughout the year. As with the Lowes, the proximity of the sea was a particular attraction.

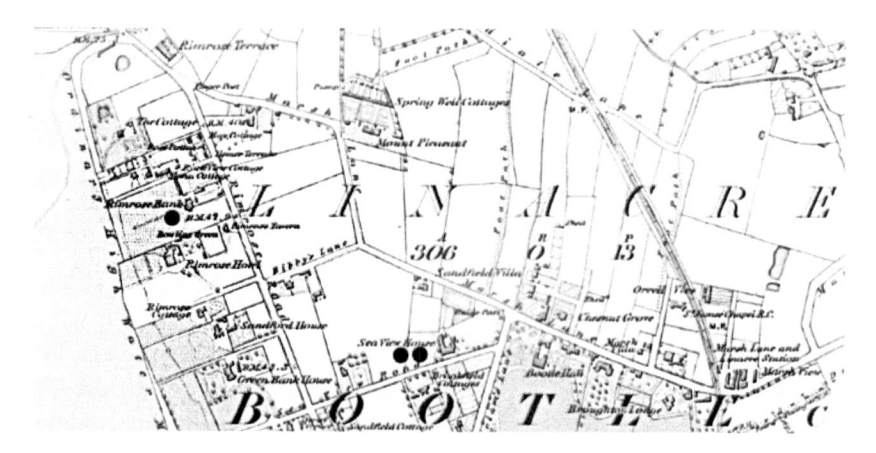

Fig. 16 Location of the two schools in Bootle.

The area of Linacre in close proximity to the sea was not extensive but it has proved difficult to identify the establishments. The Edmondsons were located in Marine Bank, Linacre in the neighbourhood of Bootle and Seaforth, near to the bathing machines, implying that they were next to the shore.[5] The above OS map, dating from the 1840s, does not show Marine Bank. There is, however, a large property called Rimrose Bank in Rimrose Road which ran parallel to the shore (one dot). Perhaps that was where they ran their seminary. At right angles to Rimrose Road and a little further south was Sea View Road. A little way inland on this road was a very large property called Sea View House, certainly large enough to accommodate the needs of the Lowes (two dots). The Lowes were a family of fourteen and needed room for servants and boarders. Sea View House was in the tenancy of Thomas Woodward, a corn merchant from 1825 until 1832 and in 1833 it was run as a prep school for boys by John Fleming. The dates that Woodward was in residence at Sea View coincide with the establishment of the Lowes who must have left for Seaforth by late 1833. It was quite common for multiple tenancies at the time, even in large properties so this is a possible location for Eliza's school.

---

5. Bathing machines were an eighteenth-century invention to preserve modesty. Bathers would climb in, change into swimwear and be drawn into the water inside the wooden caravans, from where they emerged down steps into the water. Machines were often pulled by horses.

Fig. 17 (top) Bathing machines.
Fig. 18 (bottom) Seaforth House.

Above at Fig 17 is another Herdman painting. It is dated 1830 and shows horse-drawn bathing machines on the North Shore. In the distance can be seen ladies stepping out from the machines into the water and beyond this a windmill, possibly that shown on Fig. 14 The North Shore, p. 58. Herdman published a first edition of *Pictorial Relics of Ancient Liverpool* in 1843 in which he wrote of the mansion shown in the painting above: 'It was a public house of great resort, having a fine view of the river and of vessels entering the port'. It was once owned by a Dutch settler called Van Dries and there is a street in the area today named after him.

THE SCHOOL IN SEAFORTH

At the beginning of the nineteenth century, just north of the area in the map earlier (see Fig. 18), was a sparsely inhabited area, a hamlet with a few cottages and sandhills populated largely by rabbits. This was all to change when the wealthy merchant John Gladstone, father of four-time Prime Minister William Gladstone, built a grand country mansion there in 1813 (see Fig 17). According to local historian Allan Johnston, Gladstone intended to set himself up as a country gentleman and, as such, to be a benefactor of the local populace. He built cottages, a parsonage, a farm and a church. His country mansion was richly planted with trees and shrubs, fruit and flowers and had a clear view out to sea, which lay only a quarter of a mile away. The original painting is by John Preston Neale from the British Library's 'Mechanical Curator' collection and dates from 1818.

Gladstone named his mansion Seaforth House because his wife was related to Lord Seaforth. As the area became more desirable and was built up, it became known as Seaforth, a name it retains to this day. Next, John Gladstone built St Thomas' Church and brought the Reverend William Rawson to live in the parsonage, where he set up a prep school which William Gladstone attended. When Rawson arrived to take up his position as minister of St Thomas' Church, he declared: 'Well, I don't know where I am coming to, but there is no fear of my dying of hunger.'[6] This was a reference to the rabbits that he would have met en route from the ferry.

Rawson was known to the Lowe family and it was he who officiated at the funeral of Eliza's father in 1827. The family must have attended Rawson's church in Seaforth. Amongst the 20 or so letters that Edward Lowe wrote to William Gladstone is one in which Lowe mentions a childhood memory. It is a rather touching account. On 19 July 1865 Gladstone visited Liverpool where he made a speech and Lowe took the opportunity to make contact and tell Gladstone of the Seaforth connection. Apologising for 'obtruding upon him', he wrote:

> that it has happened to me that from my infancy you and Oxford have always been identified in my mind. It was when a very little boy who used to play among the 'Sandhills of Seaforth' that I was lifted

---
6. Quoted in Allan Johnston, *Seaforth: House and Hall*, private paper.

Chapter 4. Eliza's School in Bootle and Seaforth

up in Seaforth Church to look over the back of the green baized pew at young William Gladstone who had just come down from Oxford honours thick upon him. I did not know what an Oxford class man meant but I was told and remembered that you were one. It may be this childish incident, most vividly remembered that has strengthened through life the interest with which I have followed your career.[7]

This must have been in 1831 when Gladstone graduated with a double first from Oxford. Edward Lowe would have been eight at the time. Linacre bordered Seaforth and so a young boy living in Linacre would play on the sands of Seaforth and the family would have walked to the nearby church.

The Gladstones moved back to Scotland some time before 1834 and Seaforth House was rented out. It seems that land belonging to the house was gradually sold off and houses were built between the house and the sea. The map (see Fig. 19), published in 1850, of a survey undertaken between 1845 and 1848, shows a row of substantial houses called Claremont Place, on Crosby Road, between Seaforth House and the sea and around the corner into Church Road. Some of the houses in Church Road were described by Jane Carlyle, wife of the renowned historian and social commentator, Thomas Carlyle, during one of her frequent visits to the Paulets who rented Seaforth House. She enjoyed the area so much that she was thinking of finding a house to rent in Seaforth for herself in the summer months:

I went in the afternoon to look at really good houses just for curiosity – you remember those handsome villas in front of Seaforth House two and two, together – well – they are as large handsome houses as heart could desire with stable and coach house and all sorts of 'curiosities and niceties' and the rent of these is only sixty five pounds.[8]

Church Road is the road in which St Thomas' Church was built; the road is still there today.

It was into one of the properties in Claremont Place that the Lowe family moved and where Eliza continued her school. By this time her mother Maria had died and her elder brother Charles was established as a partner in the solicitor's practice of Duncan, Lowe and Ratcliffe in Exchange Street, Liverpool. Gore's *Directory of Liverpool, 1835* records Eliza as running a boarding school in Seaforth and lists Charles, described as an attorney, in

---
7. *Gladstone Papers*, MS 44407, British Library, f. 43.
8. From www.carlyleletters.dukejournals.org, 15 September 1845. Accessed 20 December 2020.

the same property. The family seems to have established itself in the area as shown by a newspaper report that appeared in the *Liverpool Mail* of 5 October 1839. The paper reported the laying of a foundation stone for a new church in Waterloo (situated adjacent to Seaforth): 'It was intended that the pupils of the respective seminaries in Seaforth, conducted by Rev. W. Rawson, Mrs Davenport and Miss Lowe should have walked in procession to the ground. . . . [I]t was impossible for ladies to venture abroad.'

The weather was atrocious and the ceremony had to go ahead minus the pupils and their teachers. It is a lengthy report and includes full details of the prayers, readings and speech made by Rawson. In the middle of the report, in brackets, is a paragraph in which the reporter records thanks to Mr Lowe of 'Radcliffe, Duncan and Lowe' for his assistance in reporting Rawson's address: 'of which from the rain, and our position at the time with reference to the speaker, we could scarcely note a word.'[9]

Eliza's brother must have been a keen supporter of the project and wanted Rawson's address to be accurately reported. He was keen on contributing to the papers as will become evident later in this chapter. He would certainly have had inside information about the intended attendance of Eliza's pupils.

THE LOCATION OF ELIZA'S SCHOOL

Fig. 19 Map showing location of Eliza's school.

By means of a study of the census records, newspaper reports and maps, such as the above, it is possible to locate exactly which Eliza's property was. It was the one marked with a black spot. All of this land was originally part

---

9. The firm was Duncan, Lowe and Radcliffe. Perhaps in haste to deliver copy the reporter got the name of the firm wrong.

Chapter 4. Eliza's School in Bootle and Seaforth 67

of Gladstone's estate. It can be seen that her property and the one on either side were on land once part of what looks like a shrubbery belonging to Seaforth House and in fact by 1871 (after Eliza had moved to Middlesex) the property was called 'Shrubbery'.

It is likely that Eliza was the first to occupy the property. The houses cannot have been built until the early 1830s since the Gladstones were still in residence. She was well established there by 1836. In addition to the entry in Gore's *Directory* of 1835, there exists a letter from a pupil at the school in Seaforth dated April 1836 (see Chapter 6).

Bankruptcy of Charles Lowe

In 1841 something of a bombshell landed. A fiat for bankruptcy against elder brother Charles was issued and he was ordered to appear on 12 July and 10 August 1841 to face proceedings at the Clarendon Rooms, South John Street, Liverpool.[10] On 27 August two weeks or so later, a detailed notice of sale appeared in the Liverpool Mail. From this notice it is clear that Charles Lowe had bought a large amount of land from John Gladstone on which he had begun to build speculatively. The map below (Fig. 20) marks all the properties in his ownership. The sale details record five houses and three plots

Fig. 20 Map showing Charles Lowe's properties.

of land suitable for building houses. The one house which was not recorded as newly built is that which was 'in the occupation of the Misses Lowe' (plot 3). All the properties were said to have been built to a high standard by Samuel and James Holme, a well-known and respected firm. They built St George's Hall and the County Sessions House, two fine buildings in the centre of Liverpool which still stand today. One large plot of land was also said to be in the occupation of the Misses Lowe, on the map above marked 8.

10. Reported in the *London Gazette*, 29 June 1841.

The buildings on either side of the Lowe house (see Fig. 20) were possibly part of her establishment. In 1841 there were 44 people listed in the census as resident with Eliza as head of the household and it would be difficult to accommodate 44 people in one house. The sales particulars of 1841 list offices as part of the property and this would seem to imply separate buildings. In 1851 there were 29 people listed as resident in the census, in 1861 32 and in 1871 just fourteen. Perhaps the buildings were gradually sold off and the number of pupils fell because of lack of space. Certainly by 1871 the properties were in single occupation.

All of this means that Eliza's school in Seaforth was situated in what was a very large landscaped park with ample buildings to carry on a substantial school.

Charles seems to have rented the houses out and Eliza was no exception. Interestingly, Eliza signed a lease for the property on 12 July 1839, with a term of fourteen years at an annual rent of £175, rather more than the £65 Jane Carlyle cited for properties along Church Road. This lease secured the property for her after Charles' bankruptcy.

In 1845 a notice of sale appeared again; this time for her property and one other property, also rented with a lease.[11] The sale particulars are (naturally) effusive:

> Both Houses are also surrounded nearly all round with Stone walls. They command a beautiful view of the River Mersey, and the Welsh Coast for many miles; and they are secured from annoyance by buildings on the land opposite, the same being subject to restrictions which preclude the erection thereon of any Houses except single Villa or two Villas under one roof.

It may be that 1839 was the year when things started to go wrong for Charles. Perhaps this was why he arranged that year for a lease to be signed securing Eliza a period of fourteen years in the property. He was not without ability and foresight. He had held a partnership with a respected firm of solicitors for some time. However, his bankruptcy led to the dissolving of his partnership with Duncan and Ratcliffe and effectively the end of his career as an attorney and as a property speculator, in Britain at any rate.

A year after the bankruptcy proceedings, on 8 April 1842, a court case was reported in *The Legal Guide*.[12] The case was an action on behalf of the

---
11. *The Liverpool Standard and General Commercial Advertiser*, 1 July 1845.
12. *The Legal Guide* was a weekly periodical which ran between 1838 and 1843. The

Chapter 4. Eliza's School in Bootle and Seaforth

Crown Building Society against solicitors for failing to carry out adequate searches on a property for which they had granted Lowe a mortgage. A proper search would have revealed that Lowe already had a mortgage on the property, one which took priority in the event of the borrower reneging on payments. The solicitors, who were Lowe's friends and had been recommended by him, were found negligent and ordered to pay £1,340 to the Society, a very large sum. The solicitors had trusted Lowe and not subjected the mortgage to proper scrutiny. The details were not entirely clear but Lowe had engineered the loan fraudulently, and the solicitors paid dearly for their trust in him.

In the week following reports of the case were carried in many local newspapers across the country: in Durham, Hull, Taunton, Shrewsbury, Carmarthen, Newry and Londonderry, to name a few. It was even covered in *The Times* on 12 April. Some of the reports went into minute detail and it is clear that the case excited great interest.[13] The solicitor defending Lowe declared that 'he felt greater anxiety than in any case with which he had been connected'. It was important to the legal profession that trust was not lost and, equally, the same could be said for the building societies which were springing up all over the country. The impression was given that all concerned in the case were honest and reputable men. So, the case was summed up as 'one of those slips to which the most careful are occasionally liable'. Even the prosecuting solicitor spoke of Charles Lowe in delicate tones and in a way that solicits pity. He was after all one of them. He declared: '[of Mr. Lowe] he wished to say nothing harsh, as he was a fallen and, he hoped, a repentant man'.

Lowe had been honest about his creditors to the solicitor who acted for him in the bankruptcy proceedings a year earlier. He told the solicitor about the two mortgages on the piece of land and gave details of those involved. The solicitor then called together the two parties owed money, in an effort to broker some sort of deal whereby the loss was shared and his client spared exposure for his wrongdoing. He is reported as saying at the meeting that, if agreement was not reached, 'he should advise Lowe to leave the country'. As has been shown, the case did go to court and Lowe's wrongdoings were fully exposed.

After the court hearing Charles Lowe moved to live with his brother John Manley Lowe who was serving as a priest in St Ambrose Vicarage in rural

---

case was reported in Vol 7, p.379. See https://en.wikisource.org/wiki/The_Legal_Guide, accessed 20 December 2020.

13. The following quotations are taken from *The Liverpool Standard and General Commercial Advertiser*, 12 April 1842.

Grindleton, at the time in West Yorkshire. However, in December 1843 Charles left from London for Australia. A family letter dated 2 December 1843 stated:

> Charles Lowe is expected today or tomorrow to take leave, he is to sail on Tuesday morning for Australia, where he is going to commence business as an attorney; his creditors have withdrawn all opposition, & a sum of money has been raised by his friends to pay his passage out & give a few pounds on his arrival at his destination – he is whilst in London to stay in Montague Place, & his Brothers John & Edward have been invited here (11 Montague Street).[14]

The worry about Charles had affected the family. The letter continued: 'Mrs. Lowe [the wife of William Lowe in whose house nephew Charles was staying] has had a very sharp attack, yesterday she had leeches for the third time. I have not heard how she is this morning. Aunt Clarke is much worried, both by Mrs. L. being so ill & by Chas. Lowe's business – so I hope she will be better off when he is fairly off.'

Family and friends had done their best by Charles. The Landor family records state: 'In addition to educating her younger brothers and sisters, Eliza rather romantically took upon herself the payment of her brother Charles' debts'.[15]

Perhaps this explains the eighteen-month period before Charles set off for Australia. It took time for Eliza to raise enough money to satisfy the creditors. The hope must have been that he would begin a new life, free of debts and able to regain his reputation.

The following section is something of a digression from the story of Eliza. It gives a fascinating but rather sad picture of the life of an elder brother who through his own misdeeds was forced to leave both his own daughter (who was brought up by Eliza) and the family for whom he must have felt some responsibility.

Charles Lowe in Australia

It seems that, immediately on arrival in Sydney, he set about establishing himself in business, charitable and church affairs, and was quick to write to the press. On 16 July 1844 a notice appeared in the *Sydney Morning Herald* announcing that Charles Lowe, 'formerly of the Inner Temple, London' had lodged an application to be admitted an attorney, solicitor and proctor of the Supreme

---

14. Tim Tomlinson, private papers; written by Frederick Lowe, son of Charles' uncle, William Lowe, to whom Charles had been articled.
15. Tim Tomlinson, private papers.

Chapter 4. Eliza's School in Bootle and Seaforth

Court of New South Wales. His place of residence was the Hermitage, Rose Bay, Port Jackson, Sydney.[16] The passage from London would have taken six months so Lowe had wasted no time in starting off his new life.

He very soon made his presence felt in Anglican circles. In 1845 he was writing letters to the newspapers on behalf of the Church of England Lay Association of which he was secretary. In July 1845 he resigned the editorship of a church newspaper, the *Southern Queen*, citing professional commitments and hinting at impropriety on behalf of some of his fellow Anglicans. An ardent Protestant, he wrote to the newspapers on behalf of the 'Diocesan Committee for promoting Protestant knowledge and propagation of the Gospel according to Cranmer', provoking a mocking response from 'an Anglo-Catholic'.[17]

He was appointed a marshal to the Vice Admiralty Court in 1848, defending himself in the press against the writer of an article which referred to 'the manoeuvring of a certain legal practitioner'.[18] In the same year a notice appeared announcing the creation of 'The Australian Benefit Investment and Building Society', applications to be sent to Mr Charles Lowe, Secretary, *pro tem*, of the Provisional Committee. He was also deputy chairman of the Sydney Fishery Company's Wharf and wrote to the press asking for support for wives and children of soldiers.

However, things began to go wrong. A hint of what was to come was a charge of assault and battery against him, reported in the press under the heading 'Police Register' on 24 February 1855. The sub-heading was 'Grand Legal Fracas' and concerned an admitted assault by Lowe on a Mr Shuttleworth whom he had invited to his office and from whom he demanded payment for a transaction he had completed on his behalf. The men had been reconciled but Lowe had to pay costs and a fine. The report ended: 'A little coquetting hereupon took place across the table, the result of which was that the legal foes shook hands, and shed tears, after the French style of fraternisation, and the curtain fell upon one of the rarest police farces of the season.'[19]

Six months later things had become serious. The *Sydney Morning Herald* announced that Mr Charles Lowe had left New South Wales and named

---

16. In 1868 details of the property for sale described it a 'suburban marine retreat'; *Sydney Morning Herald*, 6 February 1868. The villa was suitable for a small family, with several outbuildings such as a laundry and apartments for servants. It enjoyed spectacular views from the wharf which belonged to the property. The fact that extensive improvements had recently been carried out indicates that when Lowe was resident it was less desirable. However, a grand address suited him.
17. *Freemans Journal*, 20 March 1851.
18. *The Australian*, 2 February 1848.
19. *Bell's Life in Sydney and Sporting Reviewer*.

three men as his joint attorneys, together with an address. Two days later the same paper reported that there was great excitement in the city on account of the abscondment of Mr Charles Lowe.

Charles Lowe had ridden to Adelaide in South Australia (a distance of about 850 miles) where by 1859 he had started up in business again. However, in 1861 he was summoned to address a charge of insolvency. Lowe gave a long, disjointed and inconsistent account of his affairs. He did not know whether he was declared bankrupt in Sydney, but he thought so. He did not keep proper accounts but recorded transactions in a journal; he did not know what was meant by 'proper solicitor's books'. He thought he could satisfy his creditors but was never able to raise sufficient funds. As in Liverpool he was honest about his situation but his affairs were chaotic.

In Adelaide he continued to be full of good intentions. However, by now the locals had the measure of him and the following letter appeared in the press on 13 May 1864:[20]

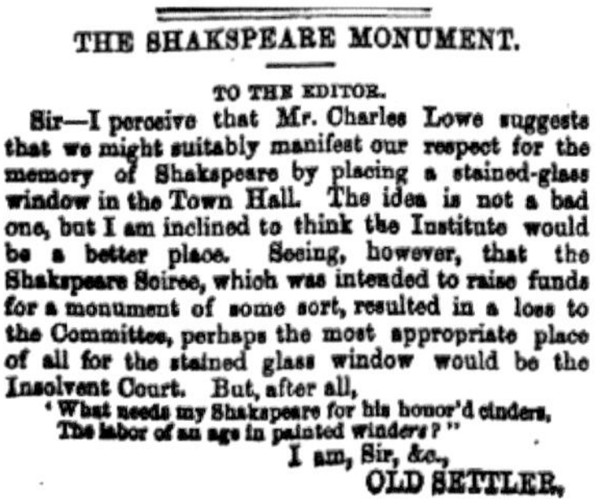

THE SHAKSPEARE MONUMENT.

TO THE EDITOR.

Sir—I perceive that Mr. Charles Lowe suggests that we might suitably manifest our respect for the memory of Shakspeare by placing a stained-glass window in the Town Hall. The idea is not a bad one, but I am inclined to think the Institute would be a better place. Seeing, however, that the Shakspeare Soiree, which was intended to raise funds for a monument of some sort, resulted in a loss to the Committee, perhaps the most appropriate place of all for the stained glass window would be the Insolvent Court. But, after all,

'What needs my Shakspeare for his honor'd cinders,
The labor of an age in painted winders?"

I am, Sir, &c.,
OLD SETTLER.

Fig. 21 'The Shakspeare Monument'.
(See transcription below.)

The Shakspeare Monument
To the Editor
Sir - I perceive that Mr. Charles Lowe suggests that we might suitably manifest our respect for the memory of Shakspeare by placing a stained-glass window in the Town Hall. The idea is not a bad one, but I am inclined to think the Institute would be a better place. Seeing, however, that the Shakspeare Soiree, which was intended to raise funds for a monument of some sort, resulted in a loss to the Committee, perhaps the most appropriate place of all for the stained-glass window would be the Insolvent Court. But, after all,
'What needs my Shakspeare for his honor'd cinders
The labor of an age in painted wind*ers*?"
I am, Sir, &c.,
OLD SETTLER

20. *South Australian Register*, Adelaide.

Chapter 4. Eliza's School in Bootle and Seaforth

Two years later the press reported an incident in court where Lowe voiced loud objections to having to share a table with the reporter of the local paper. As a member of the Bar he thought he had precedence. The reporter refused to give way so Lowe retired to a washstand. *The Southern Argos* felt compelled to write an article taking issue with him for his behaviour, referring to the 'vaporings of Mr. Charles Lowe'.[21] Two years earlier another correspondent had written of his 'fiery, fussy, spluttery epistles'.[22]

In 1863 he married again (his first wife had died shortly after giving birth to his daughter) and things seemed to settle down. He continued to work as a solicitor, in Strathalbyn, Kooringa, and in 1877 he moved back to Adelaide where he died in 1883, aged 81.

Charles Lowe had had advantages in life. He had received a good education, qualified as an attorney, had a supportive family and friends. He had a chance to redeem himself after a disastrous career in Liverpool yet it seemed he was not a repentant man. Nor was he aware of the chaos and antipathy that he aroused, both in his professional and public life. He had strong opinions which he regularly and eloquently expressed in the press. He used pseudonyms from time to time, but then gave the game away with a reference to his address or even his name. He was a man of great nervousness which led to irritation and loss of self-control. The press mercilessly ridiculed him but he carried on regardless. Yet he had principles and must have had charm to persuade so many people to believe in him and support his endeavours. In the end he was incompetent and disorganised and too proud to admit it.

How much of all this was known in England? We know that he was told of the death of his daughter in 1870 because he arranged for a notice to be put in the paper in Adelaide. Eliza's sister Charlotte made a bequest to Charles's widow Annette Elise in her will of 1890. Evidently the family kept in touch, at least on significant matters. The Australian press reported that Charles had given a lecture on middle-class education to the Liverpool Philomathic Society early in January 1868.[23] Perhaps he brought his new wife over to meet the family.

---

21. *The Southern Argos*, 7 July 1866.
22. *The Southern Argos*, 26 May 1864.
23. The Philomathic Society was founded in Liverpool to promote discussion of cultural matters amongst those employed in business and commerce. The speech was reported in the Australian press in full, with the usual sarcasm directed towards Lowe, who had clearly contributed his speech to the paper. See the *South Australian Register*, 20 March 1868.

To Return to Eliza's School in Seaforth

By 1841 Seaforth was growing fast and had attracted several schools, located in private houses that must have been substantial in size. Bootle was losing its cachet, as merchants and professional men moved further away from the industrial areas connected with the city and the docks, and the existence of Seaforth House (and later a similar property called Seaforth Hall) lent an air of exclusivity to the area. The attraction of a large property built to Eliza's requirements would have been considerable. Her school was by this time very successful and she was able to pay the large rent required. She also provided a first secure tenant for Charles.

As has been stated, the census of 1841 shows an astonishing number of people present on the night of the census, 44 in all. Head of the household is Eliza Lowe, aged 37, followed by Mary Lowe, 33, and Charlotte Lowe, 22. They are listed as Ladies' School Mistresses. Underneath, listed as teachers, are Frances Sherrett, 40, Josepha Facers (unclear), 26, Marion McPherson, 18, and Clementine Favarger, 28, the French teacher. Then follow 30 girl pupils, aged between ten and 20. Finally, there are seven servants ranging in age from eighteen to 32. Of the 30 pupils eighteen were born outside Lancashire and only twelve within.

One four-year-old, Susan Lowe, is also listed as a pupil. Susan (or Susannah) was the daughter of Charles and his first wife Susannah. On the baptism certificate her parents were listed as residing in Falkner Terrace, Liverpool, an impressive row of Georgian houses still standing today. It was a fashionable area in the mid-nineteenth century.

After his wife's death Charles may have come to live with his sisters for help with bringing up his daughter. Susan remained with the sisters for the rest of her short life. She was there in 1851 and with her aunt, Mary Manley, visited her uncle George Lowe in Burton in 1861. Her death, in 1870 aged 34, was registered in Southgate where Eliza ran her school after leaving Seaforth. Her burial, however, took place in the churchyard of Abbots Bromley where Eliza and five of Eliza's sisters were also laid to rest (see p. 142).

There were six boarding schools in Seaforth, of which Eliza's was the largest. William Rawson's school was located on Church Lane, not far from Eliza on Claremont Place. (See the map on p. 66, Fig 19.) His school was a prep school for boys mainly preparing for the prestigious public schools. In 1841 he had 21 pupils with a household of 36. He had to accommodate four pupils in a separate School House with two teachers and a male servant. Ann Davenport ran a school (said to be in Seaforth Village) with 33 boys, mainly aged between seven and ten. In all there were 43 persons listed.

Chapter 4. Eliza's School in Bootle and Seaforth

Yet another school was run by Jane Conway in Moss Bank, just to the southwest and close to the shore. Her school is listed as a ladies' boarding school. She had fifteen girls aged between ten and sixteen and a household of 24 persons. There was also a smaller school for girls around the corner from Eliza in Church Road and, around the corner again, close to Seaforth House, was another, Marshfield House.

The 1851 census reveals a scaled-down operation. After the dramatic events of 1841 the sisters were able to continue with their school, but it must have been a personal blow and possibly had an effect on the reputation of the school. Eliza and Charlotte were present, cited as principals. Their sister Mary must have been visiting elsewhere. There were two teachers, one an 'assistant governess' and one a 'musical governess'. None of the four listed as teachers in 1841 was still employed. There was one assistant pupil-teacher, aged eighteen, and there were six house servants, none of whom was there in 1841, and eighteen pupils. A household of 29 persons in all, including Susan Lowe, now aged fourteen. Of the eighteen pupils, eight were from Lancashire and ten from outside the county. The servants were drawn mainly from outside the county, in both years only one servant was born in Lancashire.

The 1851 census lists places of birth (where the 1841 only asked if born in or outside the county). This reveals some interesting facts. The two governesses were from Liverpool. Of the six servants only one was local, from Kirkby; four were from Shropshire (the county in which Eliza was born) and one from Cumberland. Three pupils were from Wigan (Lancashire), two from Liverpool, two from Manchester, one from Ireland, one from Scotland, two from Halifax, two sisters from Warwick, one from Macclesfield, one from Leicestershire, two from Middlesex and one from Rio de Janeiro, the latter 'a British subject'. As in 1841 only a small number were from the local area.

On either side of her school in 1851, in Crosby Road, lived a broker in oils and tallow and a shipbroker, both affluent merchants. The shipbroker, his wife and her two sisters had two servants to look after them, a cook and a housemaid. The area, as we have seen, was not for the poor. Also living in Crosby Road was a sugar refiner, a corn trader, an attorney and accountant and his wife who ran a school for boys aged between seven and ten (a household of 29 persons), a stockbroker, a tea dealer, a surgeon, the Portuguese Consul and a timber merchant.

A map showing the layout as surveyed in 1857 reveals that little development had taken place in relation to what was for sale in 1841. The land behind Eliza's house (plot 8 on the map on p. 67, Fig. 20) was still undeveloped. Of the eleven houses suggested for the area over the road (plot

Fig. 22 Riverslie House.

6) only one had been built. Two houses had been built on land taken from Seaforth House and that is all. The land was on lease from Lord Sefton and there were problems with the terms of the lease which may have made it a risk to a developer. It was lack of attention to the terms of the lease that may have led to Charles Lowe's difficulties.

The area of Crosby Road (now Crosby Road South) has undergone many changes since the mid-nineteenth century. However, Crosby Road South retains much the same configuration and it is the same for Church Road which adjoins it. There remains one very old property, now a nursing home, just down the road from where Eliza's school was situated. It is just off the current building line and was erected in the nineteenth century for the Liverpool harbourmaster. It is a listed building currently owned by a businessman in China. The exact date when it was built is unknown, but it was certainly there in 1871 as the property is listed by name in this census and is occupied by a Charles Smith and his family. The photograph above of Riverslie House gives a feel of the grandeur of the houses that were once on the road where Eliza ran her school.

In recent times the site of Eliza's school was occupied, oddly enough, by a primary school, Rawson Road School, until its closure in 2005.

Chapter 4. Eliza's School in Bootle and Seaforth

Fig. 23 The site of Eliza's school in 2020.

Several local roads have been given names reflecting the area's past: Rawson Road after the long-serving vicar, Reverend William Rawson; Barkeley Drive after Barkeley House which adjoined Eliza's property; Elm Drive after Elm House and Elm Cottage, houses near to Riverslie. The photograph above, taken in April 2020, is of the site where Eliza's school was situated; all subsequent properties on the site have been demolished and cleared and the site lies vacant.

1851 is the last census entry for Eliza in Seaforth. The terms of the lease would have expired in July 1853 and she needed to seek pastures new. A later chapter explores her next venture and a new location.

CHAPTER 5

The Langton Connection

This chapter tells the story of the Langton family who had a long connection with Eliza and her school. Much of the chapter is taken up with Eliza's great friend, Anne Langton, whose nieces were pupils at her school and who kept in touch with Eliza throughout her life. Pupils such as the Langton girls were the mainstay of Eliza's school. The chapter ends with brief accounts of the lives of two pupils of Langton descent who attended Eliza's school and of Gertrude Langton who supported S. Anne's in the early days.

Towards the end of the eighteenth and into the nineteenth century the Langtons ran a successful business importing hemp and flax, which was used in making ropes and sails for the shipping industry. Thomas Langton (1770-1838) was the youngest of six sons of an aristocratic family, brought up in

Fig. 24 Blythe Hall.

Chapter 5. The Langton Connection

Ash Hall, Kirkham in Lancashire. Thomas went on to have three children, William, Anne and John. Anne (1804-93) spent her first eleven years, along with her elder brother William and younger brother John at Blythe Hall, near Ormskirk in Lancashire. Blythe Hall is a Grade II listed building, built in the late sixteenth or early seventeenth century and is best described as a grand country house, an idyllic place in which to grow up. Anne had private lessons in French, Latin and also in music, learning to play the organ.

Trip through Europe

In 1815 Anne's father and her mother, Ellen Currer, the daughter of a Yorkshire parson, embarked on a five-year journey across Europe taking their children and a servant with them, leaving the business to be managed by others. This was to be a memorable journey, one rich in cultural experiences and one in which Anne regularly had art lessons and learned languages. Archaeology was another interest of the Langtons and time in Italy (following a year in Switzerland and then Germany and Austria) meant that Italian was one of the languages encountered as well. Anne's brother William, late in life, wrote verse in Italian.

Financial Difficulties

News came that the business was in difficulties, so Thomas returned, on the way living in Paris for a spell. In 1821 they took up residence in Liverpool but after the financial crash of 1825, like the owners of many other businesses, Thomas had to sell up; the family moved to a rented house in Bootle.[1]

The furniture had to be sold and son John was only able to finish his degree at Cambridge in 1829 thanks to a relation who paid the bills. The Lowes were at this point in Bootle, perhaps, as has been suggested, also because of financial difficulties.

Fig. 25 The Langton house in Bootle.

John Langton rented the house next door and tried to make a living from teaching, there being no money for him to study law. His father equally had little success in making a new career which would support

---
1. This sketch was drawn by Anne herself and is held in the Archives of Ontario.

the family. They were kept afloat by William, who forged a career in banking in Manchester and who gifted them £200 a year. In 1833 John made the decision to emigrate to Canada. In 1837, despite being offered more support by William to stay in England, Thomas and Ellen Langton, along with Ellen's sister Alice and Anne herself, travelled out to a property selected by John near Sturgeon Lake, Fenelon Falls, in Upper Canada.

Anne Langton, the Artist

Before emigrating to Canada Anne had begun to create miniatures, perhaps inspired by the artist James Ward RA, who had given her lessons. One of her landscapes has written on the back, 'drawing done under Mr. Ward'. Ward had given lessons in Liverpool during the 1820s.[2] Throughout her life she drew and painted, although, as was the norm for the time, not with the explicit intention of making a living from her art.[3] However, she did begin to sell her work after times became hard for the family and exhibited one miniature in 1831 and another in 1832 at the Liverpool Academy.

Harriet Lowe

One of the last miniature portraits that Anne completed before emigrating was of Harriet Lowe, one of Eliza's younger sisters, and this is the only representation of any of the Lowe sisters that I have been able to find.

Harriet seems to have been in Liverpool at least until the late 1830s and is referred to in a letter from a pupil set out in the next chapter. By 1851 she was running her own school near Ottery St Mary in Devon where her brother Edward Lowe was curate of the parish between 1847 and 1849. Harriet later went as a governess to France and became a Roman Catholic. She was a woman of great faith. From Oise, just north of Paris, she wrote to her old friend William Landor:

> If it were not for the 'place of refreshment, light and peace' that is beyond the grave, this world would be too sad for any of us, but *there* will be no withered leaves; all that was intrinsically good will be made perfect, and all that was tinsel we shall never wish for. . . . I like France in many respects, & have met with much

---

2. It is possible that he was engaged at Eliza's school. She employed a well-known artist when in Middlesex some years later.
3. For a thorough treatment of her life and work, see Barbara Williams, *A Gentlewoman in Upper Canada: The Journals, Letters, and Art of Anne Langton* (Toronto: University of Toronto Press, 2008).

Chapter 5. The Langton Connection

Fig. 26 Miss Harriet Lowe.

kindness in many ways. But how different the two nations are. It is not pleasant to be poor, but it is good to be so, I do believe, for the momentous trifles that occupy the rich in the fashionable world fill me with astonishment. I *would* be interested in them & I cannot.[4]

Anne Langton's Friendship with Eliza Lowe

Anne Langton, as has been said, was also a close friend of Eliza. A long and remarkable friendship developed between the two women who were of much the same age, a friendship which I now go on to explore and one which also gives a picture of how Eliza was able to attract pupils to her school. Perhaps Eliza and her family gave support to the Langtons at their time of crisis and this led to their friendship. In her account of the life of her family, Anne wrote: 'It was not until some time after we went to Bootle that my intimacy with Miss Lowe began, which continued very steadily whilst we remained in England, and how it was renewed, and what new ties arose between us, all my nieces know full well.'[5]

---

4. Tim Tomlinson, private papers.
5. Anne Langton, *The Story of My Family* (privately published, Manchester, 1881). A copy of the original is held in the Thomas Fisher Rare Book Library, University of Toronto. Digital copy was sourced in November 2019 from archive.org/details/alberta_01299. All quotations which follow are from this source.

The reason why her nieces knew 'full well' about their friendship was that they all attended Eliza's school. The first was Ellen Langton, daughter of William Langton, aged fifteen at the time of the 1851 census.

Anne wrote letters from Canada and kept a journal. Later, in response to a request from her nieces and nephews, she completed a book about her family. From these sources I concentrate here on those aspects of Anne's life which relate to her visits to England and her friendship with Eliza Lowe.

Although she always returned to Canada and her family duties there, Anne made several visits to England. The first visit took place in 1849, along with her brother and his wife. She writes: 'I went for a succession of visits amongst my friends in Liverpool, Miss Lowe, Mrs Langton and Sandown.'

Sandown Hall was a late-Georgian mansion in Wavertree, Liverpool. It was the home from 1827 until his death in 1882 of Hugh Hornby, a wealthy merchant with a particular interest in Russia. The Hornbys were another large and wealthy family based in Liverpool and whose antecedents, like the Langtons, were from Kirkham, Lancashire. Thomas Langton, Anne's father, had one surviving sister, Cicely, who married Thomas Hornby of Kirkham. Hugh Hornby of Sandown was their son. Cicely Hornby was therefore Anne Langton's aunt and visits to Sandown were to her cousin Hugh.

Hugh's brother Joseph was a business partner and together from the early 1820s they had offices at Exchange Street East in Liverpool, close to where Samuel Lowe, Eliza's father, had offices. The Hornby brothers at this point lived in Everton too, in Northumberland Terrace, not far from the Lowes in Everton Crescent. It looks likely that the Hornbys were well known to the Lowe family and perhaps clients of Samuel.

By 1846 Joseph Hornby had commissioned the famous architect, Harvey Lonsdale Elmes to build him a mansion in Woolton, south of the city centre. Druid's Cross was a fine mansion and was where he brought up his family. Elmes was the architect of St George's Hall, a neo-classical building of enormous proportions and grandeur which still stands today. Joseph's daughter, Anne Mary Hornby, appears later in this chapter laying the foundation stone for S.Anne's chapel in Abbots Bromley.

The Offer of a Teaching Post with Eliza

In 1849 Anne Langton visited Ireland where it was all talk of rebellion and disturbances. This was the period of the Irish potato famine and in 1848, following revolution in France, there had been a failed attempt by a group known as the Young Irelanders to start revolution. From her base with her brother William in Manchester, she made visits to friends and family in

Chapter 5. The Langton Connection

Yorkshire and Lancashire. After a year she began to think about returning to Canada. Family and friends, however, urged her to stay. She went into some detail to explain that she came close to taking a position in Eliza's school. She wanted more than to 'fritter her life away' at William's expense in Manchester and so was attracted to the idea of helping the Lowe sisters; she talks of 'oft-repeated arguments with my friend Miss Lowe'. Speaking of Eliza, she wrote: 'Whereupon she replied, "Come to us, our assistant governess is just leaving, you can supply her place" laying before me the advantages of such a course. . . . [A]fter I went home, she wrote to me with the same proposal. . . . Show it to William and ask for advice.'

William and others all advised that she accept Eliza's offer but in the end letters from Canada saying she was needed there tipped the balance; she returned to Canada in 1850 and 'disappointed Miss Lowe'. Clearly the friendship with Eliza Lowe meant a lot.

Anne's Nieces at School with Eliza

The connection continued. In 1854 her brother John Langton visited England to discuss business affairs with his brother William; he took his niece Ellen, William's eldest daughter, back with him to Canada for a cultural tour. Ellen (the first of the Langton girls to attend Eliza's school) would have finished school by then and was aged eighteen. Anne wrote: 'He brought our niece Ellen (now Mrs Herbert Philips) back with him. Some of her friends rather marvelled at her heroism in being willing to accompany him . . . she was quite the first person I had ever welcomed from England.'

Ellen was rewarded for her heroism with a trip to Niagara Falls and to Quebec where she was unwell and not able to enjoy the round of dinners, evening parties and other gaieties.

Equally heroic was another Ellen, the daughter of John and Lydia, born in Canada in 1848. She accompanied Anne on a journey in 1859 on the ship *North American*, arriving in Liverpool where brother William met them and took them by train to his large mansion, Litchfield Hall in Manchester. According to Anne the eleven-year-old enjoyed meeting her cousins with whom she soon became friends. Anne wrote: 'It had always been intended that Ellen should go to school but to a more economical one than that of my friend Miss Lowe.'

However, William insisted that she go to Miss Lowe's school, where his own daughters had been, saying that he would cover the cost. So, after Christmas 1859 Ellen went with her cousin Frances to Miss Lowe's school, now in Southgate, Middlesex. It is possible that Ellen did not fit in very well there, a Canadian amongst English young ladies. Anne wrote: 'Ellen was . . . chary of her admiration both of persons and of things, and, I think, was afraid of being unfaithful to her own friends and country.'

This Ellen was treated to a tour with Anne too. Anne took her to visit friends in the Lake District in the holidays, along with cousins William and Katie. Later that year Anne went for an extended period to the school in Southgate: 'I went to see my friends, the Misses Lowe, at Mayfield, Southgate and stayed with them for the remainder of the holidays, and likewise for the whole of the succeeding term, only coming back with the girls for Christmas.'

In February the next year William's daughter Ellen was married to Herbert Philips; Frances and cousin Ellen were bridesmaids. In 1862 Anne was still in England. Ellen remained at school with Miss Lowe for a time, not returning home to Canada till 1865, following a visit to Paris with her brother Tom.

In 1868 Anne repeated the trip to England, this time going in the spring with Agnes, a younger daughter of John and Lydia. William paid for this niece too to attend Miss Lowe's school in Southgate. Just after Easter, Anne took Agnes to see the sights in London before 'depositing her with my friend Miss Lowe' at Mayfield. Anne then stayed with her friends for a few days. In the summer holidays she took Agnes off to relations, staying in the family mansion, Barrow House, in Cumbria.

Fig. 27 Barrow House.

Skinner Zachary Langton

Anne stayed on at Barrow House until Agnes finished school in summer 1870. Living at the property at the time was Skinner Zachary Langton, 1797-1884, another of Anne's cousins. Skinner was a JP in Cumbria at the time Anne visited, but had been born in Southgate, London where his father,

Chapter 5. The Langton Connection 85

Zachary, a brother of Thomas Langton, ran a business. Zachary Langton, Skinner's father, was a master of the Skinners' Company and a member of the Common Council, a respected and wealthy man.[6] On the eve of the trip to Europe, mentioned at the beginning of this chapter, Thomas Langton and his family took lodgings near his brother's home in Bedford Row, London. On the spur of the moment Zachary decided that his oldest son Skinner should join his brother on the Grand Tour. It was thought that they needed someone fluent in French and German in the warehouse.

Anne and Skinner had therefore spent formative years together and may have felt like brother and sister. Skinner had children, too, so more cousins to be introduced to Anne's nieces. At this point Anne went for a last visit to Mayfield. She wrote: 'It reminded me of my former sojourn there when Ellen was at school, and it was pleasant to see some of her former school fellows.'

In 1872 William Langton was living in another large country house in Manchester, called Hopefield House.[7] It was smaller but still grand. True to form, Anne Langton painted it during this visit:

Fig. 28 Hopefield House, Manchester.

Hopefield House, near Eccles, on the outskirts of Manchester, was the home of William and Margaret Langton from about 1873 until his retirement from banking in 1876. A note on the back of this sketch reads: 'by Miss Anne Langton for Jack' (John and Lydia's fifth child, who was now in England studying at Owens College in Manchester).

---

6. The Common Council still exists today; it is the main decision-making body of the City of London Corporation, which administers what is known as the Square Mile, the historic centre of the city. The Skinners' Company also still exists today and is largely a members' club with considerable charitable functions.
7. Watercolour over graphite. Reference Code: F 1077-9-1-15, Archives of Ontario. I0008461.

Visits to Abbots Bromley

In the summer holidays of 1870 Anne visited her friends in Abbots Bromley:

> I went once more to see my friends the Misses Lowe. This was at Abbots Bromley, where they had purchased a house (the Crofts), with the view of its being a home for them when they were able to retire from the school. They were now spending only the summer holidays there. This was the last of my visits whilst I remained in England, and the last I was ever to pay to my old friend. When I came home the next time, she had attained to a more perfect rest than the one she contemplated enjoying at the Crofts.

1874 found Anne Langton back in England. She visited the two remaining Misses Lowe, Mary Manley and Charlotte, enjoying peace and rest in their comfortable home at Abbots Bromley. Not so comfortable was a trip with Charlotte later that year in a horse-drawn carriage when the pony ran away. For a good mile the pony galloped out of control only coming to its senses just in time. Later that year she visited Chatsworth and Haddon Hall with her niece Ellen Philips who had been at school with Eliza in Seaforth. The Lowe sisters must have spoken to Anne about the new school at Abbots Bromley called S. Anne's and the chapel to be dedicated in honour of Eliza.

The Laying of the Foundation Stone of S. Anne's Chapel

Indeed, Anne Langton was present the next year to attend the ceremony to lay the first stone of S. Anne's Chapel at Abbots Bromley. On 27 May 1875 she travelled with Ellen and Herbert Philips on the train with other guests. The date was little over one year after the founding of the school. Edward Lowe had moved fast. Anne gave a vivid account of the service, which I give here in full:

> The first stone of the Memorial Chapel to Miss Lowe was to be laid on the 27th. Others of the family, who wished to be present, met us in the train, and we were a large party to add to the assemblage for the occasion. The chapel was to be in connexion with St Ann's School [sic] for girls of the middle class. My cousin, Anne Mary Hornby, laid the first stone of the chapel and Mrs. Selwyn, the wife of the Bishop of Lichfield, that of a new wing for the school. The Bishop himself read the prayers and spoke afterwards. A collection,

Chapter 5. The Langton Connection

for the work in hand, was made on the ground, and afterwards there was luncheon, spread in a large marquee, with more speeches. To all present it was an interesting day. Bishop Selwyn was a remarkable personage from his work in New Zealand and Polynesia.

The event was reported in the local newspaper:

> The portion of it first to be erected, viz., the choir and sanctuary, is to be raised as a memorial of the late Miss Lowe . . . by those who have been under her instruction. At the time of her death Miss Lowe was deeply interested in the project then entertained by her brother, the Rev. Provost Lowe for the foundation of the school at Abbot's Bromley, and her old pupils naturally thought they could not more fittingly express their love and reverence for her than by uniting to build a chapel to her memory in connection with the school. In the carrying out of this purpose many gratifying and touching instances of self-denying liberality have been exhibited.[8]

Miss Hornby read the prayer at the laying of the foundation stone, which included mention of Miss Lowe, and the paper reported a touching tribute to Eliza given by Edward Lowe which will be considered in Chapter 11.

It seems that there was a large contingent of Langtons present in honour of Eliza Lowe. The choice of Anne Mary Hornby to lay the stone of the chapel is intriguing. She was the daughter of Joseph Hornby of Liverpool, living at Druid's Cross, mentioned earlier in this chapter. She was born in 1825 and thus of a similar age to Edward Lowe. Did she attend Eliza's school in Seaforth? The paper quoted above stated that Miss Hornby had long been 'an intimate friend of the late Miss Lowe' and she had 'hastened to England to be there on that day'.[9] Doubtless the Langton family had contributed financially to the founding of the school but Anne Hornby must also have had a personal interest.

This chapter finishes with three short cameos. The first two are of Langton girls who attended Eliza's school and the third is of one who was a supporter of S. Anne's school. It gives insight into the life of two girls who attended her school and into the way in which Edward Lowe was able to exploit the Langton connection to raise funds for S. Anne's school.

---

8. *Staffordshire Advertiser*, 29 May 1875.
9. Ibid.

Ellen Philips

Something of Ellen Philips, née Langton, has already been told. The daughter of Anne Langton's brother William, she was the fifteen-year-old pupil at Eliza's school in Seaforth who went on to marry Herbert Philips and live in Manchester. Herbert was by all accounts a wealthy businessman and one who devoted his life to good causes. He was highly respected and sought after in Manchester. It was said of him that there was hardly a good cause in the city with which he had not been associated. He was keen on physical activity for the working classes and had provided a gym in Ancoats, a poor area of the city. He promoted the Open Air Society, was a senior magistrate at the time of his death and an honorary freeman of the city. He was presented with a silver tankard for his endeavours in building a new church in the Ancoats area and was interested in church reform. He had also been involved in discussions to do with the Forster Act of 1870 which set up boards to provide education where the churches were not able to meet the needs of the population.

His wife shared his interests. An obituary for Herbert referred to Ellen in this way:

> He had an amiable and willing co-adjutor [in relation to charitable work] in his wife, the daughter of Mr. William Langton of Manchester, who herself became an ardent philanthropist, liberally supporting such institutions as the Society for the Prevention of Cruelty to Animals, the Sick Poor Nursing Institution, the Cattle Trough Association and the Girls' Lodging House and Free Register for General Servants.[10]

For some charities she worked jointly with Herbert. For example, she was treasurer of the Manchester and District Home for Lost Dogs, while Herbert was chairman.[11] Independently she was honorary secretary of the Manchester Ladies' Association for the Protection of Girls, where she gave reports of the girls' lodging house that they supported in Cheetham. Ellen was also a leading member of the Women's Christian Temperance Movement in Manchester. They had no children.

Thomas Worthington was commissioned to build the Philips a house, Sutton Oaks in Macclesfield, Cheshire. It was completed in 1875 and is a Grade II listed building, until recently a nursing home. It is described in the Historic England's official list of protected sites as 'a good example of

---

10. *Manchester Courier*, 11 November 1905.
11. *Manchester Courier*, 16 March 1899.

Chapter 5. The Langton Connection

one of Worthington's small country mansions of Manchester'. Worthington was one of the foremost architects working in Manchester and several of his works remain today as listed buildings, including some fine public buildings.

Fig. 29 Sutton Oaks.

Ellen Philips was also a writer. She wrote a memoir of her husband following his sudden death, which was published for private circulation. She edited Anne Langton's journals and letters, a limited edition for private circulation only. This was published in 1904, a year before Herbert's death.[12] She also edited the letters of her grandfather, Thomas Langton.[13] She was both a faithful supporter of her family, following the example of Anne, worked for better conditions for the less fortunate and had the skills and contacts to see her writing through to publication. Her education bore fruit.

Louisa Birley Tonge

One more pupil from Seaforth had a Langton connection. This was Louisa Birley, listed on the 1841 census. She was born in October 1828 at Ford Bank in Lancashire. The Birleys were another extremely wealthy and influential Lancashire family with ties by marriage to both the Langtons and the Hornbys. They were mill owners. Louisa was related to both families as her grandparents were Hornby on one side and Langton on

---

12. Ellen Philips, ed., *Langton Records: Journals and Letters from Canada, 1837-1846* (Edinburgh: R. & R. Clark, 1904).
13. Ellen Philips, ed., *Letters of Thomas Langton to Mrs. Thomas Hardy, 1814-1818* (Manchester: J.E. Cornish, 1900).

the other. She was the fourteenth of eighteen children. She married the Reverend Richard Tonge in 1867 when she was 38 or 39 years old. Richard Tonge attended a private boarding school in Pendlebury and then studied at Cambridge where he was ordained. He went on to become rector of St John's Church, Heaton Mersey, and St Ann's and St Mary's Church, Manchester, and was elected honorary canon of Manchester Cathedral. He may have been a descendant of Richard Tonge of Tonge Hall which was sold in 1726 to pay debts.

He appears to have led an exemplary life and took part in disparate church affairs outside his own parishes. He was honorary secretary of a society dedicated to visiting working men, concern being felt that so few attended church, and secretary of the Diocesan Building Society, helping to build Welsh churches in Manchester. He was keenly interested in education and promoted high schools for girls in three areas. He was also secretary of the Diocesan Board of Education. A particular interest of his was the family history of the Tonges. He made extensive notes and transcribed inscriptions from graves.[14] His obituary records that a large number of friends were present at his funeral and many represented associations with which he was involved.

They had four children together; one twin girl died only a few days old and the second a few months later. Their son died aged 26, while Louisa was still living, and their remaining child, a daughter, Agnes, survived to go on to marry the Reverend Walter Gough who was vicar of St Peter's Church, Leck in Lancashire.

The *Manchester Courier* reported the death of Louisa, perhaps significantly including her (well known) maiden name:

> The death is announced of Mrs. Louisa M. Birley Tonge, widow of the late Canon Tonge of St Ann's and St Mary's Manchester. Respecting her a correspondent writes: 'Little need be said; there will be no "storied urn or animated bust" – only the record of a simple, holy life, as maid, wife, mother, widow, as one who spent her time doing "what she could" with a silent Christian influence. Her deeds will live after her.'[15]

It is difficult to know what to make of this. It is written in the respectful tone that is conventional for obituaries. However, the writer searches around for anything at all to say, grateful for one correspondent who at least knew some basic facts. 'Doing what she could' sounds rather disparaging as if there was nothing of note in her life. Yet, bearing four children as an older

---

14. See www.tongefamily.info/, accessed 15 January 2020.
15. *Manchester Courier*, 6 April 1906.

Chapter 5. The Langton Connection

woman and losing two babies must have taken its toll. Ellen Philips had no children and clearly devoted herself to both her husband and charitable work. Louisa's life took a different turn when she found herself pregnant very soon after her marriage. Her silent witness and lack of great deeds however merited an obituary. A woman who 'did what she could'. Probably typical of many women of the time who found themselves unable to pursue a career other than the important one of raising children.

Gertrude Langton

A final connection between Eliza Lowe and the Langton family is found in a letter dated 13 October 1876. It was written by Miss Gertrude Langton from her home in 12 Abercromby Square in Liverpool to Edward Lowe. She must have been included in the list of ladies to whom Lowe wrote asking to become local secretaries with the job of raising funds for his new school in Abbots Bromley.

She wrote:

> I have much pleasure in sending a donation of £2.2s. to the Fund of the School at Abbots Bromley, but regret that owing to many local claims upon my time, I am unable to undertake the office of Lady Secretary in Liverpool. I enclose a Post Office order for £2.2.0s. and remain Very faithfully yours, Gertrude Langton.[16]

Gertrude Langton was the daughter of Joseph Langton, a successful and respected banker. He was the first manager of the Bank of Liverpool. In the Barclays Bank archives (who took over the Bank of Liverpool) there is a reference to him:

> The first manager was the highly respected Joseph Langton, who was previously sub-agent of the Bank of England's recently opened branch in Liverpool. At his death in office in 1855, the Bank of Charleston (one of the Bank's important correspondents in the American South), testified to Langton's 'many and important services . . . rendered to this Bank by his judicious management of their business entrusted to his care'.[17]

Joseph Langton was a nephew of Thomas Langton, and so Gertrude was another of Anne's nieces, though whether she attended Eliza Lowe's

---
16. Guild of S. Mary and S. Anne archives.
17. https://archiveshub.jisc.ac.uk/data/gb2044-bb25/2, accessed 28 December 2020.

Fig. 30 Gertrude Langton's house.

school is not known. Nevertheless, the connection was there and Edward Lowe was not slow to exploit it. Gertrude never married but she gained a reputation as a generous philanthropist, giving liberally to St Margaret's School in Anfield, a school which still exists today, in different form, in another part of the city, Aigburth. One of the houses at the school is named Langton after her. Abercromby Square was, in the middle of the nineteenth century, one of the most desirable areas to live in, being closer to the city than Everton but on a hill and with a lovely garden in the square. Four years after Gertrude wrote this letter, the first bishop of Liverpool came to live at 19 Abercromby Square, a house of which it has been said: 'It is perhaps the grandest surviving 19th century city house in the city centre.'[18] Number 12 (see Fig. 30) is also a listed Grade II building and today part of the University of Liverpool. It also happens to be where I was a student of Classics between 1966 and 1969.

---

18. Joseph Sharples, *Liverpool: Pevsner City Guide* (Pevsner Architectural Guides: City Guides) (New Haven, CT: Yale University Press, 2004), p. 217.

Chapter 6

The Lucy Landor Reminiscences

This chapter is based largely on the *Lucy Landor Reminiscences* lodged at Staffordshire Record Office. These papers consist of family letters and a record of interviews with Lucy Landor conducted and transcribed by Walter Noble Landor, a noted antiquarian and a nephew of Lucy. Lucy Landor and her two sisters, Frances and Cecilia, were pupils of Eliza at her school in Bootle and Seaforth and amongst this record are fascinating details of life in Eliza's school. Lucy also kept a journal, referred to as the 'Commonplace book of Lucy Landor', a detailed record of her reading and thoughts for the year 1835-36, and for a period in 1841.[1] Her papers are invaluable for giving an insider account of life at the school, the background of some of the pupils and the lives they went on to lead.

The three Landor girls were daughters of Walter Landor and his wife Sarah Hicken. The Landors were a well-to-do family, who lived in Rugeley, Staffordshire, and who were related to the Landors of Warwick, of whom the most famous was Walter Savage Landor, the poet, writer and friend of Charles Dickens. Lucy wrote of a visit made by Walter and his brother, Robert Eyres Landor, to her father in Rugeley. She was more impressed by Robert than Walter, the former living a model life as a parish priest and the latter a somewhat dissolute and disorganised life, but who was to become far better known as a poet and scholar. Robert struck her as the most wonderful and delightful talker. He spoke of his travels in Italy, bringing every scene to life. He made a far greater impression on her than did Walter, of whom she remembered only his tremendous laughs.[2]

The connection between the Landors and Eliza and her school may be related to the appointment of Eliza's uncle John Clarke as headmaster of Rugeley Grammar School. Lucy's father was solicitor to the trustees of the

---

1. Lodged in the Staffordshire Record Office in Stafford.
2. See *The Reminiscences of Lucy Elizabeth Landor, 1816-1898* in Warwickshire Record Office.

school, who were responsible for appointing him.[3] In an interesting letter from William Lowe,[4] an elder brother of Eliza's father, it appears that the Landors were 'zealous friends of Mr. Clarke' and on the evening of his appointment to the school John Clarke and his wife were invited to dinner with Walter Landor.[5] Perhaps there was encouragement from the Clarkes for Walter Landor to entrust his daughters to niece Eliza's school.

I begin by considering letters from and to school written by Lucy and other members of Lucy's family.

Politics at School

The first letter is dated 18 October 1831 and sent to Lucy by her younger sister Frances. Lucy, aged nearly fourteen, had just arrived at school with the Lowes in Bootle. Frances, aged twelve and a half (she has carefully written her age at the top of the letter) wrote giving news of the family. She also wrote about important current affairs:

> As to the Reform Bill, most of the higher classes are against it, but many of the poorer people, here, as in other places, have taken it into their heads it is to better their condition marvellously and consequently they are very furious against all who differ from them in opinion, especially Mr. Burton, who I hear has been hanged in effigy this morning, but there have been no riots here.[6]

There was great unrest at the time. A procession in Huddersfield took place on 5 November that year which ended with the burning of an effigy of a bishop.[7] Frances also mentions that the Ducal mansion built on the site of the by then largely demolished Nottingham Castle has been burnt down by protesters. The Landor girls were keenly interested in politics.

---

3. Toye, *Rugeley: 150 Years of a Country Town*, p. 91.
4. Lowe, also a solicitor, was attorney to Henry Paget, Marquess of Anglesey, an aristocratic landowner in Staffordshire and also the patron of Abbots Bromley. Perhaps he was 'leant on' also in relation to the appointment of John Manley Lowe to the parish. The letter is dated 20 November 1809 and is to be found in the Staffordshire County Record Office (see also p. 70).
5. See p. 51-2 for poems written by the Clarkes on the topic of dinners out.
6. *Carbon copy of Lucy E Landor's reminiscences*, Staffordshire Record Office, D(W) 1885/20/6. Unless otherwise stated all quotations are from this source.
7. *Poor Man's Guardian*, 19 November 1831. This weekly London newspaper, which appeared from 1831-35, was a challenge to authority on behalf of the lower classes. The article says that 20,000 people joined the procession. This may be an exaggeration but it is likely to have been based on fact, perhaps even the story that is referred to in Frances' letter.

Chapter 6. The Lucy Landor Reminiscences

Italian Lessons

Two days later Lucy's mother Sarah Landor, wrote to her daughter at school in Bootle, on 20 October 1831: 'I expect you will be quite an Italian scholar by the time you return. You must have had a very pleasant evening on Miss Lowe's birthday.'

This tells us two very interesting things about the school. The first is that pupils learned Italian – but who taught it? In the 1841 census there was a French teacher, who may have taught some Italian, but there was never an Italian governess. Alice Rathbone, a pupil at school with Miss Lowe in Middlesex in 1871, learned Italian so it was not necessarily a one-off in Bootle. Mrs Clarke, Eliza's aunt, might have been the teacher but my guess is that it was Eliza herself. Her younger brother Edward Lowe, as canon of Ely many years later, published his own verse translation of Dante's *Divine Comedy*. It is likely that he owed all his early education before going up to Oxford to Eliza and perhaps it was with her that his grasp of Italian was nurtured along with Lucy Landor and other fee-paying pupils.

Friendliness

The second interesting thing about Sarah Landor's comment is that a party for Eliza's birthday makes the school sound like a close-knit family. Eliza Lowe was happy to entertain her pupils and give them a good time. As the plaque in S. Anne's Chapel put it; she was 'a friend of youth'. Chapter 2 has illustrated how this was the norm for private schools at this period.

Teachers sat with their pupils at breakfast (and presumably other meals) as one would sit with parents at home round the table. Friendliness was important to Eliza and it seems to have been valued by her pupils. Cecilia, Lucy's youngest sister, who also attended the school some years later, wrote home: 'We have set up an amiability prize in imitation of Miss Edgeworth's Cecilia and Leonora and we are to vote every week by putting names in a box, but unknown to all the others. This is amongst ourselves and quite distinct from Miss Lowe's extra prize.'

This appears to be a reference to characters in *The Bracelets or Amiability and Industry Rewarded*, one of the many short stories and novels written by Maria Edgeworth. The story must have had great appeal for the girls. Maria Edgeworth (discussed in Chapter 2) was a very successful and well-known writer, who lived in Ireland for most of her life, although she also travelled widely with her father. She was an eminent intellectual who wrote on class, race and gender as well as education. Eliza Lowe was clearly influenced by her writings.

Cecilia referred to Miss Lowe's extra prize and that theirs was quite distinct. However, it is likely that Eliza Lowe modelled her prize on the story in *The Bracelets*.

All this fits in with the picture of a school being run on family lines; but it also echoes the character-building aspect of education so important for both Maria Edgeworth and Emily Shirreff.

Some years later, on 25 April 1836, Frances Landor wrote again from home in Rugeley to her sister at Miss Lowe's, now moved from Bootle to Seaforth: 'How do you find Emily (Lowe) and all her sisters and Mrs Clarke? I suppose they have not heard by chance from Maria, since she set sail? You may have every facility for becoming acquainted with Pericles and Aspasia (by W.S.L.) as they are a present.'

This looks as though Lucy has recently arrived back in Seaforth. She would have been 20 and it may be that she helped with the teaching. Her journal (discussed shortly) mentions a teaching week. Frances had sent Lucy a present of cousin Walter Savage Landor's latest book, published that same year in two volumes; perhaps Lucy had asked for a copy. *Pericles and Aspasia* was something of a tour de force. It consisted of imaginary letters and poems giving a flavour of classical Athens and discussed artistic, literary, political, philosophical and religious topics. It would be interesting to know if Lucy planned to use some of this material in her lessons. Emily Shirreff would have approved (see Chapter 2). Emily and Maria were two of Eliza's five sisters. At this point Maria was 30 years old and recently married to William Mosley who worked for the East India Company. She has clearly left for India. Frances displayed an easy familiarity with the Lowe family, whether because of the family atmosphere at the school or because of family connections or both, one cannot tell. The Lowes and the Landors visited one another regularly as the closest of friends. Indeed the Landor girls wrote to the Lowe sisters more as familiar friends than teachers. Fanny received a letter from Harriet[8] at Seaforth thanking her for her gift of slippers:[9]

> My dear Fanny
>
> Blessed be the good genius which prompted you to send me so kindly a remembrance. Heart and *sole* I thank you. . . . Eliza is not well at present and everyone is busy. We are delighted always to have letters from any of you. They can never come to often. I will not always write you such a stupid affair as this, but we feared you might be anxious, & in that case a stupid one is better than none. My feet are luxuriating in their woolly cases.

---

8. Here as 'Harriett'. There is inconsistency in the records about the spelling of her name.
9. Spelling as in original, letter undated.

Chapter 6. The Lucy Landor Reminiscences

>   With love
>   Ever dear Fanny
>   Your attached friend
>   Harriett

Lucy Landor wrote to her sister Fanny at school in Seaforth in 1845. Fanny would have been 26 at this point and perhaps helping with the teaching or just paying a visit:

> Tell dear Harriett (I think I may venture on this much) to keep up a good heart . . . show Harriett this & let it serve as an apology for breaking my promise of writing to her on Friday, unless anything new occurs. We have been most fortunate in our weather & were very glad indeed to catch glimmerings lights of yr. progress thro the medium of Mamma. How is Eliza? We shall have mountains to tell each other; kindest love to Mrs Clarke, & all the sisters who may be at home when this reaches Seaforth.

History Discussions

In her letter of 25 April 1836 to Lucy in Seaforth, Frances embarked on a long discussion of *Raumer's England* which she had been reading. Ludwig Raumer was a famous German historian who was much travelled and wrote down his 'history' as he moved about. He became Professor of Political Science and History at the University of Berlin in 1819. In 1835 he published *A Series of Letters Written to Friends in Germany during a Residence in London and Excursions into the Provinces*. A year later an English translation was rushed out and so Frances must have received the translated edition 'hot off the press'. Frances tells her sister that his ideas are somewhat radical:

> Have you seen Raumer's England, translated by Mr Austin?[10] Mamma ordered it into the Library and Mr. Wright is so shocked at its liberal principles that he talks of not allowing it to circulate. The writer is evidently a sensible man and one who has long studied the English constitution, he goes to the bottom of every subject, sometimes diving deeper than is altogether agreeable, for instance in the tithes, poor laws, corn laws . . . the man is not a Radical, but a well-meaning Whig, who would reform us a great deal, rather more than we would like, but retains withal a proper seasoning of respect for Sir Robert [Peel].

---

10. Frances may have made a mistake here. The translator was Sarah Austin, well known in literary circles.

The perspective of a respected foreign visitor is likely to attract attention and some of his topics sound rather sensational: the wealth and magnificence of the Church of England, the decline of the aristocracy, corrupt practices at elections, the education of women and husband-catching, for example.

Shakespeare Recitations

Frances continued in her letter to Lucy:

> Do you and Emily spout Shakespeare at one another? How is Anne? Has she begun to bathe yet? Best love from all to yourself in the first place, – then to Anne, Mrs Clarke and all the Miss Lowes, an ample proportion. Remember me to any of the young ladies who may enquire after me.

It looks as if Frances had attended the school but had now left. Frances speaks fondly of the Lowes and Mrs Clarke. It is striking that she sends 'best love' not only to her sisters but to the Lowes and their aunt. Eliza's younger sister, Emily Louisa Lowe, was born in 1816, and so 20 at the time. Lucy was the same age so perhaps they were friends. The reference to spouting Shakespeare implies that they were well acquainted with his plays and perhaps that they tried to outdo one another in being able to recite passages. Unsurprisingly then, Shakespeare was taught at the school. It is likely that Edward Lowe got his love of Shakespeare from Eliza at the same time. When, in 1854 he became the first headmaster of the Woodard middle school, Hurstpierpoint, he instituted a tradition of the boys putting on a Shakespeare play every year, one which has continued to the present day. Did Eliza get her pupils to do the same? An arrangement of Elizabeth Gaskell's *Cranford* which had been composed by 'Miss Lowe' was still in use at S. Anne's in 1904.[11]

Cecilia Landor

Lucy's youngest sister, Cecilia, also attended school with the Misses Lowe in Seaforth.

This picture (see Fig. 31) was painted by Lucy, who was an accomplished artist, as was her sister Frances.

On 18 May 1839 Cecilia wrote to Lucy from school:

> After many false alarms Mr. C. Lowe is about to take another pilgrimage to that delightful spot yclept [unclear in original] Rugeley

---

11. Rice, *The Story of S. Mary's, Abbots Bromley*, p. 222.

Chapter 6. The Lucy Landor Reminiscences

and something you will expect in answer to your many and very interesting communications. I wish you could send such a letter every day, but not always full of such bad news. . . . Can you contrive to make up a parcel to send me by Mr C. Lowe. I don't want anything very particular, though any little trifles would be acceptable, but the delight of receiving a parcel is so great,[12] – be the contents what they may, – and now I think of it I really do want some more pins and pens, for I have come to the last of the steel ones, and it is impossible to get a good quill here as in the dining room inkstand at home. Fany [*sic*] was to have her first lesson in *sailing* this morning and then to scuttle half through Wales in a day. I don't know when this will arrive at the place of its destination for it is doubtful whether Mr C. Lowe will go or not and he is a most uncertain personage. I forgot he made a very long speech at the Miss. Meeting and pulled out the little Hindu Gods in the middle, the same we saw last half year and he was so terribly nervous that he was as bad as Mr J. Dicken of Missionary Meeting memory. Never did I write such a long letter and I am so tired now I can hardly write even my own beautiful name, but I'll try.

Fig. 31 Cecilia Landor.

This letter refers to Charles Lowe, Eliza's older brother, clearly a problematic character even before the bankruptcy of 1841 (see Chapter 4). It is implied in the letter that Lucy has written previously about him, and perhaps he was the 'bad news'. However, Cecilia was happy to ask him to do her a favour.

Sailing Instruction

The reference to 'Fany' having a lesson in sailing is fascinating. This must be her elder sister Frances (see above) who at the time of writing would have been around 20 years old. After the lesson she is to set off through Wales. It is possible that she was a pupil-teacher at the school, it being common

12. A sentiment with which all boarding school pupils can identify.

for pupils of the school to stay on for a time to assist in the teaching and running of the school. Or she may have been visiting her sister and taking advantage of the opportunity to have instruction in sailing. She may, of course, just have taken a private lesson on her way to Wales. The thought that sailing was one of the accomplishments on offer at the school is not so outlandish as might first appear. We know from Frances' letter above that pupils went swimming in the sea. The sea, only a stone's throw away from the school in Seaforth, was one of the attractions of the school.

In 1815 the Dee Yacht Club was founded and the Royal Mersey Yacht Club (RMYC) in 1844. The Dee Yacht Club held regattas at Parkgate, Wirral, from at least 1827.

Parkgate attracted summer visitors for the bathing season and accommodation was provided in hotels and lodging houses. The regattas were an attraction for these visitors and interested locals both on the Wirral and across the river Mersey.

They were paid for by local subscription and organised by a committee of local gentlemen and included races for 'gentlemen amateurs', fishermen and wives and daughters of fishermen. Interestingly, in 1842 there is a newspaper report of a race for women. There were two crews, one in the *Withington*, belonging to Samuel Evans, and one in *Sarah*, belonging to George Brierley. The women were dressed in white and wore ribbons and rosettes of blue or pink to distinguish between them.

Prizes were awarded as follows:

> Withington . . . Samuel Evans . . . 1 pink £2 10s.
> Sarah . . . Geo. Brierley . . . 2 blue £1 5s.

The newspaper described the scene:

> The scene at this time was most animating, – the clear view of Flintshire's loftiest mountains – the Parkgate shore lined with spectators and equipages – the lingering sound of soft music from Stubbs' Royal Harmonic Band – and the numerous yachts dashing through the 'wizard stream' surpassed any description we can give.[13]

It seems that sailing was keenly followed, and it was common for women to be given charge of boats and join in the fun alongside the men. However, at this period there was a clear distinction between 'ladies' and 'women'. Women were working class and ladies upper or upper middle class. So, in this case the race was between working women; such ladies as were present

---
13. *Liverpool Mail*, 24 September 1842.

Chapter 6. The Lucy Landor Reminiscences 101

Fig. 32 Miss Fazakerley and her schooner.

would have been spectating. Propriety is also maintained in this account in that the boats, though raced by women, belonged to men. It was not until 1882 that the Married Women's Act allowed women to own property if they were married and the RMYC did not institute races for the ladies until 1894. The picture here shows the first lady member, Miss Fazakerley of Denbigh Castle, whose schooner is shown the background.

The pupils at Eliza's school were young ladies, of course, and so at this period of time not expected to take part alongside men in races. It is interesting to note that sailing and rowing in regattas was one of the excitements that took place in Anne Langton's life in Upper Canada as early as 1838. She says that regattas were held for both sailing and rowing boats and drew crowds. She describes one such occasion in the autumn of 1838, which must have occurred one year after their arrival. She writes:

> John [her brother] had two boats, the *Alice* and the *Fairy*. What with preparing the boats, practising with the oars, making sails, flags etc. there was a great deal to be done and much excitement about it. The flags were mostly the ladies' share of the work, we all got interested and talked of little else.[14]

The implication is that only men took part in the races. Visitors came and Anne remarks: 'Before this, I had counted ten months when I had not seen a single lady.'[15]

Here Anne means upper-class lady as she had had plenty to do with the local folk from whom they were able on occasion to employ women servants. Moreover, there is no mention of ladies using the oars. The next year a regatta was again held on Lake Sturgeon, Ontario, but a tragic accident occurred when one of the men fell overboard and was drowned. No regattas were held thereafter.

---
14. Langton, *The Story of My Family*, p. 77.
15. Ibid.

Politics Again

To return to Cecilia at school with Eliza: in amongst family news, in her letter of 18 May 1839 to Lucy, Cecilia gives an account of discussions in school: 'as Miss Lowe is become a tremendous politician herself, she gives a sanction to conversation on that subject, but the people here are so laughably ignorant of everything and everybody that to converse rationally is impossible'. She comments: 'I cannot get satisfactorily to know from Miss Lowe, whether Lord Normanby or Melbourne is premier.' Furthermore, she says she is anxious to get hold of a newspaper.

Breakfasts are amusing occasions, she says. They are an opportunity for discussion of political matters:

> Miss Sherrett[16] gives her opinion on the state of the nation 'I am really rejoiced that the Duke of Wellington has not come into power again, he is too much of a soldier to be a great statesman, indeed we require someone with more judgment . . . I fancy Sir R Peel is rather too old/too aged to take office again.' These observations she addresses to Miss Mary, who takes them all in good part, for she knows very little better.[17] Miss Lowe is the only one with any sense about her in this particular.

Eliza Lowe was probably right to show caution as to who was Prime Minister. On 7 May 1839 Lord Melbourne tendered his resignation as Prime Minister after his government's Jamaica Bill was passed by an unmanageable, narrow majority of five votes in the House of Commons. The Duke of Wellington was first invited but declined to form a new government. Queen Victoria then asked Lord Peel to form a Tory government. All would have gone well but for the Bedchamber Crisis. It was customary for the ladies-in-waiting to be the wives of the party in power and, when Victoria refused to dismiss her Whig companions, Peel refused to form a government. The reluctant Whigs were persuaded to take the reins once more. However, would Lord Melbourne return as Prime Minister? As it happens, he did, on 18 May the very day that Cecilia was writing her letter. Lord Normanby, a leading Whig, had been Governor of Jamaica and Lord Lieutenant of Ireland, amongst other high positions. It was natural to wonder whether he would take over from Melbourne. He did not but was invited to be Home Secretary.

---

16. One of Miss Lowe's teachers. Her name was Frances and she is mentioned as present in the 1841 census, aged 40.
17. This is Mary Manley Lowe, five years younger than Eliza, who worked at the school throughout her life.

Cecilia mentions that Miss Favarger, the French teacher, was very frightened about rumours coming out of France. On 12 May 1839 the *Société des Saisons*, a secret Republican society, organised a political uprising against the government in Paris. It was a failure but, nonetheless, worrying for a French native far from home and with no immediate contact with family. Cecilia's letter was dated 18 May, only six days after the uprising.

Miss Favarger also became a family friend. In a letter to Cecilia from Lucy on 16 May 1846 Lucy mentions that she had had a note from Miss Favarger thanking them for the cake. They had kept in touch since leaving school.

It is remarkable that the political crises of the day were the talk of the breakfast table in Eliza Lowe's school and told to us by a fifteen-year-old pupil, although as we have seen, the Landor girls were keenly interested in politics.

The following extract from an article in the *Liverpool Mail* was published on 16 May just two days before Cecilia's letter was written. The school was certainly in tune with the mood of the day:

> We have painful manifestations, made more clear by every noontide sun, that England, at the present moment, is in a most critical and perilous condition. To say that we have no Government is only to tell the truth. To say that we have a young, inexperienced and unprotected Queen, surrounded by wily, treacherous, libertine and unprincipled advisers, is also only saying the truth. To say that we have an unpopular and characterless ministry, hated by one portion, and despised by another portion of the people, is simply the repetition of a truism. To say that a considerable portion of the population of the manufacturing districts are in a state of revolt, are armed like traitors, and acting as desperadoes, is only to record a confession too true in all its particulars, but fearful enough to make every man of property tremble for the consequences.
>
> Such is the state of England! We shall not aggravate the incentives of her peril by doing more than briefly alluding to the sanguinary state of affairs in the metropolis of France. At the same time we dread the contagious effects; for although wise and resolute men preserved our country from the epidemic of the first revolution in France, we must question if we have the strong nerves, the same bold hearts, and the same indomitable courage to suppress that insubordination which is making war alike upon property and the revered institutions of Great Britain.

A petition

A few years earlier the Landor girls had attempted to enter politics themselves via a petition sent to their cousin Robert Eyres Landor who, as well as being a cleric and a writer was Chaplain to the Prince Regent. A letter from Robert Landor to his brother Henry, written in April 1835 stated:

> I am far less astonished by Sir R Peel's resignation than by the awful commotion in Cousin Walter's house. It is good indeed to be zealously affected in a good matter, but how these gentle dears should have been converted into such flaming politicians, is hardly accounted for even by the great occasion.

Robert reassured his brother that Lord Melbourne was back in power and there was no need to do anything about the petition. He did not say what the petition was asking for but it must have been in favour of Whig causes. Henry wrote to the girls with an amusing parody on Spenser's Faery Queen to which one of the girls ruefully replied:

> Oh may some faithful guard be found
> To save the flock from spoil and ruin
> But we were simple lambs indeed
> To look for aid from Cousin Bruin

Complaints

On 26 August 1839, Cecilia wrote to her mother pleading to be allowed to leave school at Christmas. She issued a litany of complaints and reasons as to why she should be allowed to leave. There were too many pupils, 29 with four more expected. Building work was going on and there was a lot of noise. She complained about Miss Lowe. Miss Lowe had declared that the Queen's marriage was fixed, Saxe-Coburg being mentioned. Miss Lowe was clearly right in this, but Cecilia thinks she is 'far from perfect in her version'.

She is into compound multiplication of fractions and could get on better with French and Italian at home with books. No one can understand Miss Favarger's explanations. She is desperate and says she would submit to being called Cecy at Xmas. Perhaps deliberately her sentences run uncontrollably into one another as she thinks up more and more arguments that will persuade her mother:

Now what I am driving at is this don't you imagine I shall sing well enough to leave at Christmas? for in a letter last half year on the subject & which I carefully preserve, you said plainly that it was on account of the *masters* I was staying – and this place is so disagreeable now, and there is not one girl that I really like, and we have so many teachers – for besides Miss Sherrett and her two assistants, a fourth nursery governess has arrived – and so many girls and so much to do – it is as nearly unbearable as things which *are* supportable can be.

Now Mamma I don't ask you to answer very soon, but do consider whether it is worth while staying here to be tormented and crammed both with learning and rice pudding and blown to pieces, all for the sake of accomplishments, which are not likely to be wanted, and worse than all this the girls are so extraordinarily silly in their conversation and in some cases worse than silly that there is no pleasure even in play hours, few as they are. So pray take all these miseries into consideration and just send word that I may leave at Christmas and I should be almost quite happy in spite of everything.

There is much of interest here. Her parents valued the fact that there were masters at the school. Eliza Lowe was able to call on expert masters as was clear from the school when it moved to Mayfield. Cecilia refers to accomplishments, a major justification for girls' education at this period. The reference to being blown to pieces is interesting as it mirrors the reminiscences of Anne Langton (mentioned in the previous chapter) who several times referred to the 'Bootle winds'. The house faced the coast and would have had little protection from the sand dunes.

The building work was both an inconvenience and a source of amusement for the girls:

The great gong which drove me away last night, is the only bell in the house except a little handbell, and this is in constant requisition for it is rung in the passage, and the servants have to go blundering about from room to room to find out where they are wanted, a very amusing state of things for us, if not for them.

In amongst the complaints Cecilia mentions Fanny coming:

I shall want my cloak before Fanny comes, it is very cold sometimes even now, particularly in the school room, which is partly new. However, I don't mean to sit wrapped up in my Joseph, as you might imagine by the wording. Heidleburg was much admired, but Mad^elle was very cross that there was no accompanying letter, thanks to you all, I had not the same complaint to make so I did not listen to her's.

She goes on: 'I don't think Fanny can come for two months or thereabouts, there would not be a hole to put her in, but after that there will be plenty and perhaps sooner.'

Building work was in progress and extensions to the school would mean that there would soon be room for more pupils and visitors. A 'Joseph' was a woman's riding habit so it is probable that riding lessons were provided at school (as they were later when the school moved to Middlesex).

Cecilia was not the only Landor to complain about life at school. Two years later Anne Jane Landor, a cousin of the Landor sisters (and the one mentioned in relation to bathing) wrote to her cousin Frances on 14 April 1841: 'I hope Harriet Lowe will be at Rugeley when I have finished my penance in Lancashire. Harriet goes with us to Liverpool on Tuesday as far as Warrington.'

Life at Eliza's school was clearly valued by the parents, if not always by the girls.

Interestingly, Cecilia went on to marry George Lowe, a younger brother of Eliza and the ninth child of Samuel and Maria Lowe. George Lowe was a Fellow of the Royal College of Surgeons practising in Burton-on-Trent, where the Lowe family had lived in 1819. Moreover, their daughter, Emily Landor Lowe, the fifth of their thirteen children, went on to run Mayfield school after Eliza's death and then S. Winifred's School in Bangor, founded by Edward Lowe.

I now go on to consider Lucy's journal.

Lucy Landor's Commonplace Book[18]

Lucy's journal is a fascinating document, recording her reading between 1835 and 1836 and then briefly in 1841. The journal consists of over 120 pages of closely written handwriting. The book is a good quality hardback item, measuring approximately ten by eight inches. The paper is unlined, and the book is in good condition. The ink remains clearly visible, the only difficulty being Lucy's small and sometimes illegible handwriting. She did not give reasons as to why she started it and in fact there is very little of a personal nature (reflecting Emily Shirreff's idea of a commonplace book). She aimed to note down something every day, although Sundays were generally given to summarising the sermon and there was a period in the summer when

18. Lodged at Staffordshire Record Office.

Chapter 6. The Lucy Landor Reminiscences

holidays and visiting interrupted her flow. It gives some insight into Lucy's character and is remarkable for what it reveals of her reading and interests. Perhaps she was encouraged by her time at Eliza's school to write a journal and it certainly follows the pattern recommended by Shirreff.

Her first entry was on 23 November 1835. She was eighteen at the time. She had read the life of Pitt the poet whom she compared unfavourably with Dryden, 'very inferior in signs of sublimity'. She seemed to enjoy the experience of writing a journal. On 26 November she wrote: 'How very much easier and more pleasant is it to give an account of what I read than what I do.' On 1 December she noted that some of her good resolutions were already broken, rising in the morning and her temper being particular trials: 'Oh! Cleanse thou my heart', she exclaims. Interestingly, she referred to the week being her 'teaching week'. However, no details are given. Much of the journal is taken up with the account of the English Civil War known as the Clarendon History. She writes, in relation to arguments in Parliament 'why can't they let bygones be bygones?' She comments, ironically, on the 'plenitude of their wisdom . . . concluding with a glorification of themselves'. The next day she was on to the *Life of Gray* by Samuel Johnson and that of Lyttelton in *Converts from Infidelity* by Andrew Crichton, published in 1827.

She clearly enjoyed biographies as well as history. The lives of Counts Brandt and Struensee cannot have been comfortable reading. They both ended up being executed in Denmark in the most gruesome manner. She writes about Herman Boerhaave (1688-1738), born at Leyden, theologian, mathematician, botanical anatomist and physician. She thought he was an 'excellent man' whose practice it was to devote the first hour after rising to meditation, prayer and study of the Scriptures. The politics of the period of the civil war were noted in detail and she notes the struggle for power that marked debates at the time in the Commons. She was also reading Spanish history going back to the Roman period and then under Muslim rule.

Over Christmas that year she was unwell and was forbidden to go to church but this did not prevent her reading a book on God's providence by Dr Thomas Sherlock. She summarised his arguments and seemed satisfied with them. Sherlock had been an Anglican bishop over a period of 33 years and was also a respected academic. Jane Austen wrote that she liked his sermons, preferring them to almost any. On 30 December Lucy was back to Spanish history; a short entry reads: 'the minutiae of the history of Granada is really not worth writing down'.

On 31 December she wrote:

> For more than a month then I have this journal of that I have read and of that I have done, and awful thought, of all I have ever

done and said and thought, another account has been made. If I dare not make this account, how shall I feel when it is read before men and angels! Not here, indeed, mixed up with the histories of nations and individuals, must be this journal of my own heart, but to prove and examine the heart is a duty I dare no longer shrink from. May God bless my endeavour to penetrate into its recesses and to cleanse it from defilement.

The next day, 1 January, sees her back on Spanish history and the loss of Granada to the Christian King Ferdinando. For the next few weeks she seems distracted by headaches and did not do much reading. Her thoughts turned to providence again until, on 26 February, she turns her attention to Portuguese history; by March she is reading the plays of Sheridan and the chronicles of Waltham.

Effectively at this point her daily journal comes to an end. She writes that the family went to relations in Poynton, then on to North Wales where there was much visiting to do and, finally, they returned to Rugeley. On 21 September she set out for Florence. Letters refer to trips to Germany as well. Influenza struck her down in October and it was only in November that she began to record her daily reading again. However, she notes some of her reading over the summer, which included the life of Petrarch, Dr E.V. Clarke and the poems of Coleridge. She also read Taylor's *Channel Islands*. Clarendon History was taken up again and she wrote a lot about Prince Rupert of Bohemia who fought on the side of King Charles I and served under Charles II. Then, at the end of November, 'a year since I began this book', she wrote that she could not write on important subjects 'because of what happened on Tuesday', and then 'poor, poor e'.[19]

The journal is taken up again, following many blank pages, in March 1841 when Lucy was aged 23. Geography has caught her interest. She writes about distances of various countries from Greenwich and reads about the colony of Western Australia. The journal ends with a list of the Chief Justices, including quite detailed histories of men such as Edward Coke, Bradshaw, Hyde (Lord Clarendon) and Francis Pemberton.

Lucy's journal reflects her piety and her intellectual interests. The reference to writing being more pleasant than what she did reflects the fact that her life was very much that of an unmarried lady of the time, largely a round of visiting and carrying out homely tasks. Reading and writing was her way out of drudgery, as Emily Shirreff had predicted. Certainly, churchgoing was part of Lucy's life and her personal life was a matter of great concern to her. Churchgoing was part of life at Eliza's school too.

19. I have not been able to find out what event she referred to here.

Chapter 6. The Lucy Landor Reminiscences

Churchgoing at School

Letters from the Landor girls at Eliza's school do not refer to church or religious teaching but girls will have been taken regularly to St Thomas' Church which was just around the corner from the school in Seaforth. Felicia Jennings was listed on the 1851 census as an assistant pupil which means that, like Lucy and Frances Landor before her, she was helping with the instruction. Her younger sister Julia was also listed in the same census, aged sixteen. On 31 May 1849 Felicia was baptised by William Rawson in St Thomas' Church. Listed as godparents with a note that they were witnesses were the Reverend S.P. Boutflower, Eliza and Mary Lowe. The entry stated that her parents were William and Sarah Jennings, the occupation of her father being metal founder. Below is an 1839 notice from Grace's Guide, a leading source of historical information:

WILLIAM JENNINGS,
(LATE FREETHS & JENNINGS,)
Gun Furniture Founder & Silver Caster,
LIVERY STREET, GREAT CHARLES STREET,
Birmingham.
Manufacturer of all kinds of Military and Birding Gun and Pistol Furniture, and all descriptions of Metal Blunderbuss and Pistol Barrels.
Rolled Imperial British Plate, or Improved German Silver. Round and Square Wire. Coach Harness and Spur Castings, &c.
LICENSED DEALER IN GOLD, SILVER, AND PLATINA.

Fig. 33 Business advertisement.

Grace's Guide lists his business in Great Charles Street, Birmingham. He specialised in metalware for guns and coach harnesses.

Most girls would have been baptised as babies unless their parents belonged to a denomination like the Quakers who do not practise baptism. Birmingham was a stronghold of the Quakers at the time. So why would Felicia have chosen to be baptised? The probable answer is that the school encouraged pupils to be confirmed and for this it was necessary to have been baptised. The fact that the curate, Boutflower, was a witness may mean that he was responsible for the preparation. Felicia must have personally asked Eliza and Mary Lowe to take on the role of godparents, an indication of friendship and trust.

On the Move

The lease for the property in Seaforth was due to run out in 1853 and the last time that Eliza and her school were listed in Gore's *Directory of Liverpool* was the 1851-53 edition. Her next appearance was in Southgate, Middlesex, in a very grand house called Mayfield.

CHAPTER 7

Mayfield – Eliza Lowe's School in Southgate

Eliza had to close her school in Seaforth and she chose to relocate it to Southgate in Middlesex. Southgate was a wealthy and fashionable area of north London where very little building was allowed as the Walker family, wealthy landowners, operated their own private green belt policy. One source writes: 'In the Victorian era Southgate was not subject to the same intensive urban development as much of the surrounding area and maintained its reputation as an unspoilt rural idyll.'[1]

The same source writes of 'the generally rich community of Southgate'. Much the same as Seaforth in the early part of the nineteenth century.

Certainly, the area was popular for boarding schools and there were also many short-lived day schools. According to one source there were 85 teachers in Edmonton (the district of which Southgate was a part) in 1851 with 392 children attending thirteen boarding schools.[2] The largest were Eagle Hall and College House, both accommodating 45 boarders each.

What this means is that, as in Seaforth, Eliza Lowe chose to site her school in an affluent, attractive and perhaps exclusive area and one which would appeal to wealthy parents. There was also from 1855 a nearby railway station on the Great Northern Railway line. Anne Langton commented on the joys of rail travel which she encountered on her visits back home in later years. However, why move to Southgate?

There is one interesting possibility. Up until 1855 Skinner Zachary Langton, Anne Langton's cousin whom Anne visited regularly when back in England, lived there.[3] He was born in Southgate. Two at least of his children were born and raised in Southgate too. The 1841 census lists

---
1. https://hidden-london.com/gazetteer/old-southgate/, accessed 30 December 2020.
2. Edmonton: Education: British History Online (british-history.ac.uk), accessed 30 December 2020.
3. See Chapter 5 for the description of the Langtons' tour of Europe which included Skinner.

Chapter 7. Mayfield – Eliza Lowe's School in Southgate

Skinner living with his wife and family in 'Chase on the road to Southgate'. A successful merchant, his house was big enough for his six children, a visiting Langton and six servants. A baptism record for a son Walter in 1840 says that the family was living in Oak Lodge. Walter was still living in Southgate in 1871 in an area known as Chase side, presumably in the property his father had owned. The map below, from a survey which took place between 1863 and 1865, shows Oak Lodge on a large plot of land with associated properties. It was accessed via a road or path leading off Chase road which led into the village of Southgate.

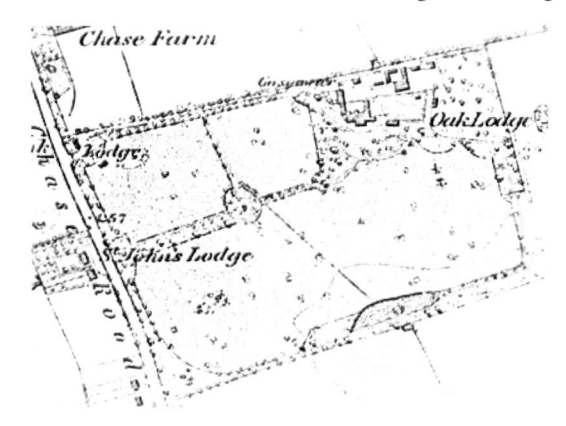

Fig. 34 Map showing location of Skinner Langton's property in Southgate.

In 1853 Skinner purchased Barrow House estate near Derwentwater and had moved there by 1855 (see p. 84, Fig 27). Skinner was an extremely wealthy man, leaving an estate of some £57,000 in 1884, the equivalent today of over £100 million, and, as we have seen, had travelled with Anne in Europe while he was a teenager. He will have known of Eliza Lowe and the Langton family tradition of sending their daughters to her school. I wonder whether he tipped off Eliza about the possibility of land becoming available or perhaps he owned the land and suggested it would be a good place for her school? The 1851 census does not mention Mayfield House; it seems that it was built after this date.[4] It is certain that Eliza and her sisters were at Mayfield in 1859, and seemingly well-established, because her Canadian niece and a niece from Manchester were pupils in that year. Eliza was experienced in employing builders and by the 1850s may well have built up a large reserve from profits. Clearly a successful businesswoman, it is not inconceivable that she had Mayfield built to her specifications as was the case with Hannah Wallis in Birkdale (see p. 32). If this was the case, then her establishment was purpose-built in both locations.

---

4. https://www.british-history.ac.uk/vch/middx/vol5/pp142-149, accessed 15 January 2021.

Mayfield House was a large property with extensive grounds, still in existence as a school in 1908. It was a short distance south of Oak Lodge. The following description locates it in relation to modern-day buildings:

> The House was sited fronting onto the High Street (formerly South Street), set back from the street, located across what is now The Close and running towards The Baird Memorial Homes on Balaams Lane. The garden was extensive, running back from the High Street along the boundary with the Walker Cricket Ground. Mayfield house was demolished circa 1924 to make way for the houses built at Mayfield Avenue.[5]

Fig. 35 Mayfield House, Southgate.

It was certainly a fine location for a school and survived as a school well into the twentieth century. Promotional postcards of the school from a later period show girls playing hockey in a large field next to a field of cows. Below is an OS map, from a survey between 1863 and 1865. The houses along the high street were also built after 1851.

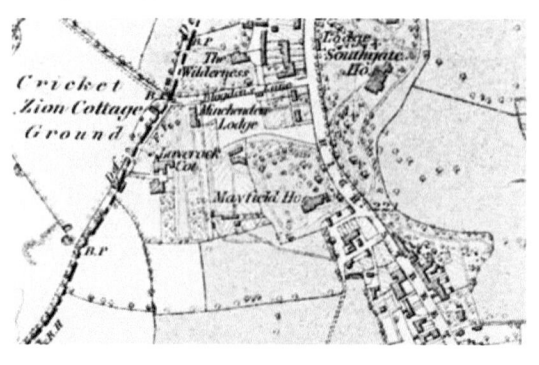

Fig. 36 Map showing location of Mayfield House.

---

5. I am grateful to Chris Horner of the Southgate Green Association for this description.

Chapter 7. Mayfield – Eliza Lowe's School in Southgate

If she did build Mayfield House, why did she choose the name Mayfield?

Before the industrial age it was common for farmers to name their fields and field names can still be seen on ancient maps. From the map of Southgate (see Fig. 36) it can be seen that there was a field called 'The Wilderness' adjacent to Blagden's Lane. This may have been so named by a farmer. If so, then Mayfield House may have been built on a field where May Day celebrations were held. One other possibility is that the house was named after a house in Staffordshire, not far from where Eliza and her family lived in Burton-on-Trent.

Fig. 37 Mayfield Hall, Tutbury.

There is certainly a similarity in size and style. Whatever the case, Mayfield in Southgate was a mansion, the property extensive and only to be sought after by the rich. It supported not only the Misses Lowe, their servants and pupils but also a lodge where a gardener lived with his family.

One fascinating piece of evidence as to the costs of running Mayfield is a receipt for £185, dated 1 October 1867, equivalent to well over £20,000 today.[6] The stamp was a fiscal stamp used for receipt of taxes and so this was her tax bill for the year. Income tax at the time was low, between one and three per cent but, nonetheless, this was an expensive tax bill. In rough terms this means that her school was as expensive as elite boarding schools are today. This is borne out by a study of her pupils which comes later.

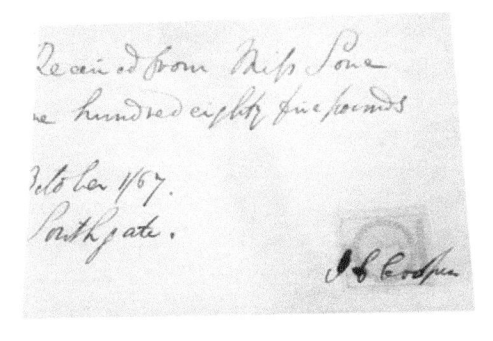

Fig. 38 Eliza Lowe's income tax receipt for 1867.

---

6. Sourced from Enfield Local Studies Library and Archive.

Well established by 1859, Eliza Lowe is listed along with her sisters in a list of subscribers to the building of a new church for Southgate.[7] The 'Misses Lowe' gave £26 5s., 'Friends by Miss Lowe', £52 10s. and 'Miss Lowe's servants' two guineas. Clearly Eliza approached wealthy friends and expected her own servants to give to the appeal. The sum of £80 was substantial, equivalent today of around £10,000. Amongst the list of contributors was W. Rathbone who gave £105, or more than £13,000 today.

This is likely to have been William Rathbone V who was a Liberal politician and once Lord Mayor of Liverpool. The Rathbone family were a wealthy and famously philanthropic family in Liverpool and it is quite likely that Eliza knew them from her time in Everton and Seaforth and also approached them for a contribution. Later, in 1871, Alice Rathbone, the niece of William Rathbone VI was a pupil at Mayfield (more of her later, see Chapter Eight).

Life at School

What was life like for pupils at Mayfield? As at Seaforth girls would have been taken to church and, just as they were intended to be present at the laying of the foundation stone for the new church in Waterloo (see Chapter 4), one imagines that they attended similar ceremonies in connection with the building of Christ Church Southgate, consecrated in 1862. As we have seen, Eliza was keenly involved in fund-raising for the church and the fact that in the church today is fine tablet in memory of the three sisters is testimony to their participation in church life.

This striking tablet, given by former pupils in 1899, is erected on the north wall in a prominent position, in between fine stained-glass windows designed by Edward Burne-Jones, the famous Pre-Raphaelite artist. Charlotte died in 1897. It is quite remarkable that former pupils, perhaps approached by Edward Lowe, would want to commemorate their teachers 25 years after they had left school. The sisters must have left a lasting and positive impression.

The tablet also bears witness to life at Mayfield. The wording 'not only from their lips but by the examples of their lives' resonates with words in the Prayer Book General Thanksgiving 'that we shew forth thy praise, not only with our lips, but in our lives'. These words come naturally to those schooled in such prayers.[8] So perhaps at Mayfield the Prayer Book was in daily use. The quotation at the bottom of the tablet reads as follows:

---

7. Accessed 25 April 2019 at Enfield Local Studies Library and Archive.
8. It is one that I had to learn at Abbots Bromley School and still remember today.

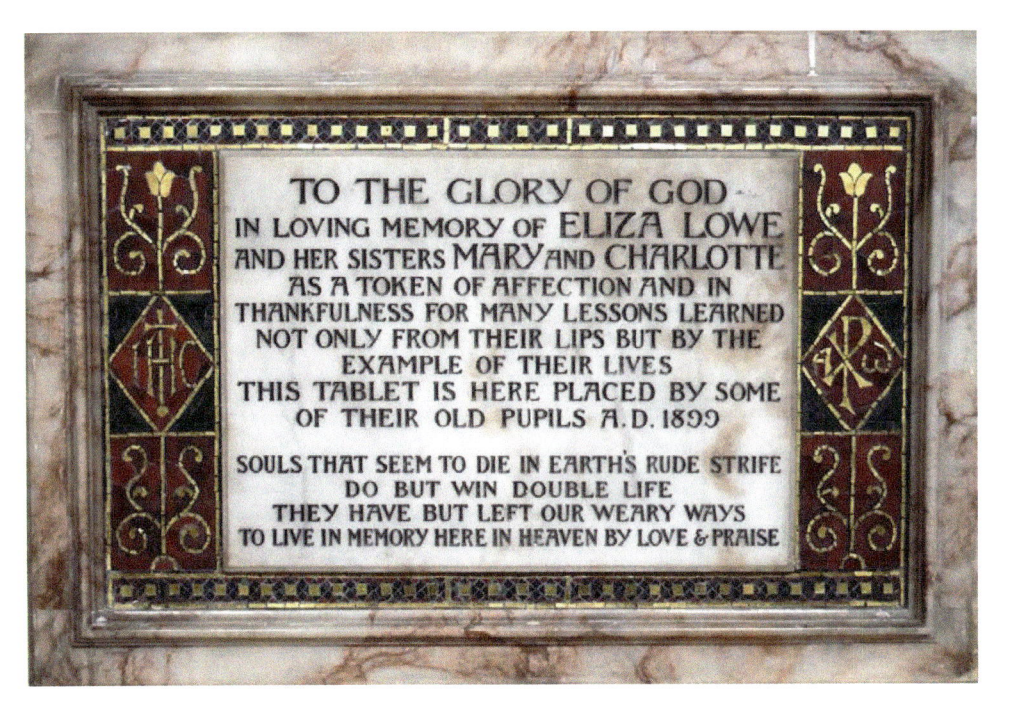

Fig. 39 Memorial to Eliza, Mary Manley and Charlotte in Christ Church Southgate.

'Souls that seem to die in earth's rude strife do but win double life. They have but left our weary ways to live in memory here, in heaven by love and praise.'

It is taken from John Keble's *The Christian Year*, first published in 1827. Keble is credited with inspiring the Tractarian Movement and this work became enormously popular in the nineteenth century. It contains verses appropriate for every week of the liturgical year and also for the saints remembered in the Anglican Calendar. These words come from the verses written for St Barnabas Day. Barnabas is mentioned in Acts 4:36-37 where he is referred to as Joseph but named Barnabas by the apostles; the name Barnabas means 'son of encouragement'. The verses develop the theme of encouragement, only naming him in the last stanza; ending with the words chosen for the memorial above. Keble refers to those saints whose joy is in bringing others to God and who rejoice more in the achievements of others than in their own. By choosing this epitaph the Lowes' former pupils clearly wanted to say something about the way the Lowe sisters lived their lives and encouraged them.

So, the girls of Eliza's school were familiar enough with Keble's *Christian Year* to remember the poem for St Barnabas and similarly with the General Thanksgiving to reflect its phraseology. As at Seaforth, girls at Mayfield were baptised at Southgate. The baptismal records for Weld Chapel[9] show that three Mayfield girls were baptised there. Lilias Dalglish on 19 April 1869, aged thirteen, Edith Ecroyd on 7 June 1869, aged nearly sixteen, and Margaret Ecroyd on 19 December 1870, aged sixteen. Lilias was the daughter of the Scottish MP Robert Dalglish who had been part of a breakaway group from the Episcopal Church of Scotland and this may explain why she was not baptised as a baby. The Ecroyd family were Quakers. Again, these girls must have been encouraged by the Lowes to be confirmed and so baptism was arranged for them.

Amongst the accomplishments (as they would have been called) on offer was horse riding. A correspondent in the *Palmers Green and Southgate Gazette* on 16 January 1931 recorded: 'Another pretty sight was to see the young ladies from the Misses Lowes' school out for their riding lessons, about 25 of them, all dressed alike in blue riding habits and high hats.'

The correspondent goes on to say that many daughters of the nobility were educated there. It was a high class and exclusive school for girls largely between fourteen and eighteen years old.

A letter lodged in the archives at Enfield enquired about an art teacher who had been employed at Mayfield. This was John Cross, quite a famous artist of the time. He was well known in the art world and had a painting bought by the royal commissioners for £1,000. He exhibited regularly at the Royal Academy. On 27 January 1861 he died, leaving a wife and young children. Friends in the art world organised a fund to support his family and amongst the list of subscribers, which included Lord Palmerston and William Gladstone, were Miss Lowe (£5) and pupils of Mr Cross at Miss Lowe's school in Southgate who gave the large sum of £60. This tells us that Eliza Lowe was ambitious in her choice of teachers, that the pupils were very attached to their art teacher and were able to persuade their parents to give money, presumably, if the cause were good enough.

Another teacher was one of the most prominent musicians of the day, Dr William Sterndale Bennett.[10] Bennett was an English composer, pianist, conductor and music educator. At the age of ten he was admitted to the Royal Academy of Music (RAM) in London and by the age of 20, he had begun to make a reputation as a concert pianist. Among those who had a high view of Bennett was the German composer Felix Mendelssohn, who invited him to Leipzig where Bennett became friendly with Robert Schumann who shared Mendelssohn's admiration for Bennett's compositions.

In 1837 Bennett began to teach at the RAM, with which he was associated for most of the rest of his life. For 20 years he taught there, later

---

9. Christ Church was built on the same site as Weld Chapel.
10. 1816-75.

Chapter 7. Mayfield – Eliza Lowe's School in Southgate

also teaching at Queen's College, London, of which he was a founding director. He was Professor of Music at Cambridge from 1856 until 1875. In 1866 he became Principal of the RAM, rescuing it from closure, and remained in this position until his death. He was knighted in 1871 and was buried in Westminster Abbey. Bennett had a significant influence on English music, as a composer, teacher, promoter of standards of musical education and as an important figure in London concert life.

Clara Schumann noted that Bennett spent too much time giving private lessons to keep up with changing trends in music: 'His only chance of learning new music is in the carriage on the way from one lesson to another.'[11]

This included travelling to teach the girls of Mayfield. Eliza Lowe was able to say to parents that their girls would be taught by the foremost musician of the day and one of London's great artists.

The census of 1861 shows Eliza at Mayfield, along with her sister Charlotte, running a Ladies' School. Eliza is now 57 and Charlotte is 41; they are the two principals listed. They have a visitor staying, Helen Barker, born in Sheffield. Jane Bickley, born in Shrewsbury, aged 40, is listed as a ladies' maid (she was also with Eliza in Seaforth in 1851); a cook; a kitchen maid and three housemaids. Also listed is one pupil, Frances Helen Reed, aged fifteen, from Middlesex. Mayfield Lodge has a gardener, George Nash, aged 61, his wife and a daughter, aged 20, a seamstress. The 1861 census recorded those present on the night of 7 April. Easter that year was on 31 March and so it is quite likely that pupils were away on holiday on that date. Perhaps the one girl left, a local girl, was waiting for her parents to come home from a trip abroad.

Ten years later in 1871 she was running a flourishing establishment. This census records 38 pupils, along with Eliza, Mary Manley and Charlotte as principals. Eliza was now 68, Mary 62 and Charlotte was 52. Governess Amelie Hartkopf, 24, came from France and there was a German governess from Hanover, Charlotte Wyneken, 49. There were six servants including Jane Bickley, still with the sisters, now aged 50. One imagines that Jane Bickley took the role of managing the other servants and that by now she was very used to the Lowe sisters whom she had served for at least 20 years. Interestingly, Jane Bickley was a witness to Eliza's will.[12]

The 38 pupils were from diverse places, including Aberdeen, Liverpool, Glasgow, Tralee, the Isle of Man, Beaumaris, Welshpool, London, Manchester and even Valparaiso. In most cases pupils came singly and one

---

11. Berthold Litzmann, *Clara Schumann: An Artist's Life, Based on Material Found in Diaries and Letters*, trans. by G.E. Hadow, 2 Vols (Cambridge: Cambridge University Press, 2013), Vol. 2, p. 132.
12. Tim Tomlinson, private papers.

wonders at their bravery travelling such long distances on their own. There were also nine pupils from Manchester and five from the London area. Pupils were mainly aged between fifteen and eighteen, with some nineteen-year-olds and only one or two fourteen-year-olds. The fact that six servants were employed in 1861 and 1871 implies that the school had a similar number of pupils in 1861.

Examples of Pupils who Attended Mayfield

To illustrate the background of pupils who attended Mayfield I have researched two sets of sisters who were at the school in 1871. The girls were from extremely wealthy families.

The Ecroyd Sisters

Edith and Margaret Ecroyd were from Marsden in Burnley. These sisters were the two eldest daughters of William Farrer Ecroyd and his wife Mary (née Backhouse). They had six other siblings born between 1856 and 1864. In 1881 Ecroyd was a magistrate, a farmer of 314 acres employing ten people and a worsted cloth manufacturer employing 600 people. He later became MP for Preston. The family lived at Spring Cottage, Nelson. Spring Cottage belied its name; it was a very spacious building in its own extensive grounds.

The Ecroyds had mills at Lomeshaye village which is an area less than a mile away from Spring Cottage. Like many Quakers the Ecroyds were concerned for their workers and built workers' houses near the mill. These properties were very advanced for the period, with gas, water and good sanitation. There was a school, a mechanics institute and a reading room, but no pub. The Ecroyds were involved in the formation of the Nelson Local Board in 1864 and various other local government matters.[13] Nelson was first recognised as a separate district at this point. William Farrer Ecroyd died at Credenhill Court, Hereford (photograph below) in 1915 leaving over £179,000. This Grade II listed building was built in the eighteenth century, enlarged in the nineteenth century and is now a rest home. It had extensive grounds.

His wife Mary died in 1867 and in 1869 Ecroyd married again to Anna Maria Foster. Would the girls have gone to Mayfield if their father had not remarried? The older of the two Ecroyd sisters at Mayfield, Edith died, aged 90, a very wealthy spinster in Torquay. Probate shows her estate valued at £23,335 18s 6d.[14] Probate was granted to a local officer and Adelaide Jane Herbert, widow. Adelaide was one of her sisters for whom there is an

---

13. I am indebted to Jean Ingham of the Pendle and Burnley branch of the Lancashire Family History and Heraldry Society (LFHHS) for this information.
14. See www.gov.uk/search-will-probate.

Chapter 7. Mayfield – Eliza Lowe's School in Southgate

Fig. 40 Credenhill Court.

entry in the Guild of All Souls. The Guild was set up in 1873 by the Anglo-Catholic wing of the Church of England with the purpose of praying for the souls of departed members.

However, the younger of the two sisters at Mayfield, Margaret, did marry. Her husband was Harry Tunstill, described on their marriage certificate in 1879 as a gentleman. He was the son of a local cotton manufacturer, William Tunstill. William Tunstill had built up quite an empire with two spinning mills and a farm.[15] Tunstill was highly popular amongst his workers because he had supported them during the cotton crisis which arose because of the American Civil War. He was also chairman of Burnley Board of Guardians and a county magistrate.[16] Following his brother Robert's death in 1902, and his father's in 1903, Harry became sole proprietor of the company. In 1904 the company was incorporated as Brierfield Mills Ltd, with Harry Tunstill as one of three directors. At this point it comprised two spinning mills (with more than 90,000 spindles in total), three weaving sheds (more than 2,000 looms) and various other properties. According to one source, Harry was at that time a principal landowner in the area.[17]

---

15. He lived at a property called Reedyford and gave money to build Reedyford Methodist Church in the area, obviously not a high Anglican as one assumes Adelaide was.
16. See https://www.heritagegateway.org.uk/Gateway/Results_Single.aspx?uid=98baa0d3-a35f-4d70-8b72-266b41105904&resourceID=19191, accessed 19 December 2020.
17. https://forebears.io/england/lancashire/whalley/marsden, accessed 20 December 2020.

Thirteen months after the marriage, Margaret gave birth to their first child, Mary Cicely, and by 1894 had given birth to seven more children. Interestingly, a governess was employed to teach the girls, while their only son, Harry Gilbert, was sent to Charterhouse for his education. There were six servants employed as help in the household. In 1909 the Tunstills had a house in Aysgarth, North Yorkshire, which was used for holidays and much visited by her large family.

Fig. 41 Thornton Lodge.

The house still exists today with some of the original oak panelling and Edwardian furniture. The site has good views and was landscaped to create a solid but no doubt comfortable residence.

Margaret was 88 when she died in Aysgarth in 1942, just a year before sister Edith Mary's death. She was a keen dressmaker and used the billiard table for cutting out patterns and cloth. She was known for her efforts in both wars and, in 1939, allowed a children's hospital the use of Thornton Lodge when a fire damaged the hospital. She had moved out at this point to stay with relatives. There was a tiled toilet opposite the study which Harry Tunstill would not allow to be used by anyone other than himself.[18]

In 1914 the Tunstill's only son, Harry Gilbert (known as Gilbert), was moved by the outbreak of war to advertise in the *Craven Herald and Wensleydale Standard* for 100 men to join him to form a troop. Shortly thereafter 87 men set off with Tunstill for York. By the time they arrived word had got around and their number had grown to 240, to be known as Captain Tunstill's men. On 8 July 1916 Tunstill led his men into action at the Somme, where he was wounded and invalided back to Britain in September that year. The story did not end happily. On the same date as the battle, fifteen years later, he committed suicide.[19]

Below are photographs of Margaret's eldest daughter, Cicely, and her younger daughter, Edith Dorothea, known as Dolly, the latter in nurses'

---

18. I am grateful to Vanessa Kilvington for information about Margaret Tunstill.
19. https://www.cravenherald.co.uk/nostalgia/nostalgia_history/11466580, accessed 20 December 2020.

uniform.[20] The the T on her lapel indicates that she was a member of the Territorial Forces Nursing Service (TFNS) and the badge, though indistinct, indicates the same. TFNS was set up in 1908 to assist in time of war and during World War I there were 8,000 TFNS nurses serving in areas of conflict. They were trained nurses, as opposed to the many volunteers who served alongside them. So, two at least of Margaret Tunstill's children served in the Great War. In the pictures below Cicely is on the left.

Fig. 42 Cicely Tunstill.   *Fig. 43 Dolly Tunstill.*

The McConnel Sisters

Another pair of sisters at Mayfield were Mary Anne and Margaret McConnel from Manchester. They were two of the eight children of William McConnel and Margaret Wanklyn. A younger sister, Lucy, attended the school ten years later, in 1881. They were from a very wealthy family too. McConnel and Kennedy, founded by William McConnel's grandfather, spun cotton using a good quality of cotton from the plantations of North America and the Caribbean known as Sea Island Cotton. On the next page is a postcard photograph of the cotton mills in 1915.[21]

---

20. http://tunstillsmen.blogspot.com/search?q=harry+tunstill, accessed 20 December 2020.
21. Wikipedia, accessed 11 May 2020.

Fig. 44 The McConnel factory in Manchester.

Their father was sole owner of McConnel and Kennedy in 1861 and, following the crisis in cotton caused by the American Civil War, diversified into quarrying slate in Wales. He formed the Aberdovey Slate Company and built the Talyllyn Railway from the quarry to Tywyn, a seven-mile stretch which still exists today. He bought Hengwrt Hall in Dolgellau as a place to stay in Wales in 1859.[22]

A brother, John Wanklyn McConnel, was vice president of the Fine Cotton Spinners and Doublers' Association of Manchester and owner of several plantations in Mississippi. He survived the sinking of the Lusitania in 1915 and gave a moving account of the sinking which was published in the *Manchester Guardian* on 10 May 1915.[23]

Lilias Dalglish

Another Mayfield girl was Lilias Dalglish (mentioned earlier). She was also the daughter of a rich businessman. Her father, Robert Dalglish MP, lived in Southgate while he attended Parliament.[24] His father had been Provost of Glasgow. Robert was an able and popular MP for Glasgow from 1857 to 1874. A delightful cartoon of him was published in Vanity Fair in June 1873 with the caption: 'The most popular man in the House of Commons'. The family business was calico printing. He ran a mill in Lennoxtown, near Glasgow, where the family home was situated. He bought a grand residence called Kilmardinny in the area of Milngavie where he entertained in lavish style and where Lilias and her brother, James Hertz Dalglish, were born. Many notable people dined there.

---

22. See http://dams.llgc.org.uk/behaviour/llgc-id:1126605/fedora-bdef:image/reference; the National Library of Wales catalogue. The picture on the website is of Hengwrt Hall, accessed 11 May 2020.
23. The account may be read at Mr. John Wanklyn McConnel - The Lusitania Resource (https://www.rmslusitania.info/people/saloon/john-mcconnel/, accessed 12 February 2021).
24. I am indebted to Ian Brown of the Milngavie and Bearsden Historical Society for much of this section.

Chapter 7. Mayfield – Eliza Lowe's School in Southgate

Lilias and James were the children of Robert's second marriage. Interestingly, James Hertz, aged nearly 16, was also baptised in Southgate, on 22 April 1870, a year later than Lilias. Robert Dalglish joined the Free Church of Scotland after the Disruption in 1843.[25] Having left the established Church, the new members of the Free Church in the local area had nowhere to meet other than in an inn where they lived in Lennoxtown. The fact that, when Lilias and James were born, their parents were not attending a dedicated church may explain why they were not baptised as babies.

Lilias married Louis Homburger in Paris in 1879. A year later a daughter was born, called Lilias after her mother, followed by a boy, Louis, in 1882. The younger Lilias went on to become a well-known and respected academic in the area of linguistics. Her interests lay in African languages and her work is still quoted today. She taught linguistics in Paris and was president of the Société de linguistique de Paris from 1940 until 1944. Having a Scottish mother, a German father and living in Paris, she had something of an advantage when it came to learning languages. Languages were viewed as important at Mayfield, so her mother would probably also have had a good command of French and German.

The next chapter tells the story of two more Mayfield pupils.

---

25. This is the name given to the schism within the established Church of Scotland. It was partly an argument about powers of patronage and partly about doctrine.

Chapter 8

Alice Rathbone and Eva Müller

This chapter explores two pupils who were great friends at Mayfield and grew up to have very contrasting lives despite both having considerable intellectual gifts. One went on to live a conventional married life, while the other became a campaigner in the women's movement. One of these pupils tells us about her experiences at Mayfield.

Alice Rathbone

Alice Rathbone was at Mayfield with the Ecroyds, McConnels and Lilias Dalglish in 1871. She was from Liverpool and a member of the Rathbone family, a wealthy and famously philanthropic family of some stature. Alice's parents were Philip Henry Rathbone and Jane Stringer Steward. Philip Rathbone encouraged the cultural life of the city and sat on many of the city's committees. He worked in insurance and was noted for his bohemian dress and artistic nature. Alice took part in the plays regularly held at their home, Greenbank Cottage, on the family estate in Toxteth Park and sometimes invited friends from Mayfield to the performances.

Amongst the Rathbone Papers in the archives of Liverpool University are a number of remarkable letters written by the young Alice, mainly to her cousin William Rathbone.[1] Her mother had suggested that she spend some time writing letters (Alice complained that her mother had no idea how much time she had to spend at her lessons) and so began a long correspondence with William, of whom she became very fond.

Amongst these letters is the beginning of an account of her time at Mayfield, which frustratingly ends after the first day:

---

1. I am grateful to the University of Liverpool for permission to reproduce these letters and the associated photographs. The Rathbone Papers are part of the University of Liverpool Special Collections and Archives. All quotations are from this source unless otherwise stated.

Chapter 8. Alice Rathbone and Eva Müller

1872, bright hot days were rare events in the year 18- when I first thought of writing down some sort of account of what happened to me at school. But that day was one of them. I will begin my narration of unimportant events by a description of myself, one of the most unimportant personages in them. I am 16, a reasonable height for my age, I have green eyes no particular features either good or bad and still wear my hair down. When I first went to school I was just 15. The night before I was out at a dance at my uncle's. What fun we had to be sure, we went home about 2am and I read till 4o'clock. The next morning I rose at 6, much against my will, and after a long journey of 7 good hours I arrived at Mayfield. I was too tired to notice anything much but I remember Miss Smith's kind face in the warm firelight and being put in charge of Alice Brown who helped me to unpack my bags and then my entrance into the crowded schoolroom, my feeling of being criticised by ? eyes at once and trying to appear at ease and write a letter. Then to end my misery came bed-time and I went to sleep, too tired even to cry.

Alice was kept busy at school, rather like the Landor pupils at Seaforth. She wrote from Mayfield, on 23 January 1872, to William to thank him for the book he had sent: 'I shall have no time to read it except at night in the house in the hour we have for undressing between nine and ten. I tied up all your music and photographs in your portfolio, only I have kept the Schumann a little longer, you said I might.'

An Essay by Alice

Perhaps because she was so busy there are only two letters from Mayfield. She was a pupil there for two years. However, there is a remarkable item in the Rathbone Papers at Liverpool. It is an essay written by Alice at Mayfield and gives an insight into what was taught there and the standard reached. The essay was entitled *Short-lived Dynasties*. This is a fine essay for a young girl, and presumably she and others thought so too and took steps to preserve it. She does not entirely stick to the point of the title, excusing herself by remarking at the start: 'The scarcity of short-lived dynasties in modern history makes this a very difficult subject to write upon.'

The next move is to argue that kings today are not really kings as they are ruled by ministers of the day:

> Ever since the succession of kings . . . hereditary great statesmen have arisen who have been the true kings. A long-lived dynasty

only means that the kings have been sensible enough to follow advice, so the people were content. Why should the state keep and pay for a man for doing nothing while the real rulers work and slave, living upon a comparatively meagre income supplied from their own purses.

She continues: 'Of course, it is natural that people should cling to old customs . . . besides uneducated people will be awed by old established customs. So why should so much money be spent on them?' Her solution is for a good statesman to become king, then be succeeded by a king elected from the remaining chief statesmen by the Lords and Commons.

Below is a photograph of the first page of the essay. It is dated November 1870.

Pencil comments from the teacher were: 'Very revolutionary. Spelling not perfect – '.

Underneath the pencil comments are initials, but it is not clear what or whose they are. There is a later comment: 'I did not ask for a *mere* verbal definition.'

Note that the comments are written in pencil rather than pen. I rather like this as it shows respect for the pupil and what she has written. A later letter mentions notes for an essay entitled, 'Some of the differences between the English constitution and those of other nations'. Clearly international history and politics were on the syllabus.

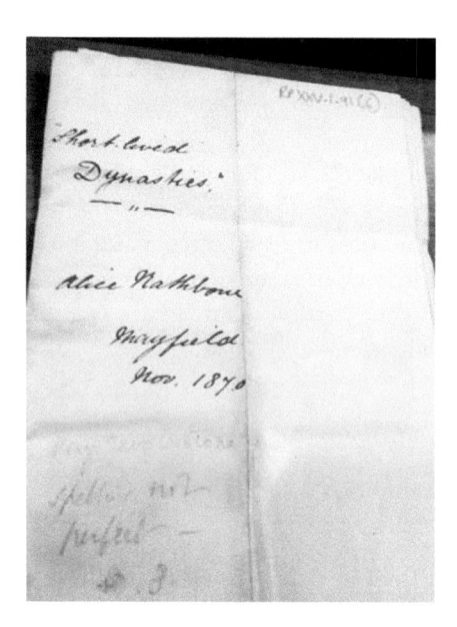

Fig. 45 Essay title page.

Letters written after she left Mayfield give some insight into her life and the influence of school.

Lessons in Frankfurt

In January 1872 she was at Mayfield but later that year she was living in Frankfurt am Main. On 14 September, she wrote to William from Frankfurt where she was staying with Fräulein Borré at 21 Taubenstrasse. She encouraged William to go into Parliament to invent some bill which

Chapter 8. Alice Rathbone and Eva Müller

would sort out drunkenness in Liverpool, as a result of which there would be processions from the Band of Hope, parades and so on and great popularity. There would be a statue of him outside St George's Hall.[2] It is a very fine letter. The new Liverpool University would be called after him. She gave him a list of things to do to prepare, imagining she is his teacher. He should learn speeches and she quoted great men of the day: Pitt, Burke, Lord Brougham, Bright, Earl Grey. She wrote: 'After 1874 I shall know such heaps I shall be quite qualified for the office of debating contradictions.'

She was one of a group of girls with Fräulein Borré. Was this an outpost of Mayfield? She told William that on his recommendation they were now reading Carlyle's essays and that the girls would always go to her for reading suggestions. She was continuing with her piano lessons and was keen for William to send her more songs. She commented that she liked a melody that William had written. She went to a concert given by Mme Schumann who played Chopin, Schumann and Beethoven. She commented that Clara's playing of Robert Schumann's *Schlummerlied* was 'like an opal, one colour but with brighter ideas flashing through'.

She was having lessons from Clara Schumann who was, to Alice's distress, leaving Frankfurt. She said: 'Dr Bennett was a good teacher – everyone said so but the two years I was at school he did not do so much towards making me attentive, and my fingers obedient as Miss Schumann has done in one month.'

The arrangement with Clara Schumann may have been put in place by Dr Bennett. Bennett had spent three winters in Germany as a young man and become very friendly with Robert Schumann. Alice did not like the Chopin piece played by Clara Schumann: 'No deep undertones like in Schumann'; and 'Don't laugh at my romanticism', she said to William. She was only seventeen at this point.

On 15 October 1872 from Frankfurt she complained that she was always being called naive: 'Aber, wie naïve .' She was able to slip into German with no difficulty.

Friendship with Eva Müller

Her great friend at Mayfield was Eva Müller. In the same letter from Frankfurt (15 October 1872) she told William that Eva was a pearl: 'No-one can have any idea how patient and good to me she was at school and how vilely I behaved to her out of jealousy. She is really clever.'

---

2. In 1899 a statue of William's father, William Rathbone VI was erected outside St George's Hall.

She goes on to say that she does not mind it if it is romantic, she loves her.

She is pleased because the Müllers are going to be in London for three months after Christmas and have invited her to stay with them and be with Eva, but her parents won't reply. Eva's older sister Ella is very clever and wants to go to college. Perhaps William can advise:

> Is Hitchin or Cambridge more likely to suit her? She doesn't wish to go where there are only governesses . . . it is such a bold step for a girl to take and cuts her off from so much. That it would be a help to know she was not the only one.

By 1872 Emily Davies, a great advocate of women's education, had moved her Womens' College at Benslow House, founded in Hitchin in 1869, to Cambridge where, situated close to the village of Girton, it became known as Girton College. Perhaps Alice did not realise that Hitchin and Cambridge were the same college. Her attitude shows how novel the idea of women going to college was at the time, both in terms of it being 'bold' and in the concern to check that teaching would not be undertaken by yet more governesses. Alice showed no inclination for a college education at this point.

She finishes her letter by telling William that, following hearing Schumann's *Faust*, she has changed her view on Goethe. A few months later, in January 1873 she writes of her bad temper and of her friend Frank (Frankie Bircham) who did good German translations at school. She comments on pictures of Napoleon and Dante and knows of Arnold's view that boys should learn to be gentlemen and Christians first.

A visit to Mayfield

At some point she and Eva were in London from where they visited Mayfield.

Alice wrote to William:

> Today we had a good time of it. Eva and I went down to Mayfield. We behaved rather badly I'm afraid. There was a guilty feeling of delight in walking up the front stairs, going in the garden without jackets or gloves, buying things at the village shops etc. The Cedars looked just as splendidly dark against the lovely bright stretch of lawn. There were girls sitting in our old haunt under the American oak and strangers walking arm in arm between the laurels in the shady walk, Frank's walk.[3] Of all the 35 girls I only knew 4. Minnie (?) turned

---
3. This was Frankie Bircham, another of Alice's close friends.

quite white when she saw us and was half hysterical with delight the whole time. Poor old girl. I was sorry to have to leave her there with those girls and Miss Wynkner. A feeling of the old vicious schoolgirl hatred of that woman came over me as she kissed me and called me 'darling'. It makes me hot and angry even now to think of the things she has said about Eva whose friend she called herself. Those she said of me were not so bad because from the first day war was declared between us. We always detested each other. Miss Charlotte we only saw for a moment coming away. All the Miss Lowes liked me, she best of all. She said in her old cordial tones 'Why, child how glad I am to see you. I wish we had you back.' Which is a great deal for her.

According to the census Charlotte Wynkner came from Hanover where there is evidence of Wynkners who had military careers in the Electorate of Hanover and one who became a well-known Lutheran missionary in the United States.

Fig. 46 Alice Rathbone.

I don't think Alice was the easiest of pupils and it is not hard to imagine her making enemies. However, it is clear that the Misses Lowe viewed her with affection and respect, as they had done the Landor sisters.

This photograph of Alice was taken during her time in Frankfurt by F. Weisbrod of 70 Bleichstrasse. As was common in early photographs, the subject looks very solemn but also thoughtful and very self-possessed. The serious look in these early photographs is often due to having to be perfectly still during the film exposure of several seconds.

In the autumn of 1873 Alice was at home, taking part in theatre productions at Greenbank Cottage. Having left school, she was still studying. She told William that she was having Italian lessons and really liked reading and translating Dante: 'I translate it with Uncle Thomas now instead of the German.' She was looking forward to Eva visiting: 'What I want to know about Eva is how she is looking and what she seems to be doing. All the while we were away Eva never lost her temper except once when I was cross and disagreeable and fractious to an unbearable degree.'

Alice's Reading

She encouraged William to keep on with Erasmus which she was also reading, along with Robert Bridges' poetry. The latter had been to visit and Alice commented that he was very different from the way in which she had anticipated him from reading his poems. A month later she was reading Robert Burns.

In a letter on 29 October 1873 she said: 'I got a letter from Ella[4] at Girton saying she was very happy. I was very glad to read Miss Davis[5] letter.' (Emily Davies was coming to visit the Rathbones.)

This letter is interesting because it marks the start of Alice's interest in going to study at Cambridge. The matter must have been discussed with Miss Davies and in a later letter (November 1874) Alice says that her friend Frankie from Mayfield days is going to take the Cambridge exam.[6] She asked William whether she should try herself. Certainly, her intellectual interests showed no sign of diminishing. She was fluent in German and comments that she was helping her uncle Thomas and Miss Raleigh. It is not clear from her letter who Miss Raleigh was.

She told William in a letter of 8 June 1874 that she was reading John Stuart Mill on communism[7] which gave her a tingling feeling of entering

---

4. Eva's older sister Henrietta was one of the first students at Girton. She went on to campaign for women's rights in Britain and in India, which she regularly visited, on occasion with Eva. There is an entry for her in the *Oxford National Dictionary of Biography*. Ella must have been a nickname as Girton College could find no mention of an Ella Müller in their records.
5. Spelling as in Alice's letter.
6. Emily Davies, an early suffragist, was the co-founder of Girton College, which moved from Hitchin to Cambridge in 1873. Davies was keen to encourage women to take the Cambridge entrance exams and it looks as though this was the purpose of her visit to the Rathbones. (See Chapter 2.)
7. This is a puzzle as Mill did not write on Communism and his work on Socialism

Chapter 8. Alice Rathbone and Eva Müller

a new world and leaving the old behind, a feeling she had not had since reading Dante. She was reading about court life in France under the old regime. That summer she visited her friends Eva and Frankie and then attended a ball with Oxford students in Penmaenmawr, North Wales where, she says, she found some German books in which she was revelling. She particularly liked J.-P. Richter's poems.

In October of that year she went to the Royal Institution in Colquitt St, Liverpool to attend lectures. These may have been extension lectures. Extension lectures in provincial centres were an important feature of university activities in the late nineteenth century. They were often associated with attempts to provide professional teaching and examinations for girls through the local examinations for schools provided by Cambridge University in conjunction with Oxford.[8] However, she thought she wouldn't bother writing the exam essay, didn't need a dressing down and would feel useless and humiliated.

A later letter, of 16 December 1874, showed that she was having a change of heart. She attended a ball in Derby, invited by Mrs Willoughby (Blanche Davy of Mayfield days), and then told William that lectures for ladies began again soon and were to go on till March when the exam took place.

There is a gap of four years until October 1878 when we learn that Alice did take the Cambridge exam and felt utterly dejected because she failed the arithmetic paper: 'it is very ignominious after working so hard at it but I failed in the Cambridge local exam through arithmetic: now I am working for next year.'

At the same time, she was able to tell William that she was reading Lessing and found him second only to Goethe.

Marriage and Family

After this the next letters to cousin William are after her marriage to William Moore, a Liverpool businessman whom she had known from childhood. Moore had taken part in plays at Greenbank Cottage so must have been a family friend. They married in 1880. In a letter to William from their home in Hoylake on the Wirral she told William: 'Mind you tell me if you see Eva and Frances'. A letter on 11 August 1888 gave news of three children, Marjorie, Gwennie and Billy who were giving her much pleasure.

---

was not published till after his death in 1879. But it is not impossible that Alice had got hold of an early version of Mill's work.

8. www.cam.ac.uk/about-the-university/history/nineteenth-and-twentieth-centuries, accessed 15 January 2021.

We never learn if Alice retook the Cambridge exam. Perhaps other events took over. William and Alice would go on to have three further children and the family would later become the residents of Greenbank Cottage, her childhood home.

Conclusion: On Alice

Alice's letters are mainly about her feelings, friendships, social life and her reading but there are a few other interesting aspects of her life that emerge. She had visited in hospital a woman whose husband drank and beat her which led Alice to say that people should not have to live together forever if unhappy.

At some point she went to the Liverpool Infirmary two days a week to learn bandaging. The family was heavily involved in philanthropic activities in Liverpool. Her uncle William Rathbone VI consulted with Florence Nightingale and was very involved in the development of nursing and hospitals for the poor. In one letter Alice said she was concerned about the plight of men in Liverpool following the strike; there was no work for them, and they would emigrate to Texas if they could get there. She referred to Father Nugent, Roman Catholic chaplain at Walton Jail, who was very concerned and active. She asked William to help.

Of her time at school it is the friendships she made that stand out and were a continuing theme of her letters. Nevertheless, she was also keen to enter into debate with William on intellectual themes and the range of her reading and academic interests was extensive. How far this interest was sparked off at Mayfield cannot be assessed but, as with Lucy Landor, she continued to read and debate well after leaving school. How far her lack of expertise at arithmetic was due to her school is also uncertain! What is clear is that she and other pupils were beginning to think about going to university and Eliza's school had been a good preparation.

Eva Müller

Now on to Alice's great friend Eva, with whom she kept in contact for many years, even after she married.

Eva Müller was born in Valparaiso, Chile, to a wealthy German businessman and an English mother. Valparaiso was a thriving commercial centre and many Europeans and Americans did business there. Her family home in London was in Portland Place and they had a country house at Shenley, Hertfordshire, a house called Hillside. There is often mention of this house in Alice's letters. Eva's early life was spent in Valparaiso where she was taught by a governess. The family travelled widely and, as a young

Chapter 8. Alice Rathbone and Eva Müller

woman, Eva mountaineered in the Swiss Alps and in later years travelled to the United States and India. Her mother had progressive political views and, with her encouragement, Eva worked, aged 20, with Octavia Hill in Marylebone where her duties were to collect rents and to look after the welfare of tenants. Octavia Hill was an influential social reformer and founder of the National Trust. Although the family was extremely wealthy, they allowed Eva to accept a nurse training post at Brownlow Hill Infirmary, a workhouse infirmary in Liverpool (where Alice learned bandaging). Eva Müller went on to have a very full and interesting life. She had a close relationship with her parents, something of which Alice was at times jealous. In one letter Alice said that Eva would never get to marry well because her parents didn't know the right people and she worried that, if she did marry, Eva would not find a suitable person.

Marriage to Walter Stowe Bright McLaren

Alice need not have worried. Eva did indeed 'marry well'. She became the wife of Walter Stowe Bright McLaren. McLaren was the youngest son of Duncan McLaren (formerly Lord Provost of Edinburgh and from 1865-81 MP for Edinburgh) and Priscilla Bright who was President of the Edinburgh National Society for Women's Suffrage and sister of John and Jacob Bright. After Edinburgh University, Walter entered into business as a worsted spinner in Keighley, Yorkshire. In 1886 he was elected as Liberal MP for Crewe and became an active Parliamentarian. Both he and Eva had wide interests in reform and acted together on many fronts. The photograph on the next page shows Eva (hatless) behind Walter on his campaign to win the Inverness Burghs seat at the 1885 General Election. Family were there to support him and also Joseph Chamberlain who was advocating a radical Liberal agenda at the time.

Eva's experiences with Octavia Hill and in the workhouse infirmary in Liverpool seem to have given her a keen desire to help the poor and vulnerable of society. A notice of her wedding appeared in the *South London Press* on 21 April 1883 and included the following accolade:

> Of the bride it may well be said that, although only on the Board[9] one short year, she has won golden opinions not only from her colleagues, but from all who have had the privilege of coming in contact with her. Her extreme sympathy with, and large heartedness towards, the poor, and her anxious care for their welfare, must have left a memory that will always remain.

---
9. This was the Board of Guardians for Lambeth.

Fig. 47 Electioneering in Inverness.

The notice of her wedding described the service at the Friends' Meeting House at Westminster. As a Quaker marriage there was no giving away of the bride or leading the bride up after the groom had entered, certainly no differences in the promises made. Bride and groom entered together and sat behind a table facing those present. All present were invited to meditate upon the seriousness of the promises that were about to be made. The vows were repeated with little ceremony and all were invited to sign the illuminated document which was the marriage certificate.[10] To complete the picture of equality there was both a minister officiating and a 'ministress' as the paper quaintly puts it, unsure of what she should be called: 'if one may be allowed to so designate the lady officiating'. In line with the spirit of the marriage service, Eva was known throughout her married life as Mrs Eva McLaren, never Mrs Walter McLaren which would have been standard practice.

---

10. 'Friends, I take this my friend, Eva Maria Müller, whom I hold by the hand, to be my wife promising with God's help, to be unto her a faithful and loving husband, until God by death separates us.' The bride then said exactly the same words substituting the word 'wife' with 'husband' and Walter's name for hers.

Chapter 8. Alice Rathbone and Eva Müller

The paper also included a lengthy description of the 'At Home' that was held a few days later at the Müller home at Portland Place. A magnificent array of wedding presents was on show. One gift not present was a horse, named Columbine – shades of riding lessons at Mayfield.

Article in the Feminist Press

One year later, on 31 May 1884, an interview that she gave in her home was reported in the *Women's Signal*, a feminist publication. This gives insight into her motives and her sense of humour. The interviewer, Sarah Tooley, after describing Eva's early life, asks her what policy she intends to adopt following her election as Vice President of the British Women's Temperance Association. Eva replies: '"My policy, briefly, is to follow my chief", accompanied with a merry laugh.'

Tooley describes the room in which she is conducting the interview, in Poet's Corner, attached to Westminster Abbey, comments on her blue-grey dress, fitting for someone who belongs to the Society of Friends and continues: 'Her manner is frank, cordial, full of good nature and absolutely natural.' This could have been written by Alice Rathbone.

Tooley's interview shows that Eva had a wide vision of what women could achieve. She expressed herself in the following passage in terms which mirror St Paul's picture of how different gifts are given for the good of all:

> All will learn together what the great possibilities for the women of today are, and will realise the many directions in which women can work, according to their respective gifts. This seems to me most important. 'One woman has the gift for public speaking, another for writing, another for organisation, another for work in the homes of the poor, and so each can choose the vocation to which her special abilities point. And, moreover, the social reforms being various, each woman while being in sympathy with all, devotes her time to the one which attracts her the most and, needless to say, that will be the one where she does the best work.'[11]

One might remark that Eva possessed all these gifts and more. It is also clear that only women of independent means, not those having to work for a living, could exercise their gifts in this way. The great possibilities that Eva lists here do not involve anything other than voluntary work although it was becoming clear that things were changing and, after World War I, jobs hitherto thought only for men would increasingly become open to women.

11. Sarah Tooley's interview in the *Women's Signal*, 31 May 1884.

Alice Rathbone's younger cousin Eleanor Rathbone went to university and would become one of the first women MPs. However, in Eva's time the great issue was women's suffrage and that, along with social reforms, occupied her time and thoughts.

Activities after Marriage

Upon her marriage she and Walter lived first in Bradford where Walter had business interests. She transferred from Lambeth to be a poor law guardian in Horton, Bradford and campaigned for improvements in the poor law and better conditions in workhouses. However, with Walter's political leanings and parliamentary ambitions, they moved down to London where their campaigning really took off. Her life became one long round of committees, drumming up support and public speaking, at which she excelled. She also published several pamphlets,[12] including *The History of the Women's Suffrage Movement in the Women's Liberal Federation*.[13] *Civil Rights of Women* was an academic study of women's civil rights and duties both in England, Scotland, Ireland and the Isle of Man (where women gained the vote in 1888). It gave painstaking details of various local and national boards or institutions, showing how widely women were already contributing to public life. She showed how married women were less able to take their part in public life, generally because property was still often in a husband's name so a wife did not count as a ratepayer. Ratepayers were usually the ones who voted to elect members to different authorities. Nevertheless, increasingly women were being voted onto boards, such as school boards and boards of guardians. They could also become county inspectors in various local government departments.

She and Walter worked with Josephine Butler, a leading social reformer and feminist of the Victorian era, on the campaign for the repeal of the Contagious Diseases Act. In 1883 Butler wrote to a friend suggesting Eva McLaren as a speaker and later Eva was to become secretary and then chairwoman of the London branch of the Ladies' National Association. She was a signatory to a petition presented to the Liberal Prime Minister Campbell-Bannerman representing the Liberal Women's Federation and was involved with Welsh Liberal Associations as well as ones in Crewe and Southport.[14]

---

12. *Civil Rights of Women*, National Society, 1888. *The Election of Women on Parish and District Councils* and *The Duties and Opinions of Women with Reference to Parish and District Councils,* Central National Society for Women's Suffrage, 1894.
13. A copy is kept at Manchester Libraries, Information and Archives, published in 1903.
14. For an account of her life and political involvement see the entry for her in the *Oxford Dictionary of National Biography*.

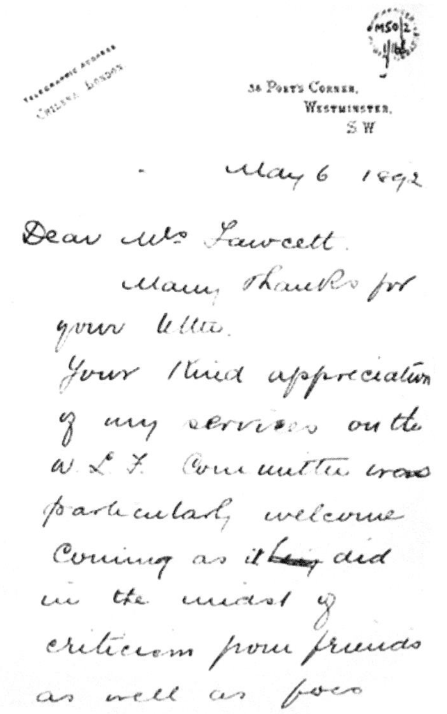

Chapter 8. Alice Rathbone and Eva Müller

All this could be both physically and emotionally exhausting. A letter (parts of which are produced opposite) from Eva to Millicent Fawcett hints at this. Note the choice of Chilena, London for their address to receive telegraphs, a link to her childhood in Valparaiso.

Fawcett had asked Eva to speak at a meeting. In the same letter, Eva replied: '[I] shall feel it a pleasure and a privilege to show that I can work with those who differ from me on some subjects if united by the bonds of sympathy in the cause of women'. At the end of Eva's letter is a lovely touch where she thanks Mrs Fawcett for her kind words about Walter.

Fig. 48 Letter from Eva McLaren.

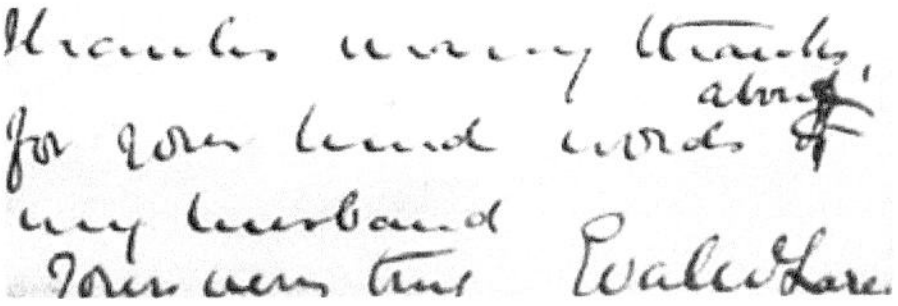

Fig. 49 Eva's signature.

Something of the toll that work took on her is also shown in two letters from Walter to Mrs Fawcett shortly after the above letter was written. Eva had agreed in the above letter to speak at a meeting and Walter writes to ask for his wife to be excused. His four-page letter shows his concern for Eva but also his concern not to let Mrs Fawcett down. He says that Eva had agreed to sell 50 tickets but pleads that they are not sent to her as all she was capable of at the time was resting. He would find a substitute speaker.

Suffragist Campaigning

After her marriage Eva took on the mantle of women's suffrage in a big way, perhaps under the influence of her husband but also in the wake of her sister Henrietta who, while at Girton, had become an ardent feminist.

Fig. 50 Walter McLaren – Bodnant Garden, Conwy.

In 1903 a split occurred between those who believed in working through constitutional channels and those who argued that force and illegal means would be the only way to gain suffrage. The former were known as Suffragists and the latter Suffragettes.

Disagreements between the two groups developed which became more strongly expressed as time went on, some women agitating for militant action which involved in some cases breaking the law. Eva was one of those who strongly opposed unconstitutional means. She wrote a letter in 1912, shortly after Walter's death, giving voice to her objections. She wrote on behalf of the Home Counties Union of Women's Liberal Associations: 'I write . . . to protest against the illegal actions of a relatively small number of women, the members of the Social and Political Union.'[15]

She and others felt that such action would jeopardise their chances of gaining the vote which in 1912 looked close to reality with a bill to that

---

15. https://www.nationalarchives.gov.uk/education/britain1906to1918/pdf/gallery-4-gaining-suffrage-case-studies.pdf, accessed 31 December 2020.

Chapter 8. Alice Rathbone and Eva Müller

effect being debated in Parliament. (The Parliamentary Franchise [Women] Bill 1912 was defeated by 222 to 208.) On the other side Emmeline Pankhurst represented the view that to restrain from active protest was to betray the cause and effectively prolong injustice. One can understand the frustration of those like Eva, who, with her husband, had worked so hard and so long for women's rights, at being told they were betraying the cause. Interestingly, Walter had taken the view that these women were plucky and should be supported.

There is a fine sculpture of Walter McLaren at Bodnant Garden, near Conwy (see Fig. 50). His older brother married Laura Pochin who inherited the mansion and gardens there. Bodnant is still today the home of descendants of the McLarens.

Life after Walter

Eva retired from most of her public duties following Walter's death in 1912. Incredibly, however, at the age of 61 she resumed her nursing career and worked at a base hospital in France during the winter of 1914-15.

One letter, written towards the end of her life, reveals that Eva missed all the meetings and activities in which her life had been spent. It also shows that she enjoyed company and a good laugh. The letter was to Vera Holme and is dated 18 February 1918. She thanks her for the photographs and hopes they can meet soon: 'I long for another laugh with you! And for another big meeting!'[16]

Eva tells Vera that the minister at Portobello (the letter is addressed from Merchiston Gardens, Edinburgh) is catching on and has invited Eva to speak at a meeting at his church. The letter also mentions that Eva is about to go on a tour with a Miss Curwen. At this point Eva was 66 and not in good health but was still engaged in suffragist activity and travelling. She ends her letter: 'May you have glorious meetings wherever you go. Yours affectionately Eva M. McLaren.'

Vera Holme was a 'larger than life' character who had spent time in prison for her suffragette actions yet was clearly on close terms with Eva who had argued strongly against the suffragette policy of militant action. All her life Eva had been a reconciler and it is therefore not surprising that she had become a close friend of Vera. The letter is very different in tone from that sent to Millicent Fawcett, perhaps because it was not of a political nature. Nevertheless, it is a puzzle that Eva makes no mention of the passing of the first Women's Suffrage Act that month on 5 February 1918.

---

16. See London School of Economics, Women's Library Archive, 7VJH/2/5/17.

Her Death

Eva's death came in 1921 at her home in Great Comp, Borough Green, Kent, following a breakdown in health and chronic Bright's disease. She and Walter had moved there in 1908 as a retreat from London. They lived alongside a great friend, Frances Heron-Maxwell,[17] with whom she and Marie Corbett had founded the Forward Suffrage Union as a focus for women's suffrage efforts inside the Liberal Party and through the Women's Liberal Federation. Jocelyne Turner in *Down Memory Lane* recalls that the McLarens and Frances were joined there by Miss Somerville, also a campaigner, who was keen on sports and crafts.[18] Shakespeare plays were performed and sporting activities were a regular feature of life there. They lived in separate accommodation but it sounds as if there was regular social interaction between the neighbours.

A local newspaper in Wrotham gave details of Eva's will.[19] Her servants, both indoor and outdoor, were left money, as were several friends and relations. The bulk of her estate, £44,696, was left to her adopted daughter, Mary Florence Campbell McLaren who lived with her at Great Comp. Eva directed her executors to 'cause my body to be consumed by the process known as cremation, instead of being interred in usual way'.

Conclusion: On Eva

Eva McLaren was a remarkable woman. Alice Rathbone's description seems apt: a pearl. She was unconventional in some ways: her wedding, instructions for her cremation, her insistence on being called Mrs Eva McLaren being examples. She was totally single-minded in her beliefs, which can be summarised as reforming injustice wherever it occurred and not only in Britain. Her range of interests and campaigns was extraordinary. Yet she was also a conventional upper-class woman who employed servants, lived in fine houses and supported her husband in all situations. She had great charm, a fine intellect and was a much sought-after speaker and writer. She was remembered by Alice as clever, patient and forgiving and in later life too she took pains not to upset others. People mattered to her and she was always loyal to those around her. Of her life at school, apart from what Alice tells us, I know nothing. However, I am sure she won Miss Lowe's amiability prize.

---

17. Mrs Heron-Maxwell was a beneficiary in Eva's will.
18. Jocelyne V.C. Turner, *Down Memory Lane* (Platt Memorial Hall, 2016), available from http://plattmemorialhall.org/warmemorial/books/.
19. *Sevenoaks Chronicle and Kentish Advertiser*, 11 November 1921.

CHAPTER 9

Mayfield after Eliza and S. Winifred's

This chapter continues the story of Mayfield and its connection with the Lowe family. It goes on to tell the story of the founding of S. Winifred's School in Bangor (later in Llanfairfechan) and of Emily Landor Lowe who at different times was head of both schools. It begins with the death of Eliza.

The Death of Eliza

Fig. 51 Eliza's grave.

On 9 August 1872 Eliza Lowe died at Mayfield aged 68, after an illness of 'much weariness and suffering'.[1] Perhaps this is why there is no mention of Eliza in Alice Rathbone's account of a visit to Mayfield mentioned in the

1. Rice, *The Story of S. Mary's, Abbots Bromley*, p. 31.

previous chapter. She died in Southgate still in harness with her sisters but was brought back to Abbots Bromley for a funeral service in St Nicholas Church and burial there in the churchyard.

The gravestone is what is known as a 'raised ledger' stone. It is rather beautiful, carefully sculpted with an intricate stone cross carved out of the upper surface, the whole tapering from west to east. The first bevelled edge, just visible on the photo, reads: 'Give thine holy angels charge concerning them.'

Underneath reads: 'Beneath until his coming again rest the mortal bodies of Emily Louisa and Eliza and Mary Manley and Charlotte daughters of Samuel Lowe Esq of Whitchurch Salop and of Maria his wife.' The opposite side reads: 'Maria Sarah daughter of the above Samuel and Mariah Lowe widow of Capt William Bayley Mosley 10th Bengal Cavalry.' On the west side of the stone it says: 'Here also rests Susannah daughter of Charles Lowe and of Susannah his wife.'

Unusually, there are no dates for any of the five sisters or for their niece Susannah. The script is uniform and quite elaborate and it appears that the inscriptions were all made at the same time. Charlotte died in 1897. It can be seen from the photograph that an identical stone is laid next to it. This commemorates John Manley Lowe who died in 1904. The script is the same font and this stone too must have been commissioned at the same time. It may be that Edward Lowe arranged for the stones to be laid and inscribed. Family meant a great deal to Edward Lowe; he had no children of his own and as Chapter 11 will show it was important to him to create fitting memorials.

The officiating minister at the service for Eliza was not the vicar of the parish, Eliza's brother John Manley Lowe, but Edward Lowe.

On her burial certificate she is listed as living both in Southgate and The Crofts, Abbots Bromley. The three sisters, Eliza, Mary Manley and Charlotte, who had worked together all their lives, intended to retire together to Abbots Bromley and it may have been their brother John who negotiated the buying of the lovely Georgian house opposite the Butter Cross in the marketplace for them (see the photograph on p. 165). After the death of the last of the sisters it became part of S. Anne's School,

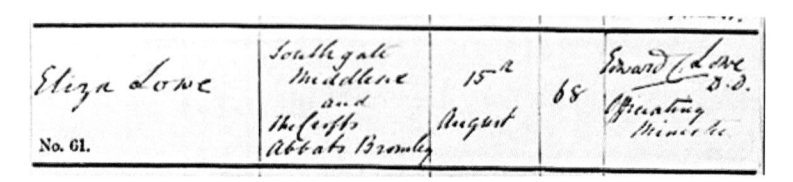

Fig. 52 Eliza Lowe's burial certificate.

Chapter 9. Mayfield after Eliza and S. Winifred's

officially Talbot House after a later Provost, but always referred to as Crofts. Yet in April 1871 Mayfield was flourishing with the 67-year-old Eliza still resident. The fact that Eliza died in Southgate shows that she was keeping an eye on things as late as August 1872. John Manley Lowe travelled down to Mayfield shortly after the funeral, presumably to sort things out there.[2]

Emily Louisa Lowe takes over Mayfield

It was intended that the school carry on with the eldest daughter of John Manley Lowe as headmistress. This was Emily Louisa Lowe, who was born in 1850 and so very young when she went to Mayfield. She may have been named after Eliza's sister, Emily Louisa, mentioned as reciting Shakespeare with one of the Landor sisters at Eliza's school in Seaforth, who had died in 1849 aged just 33. However, this Emily Louisa too died prematurely in 1873 of rheumatic fever. A letter from Lucy Landor to her sister Fanny passed on the sad news that Emmie (Emily Louisa) had died on 23 October:

> On me it fell to tell . . . the most sad news which reached this house from Mayfield between 9 and 10 o'clock. By *post* had come a better acct. of poor Emmie; within an hour, the telegram said she had passed away at 6 this morning. . . . John [Manley Lowe], they think, will be utterly overwhelmed by this terrible blow. He was so proud as well as so fond of Emmie. None of his other children, nor of their cousins seem at all qualified to take her place, indeed few, at 23, could be found anywhere to take and fill it as she seemed beginning to do, exacting the respect as well as winning the love of her pupils, and promising to make another Eliza Lowe, with in many ways superior advantages.[3]

Lucy did not have to explain what she meant by 'another Eliza Lowe' – evidence of the respect with which Eliza was held within the family. Emily Louisa Lowe also commanded respect. Friends gave gifts to the chapel in her memory and an early account of S. Anne's school states: 'On either side of the reredos are three figures in Mansfield stone. They were given by the pupils of the gifted Miss Emily Lowe who succeeded her aunts at Mayfield but died prematurely in 1873.'[4]

---

2. Letter from Mary Lowe, John Manley Lowe's wife, in Tim Tomlinson, private papers.
3. Tim Tomlinson, private papers.
4. Violet M. McPherson, *The Story of S. Anne's, Abbots Bromley, 1874-1924* (Shrewsbury: Wilding & Son, 1924), p. 31.

Maria Mosley Lowe

The family connection did not end with Emily Louisa's death. In 1873, just one month after the death of Emily Louisa, a notice of change of name appeared in *The Standard*, London. Posted by Maria Mosley, daughter of Maria and William Mosley and a niece of Eliza, it read:

> My Affection is Unalterable
> Notice: I, Maria Mosley late of Rectory-place, Loughborough, in the county of Leicester, but now of Mayfield House, Southgate, in the county of Middlesex, spinster, hereby Give Notice that from henceforth I shall on all occasions and all documents and transactions, ADOPT and USE the name OF MOSLEY LOWE instead of the name of Mosley, hitherto borne by me, – Dated this 20th day of November, 1873.

After the death of her father in 1848, Maria, aged eleven years, had arrived with her widowed mother to live with Harriet Lowe at her school in Devon. As Harriet had helped them so Maria stepped into the breach to help her family run the school at Mayfield. Perhaps she changed her name so that she could be numbered amongst the Misses Lowe.

By 1881 she had left and was running a small school in Combe Down, Bath, for three nieces and three other girls, where she was listed as Maria Mosley – quietly having given up the name Lowe. By 1891 she had joined St Thomas' Sisterhood at Oxford. The Sisters of Charity (as they were known) had been founded by the Reverend Thomas Chamberlain, a staunch Tractarian, with the task of running the three institutions that he set up during his 50 years as vicar of St Thomas Martyr. One was an Industrial Home and Orphanage for orphaned girls and girls with no means of support. These girls were trained to go into service. There was a Day School and Kindergarten called St Scholastica's for girls aged three to eighteen and boys under seven. Fees were £2 a year or one shilling a week. Then there was a school for girls of wealthier parents called S. Anne's set up in 1873 in a purpose-built school called Rewley House (after Rewley Abbey, a Cistercian convent west of the city). Religious observance was strict and in many ways this school mirrored that set up by Edward Lowe at S. Anne's in Abbots Bromley.[5] A notice in the local paper in 1905 announced that the sisters were setting up a nursery for infant orphans so that they did not

---

5. I have found no explanation of the choice of S. Anne for the chapel and school. Perhaps Edward Lowe named his school in Abbots Bromley after St Anne's School in Oxford.

Chapter 9. Mayfield after Eliza and S. Winifred's

have to be separated from their siblings. It is not clear when Maria Mosley became Reverend Mother but this was quite a job![6] In 1905 there were 90 children being looked after. Only a gifted woman could have run such a large organisation, which included sisters, cooks, matrons, housemaids and other ancillary staff.

Emily Landor Lowe

After Maria left Mayfield the running of the school passed to another family member. By 1881 another Emily, this time Emily Landor Lowe, was in charge. She was born in 1852, the daughter of Cecilia Landor and George Lowe who had married in May 1846 at St Augustine's Rugeley. In this way the connection with Eliza's school in Seaforth, attended by Cecilia and her sisters, was retained.

In 1881 Emily Landor Lowe was 29 and seems well established as head of the school with four teachers and five servants. One teacher is John Manley Lowe's daughter Charlotte, aged 23. As in 1871 there is a German and a French native speaker, the former is listed below Emily as 'partner' and is called Bertha von Wolfskeel. She was 35 and came from Konstanz, south Germany. Louisa Brassinne was also 35 and came from France. There were two Lowe girls listed as pupils: Mary Constance Lowe, born in Abbots Bromley and aged seventeen, and Lucy Caroline Lowe, born in Burton-on-Trent and aged fifteen.[7] Mary was the second youngest daughter of John Manley Lowe, the vicar of Abbots Bromley, and Lucy was the daughter of George and Cecilia Lowe and therefore a younger sister of Emily. The fact that they were not sent to S. Anne's is interesting. The census of 1881 lists two children of John Manley Lowe aged sixteen and fourteen residing in the vicarage at Abbots Bromley. Perhaps they were day girls at S. Anne's. This leaves open the question of why Mary Constance attended Mayfield.

Perhaps the longstanding family connection with Mayfield swung the decision against S. Anne's; or perhaps George Lowe, a well-respected and successful doctor in Burton-on-Trent, preferred Mayfield and was keen for his daughter to have a cousin with her and offered to pay for Mary Constance. The fees at Mayfield were nearly double those at S. Anne's.[8]

6. Tim Tomlinson, private papers.
7. Lucy Caroline went on to study at Oxford and to become a teacher. She wrote plays based on famous novels for pupils to perform, in the tradition of Eliza Lowe.
8. Edward Lowe wrote a letter to a lady supporter requesting funds for S. Mary's School building fund in in 1890 in which he tells her that the fees at S. Anne's were c. £40 p.a. and those at S. Mary's c. £21 p.a. (source Guild archives). An advert for the school at Mayfield in 1885 stated that the fees were from £75 p.a. However, it may simply mean that S. Anne's and S. Mary's were very reasonable, rather than

Mayfield had five teachers, including a native German and French teacher, five servants, large grounds and an enviable reputation. There were only fifteen pupils, still from far afield places such as Manchester, Ulverston, Scotland, Derbyshire, Nottinghamshire, Birmingham, but not quite so far flung as in Eliza's days. Just as in 1871 pupils were largely aged between fifteen and eighteen. By contrast there were 56 pupils listed at S. Anne's in the 1881 census with six servants, only four teachers and five student teachers, aged between eighteen and 20, to help. Whatever the motives, the families were supporting Emily Landor Lowe at Mayfield.

Ellen Bowyer Brown Takes Over Mayfield

From at least 1885 Emily's successor at Mayfield was Miss Ellen Bowyer Brown from Colne in Essex. For the first time Mayfield was to be run by a lady outside the Lowe family. By the early 1880s schools, including S. Anne's, were being examined by university dons and taking Oxford and Cambridge exams (attempted by Alice Rathbone following Mayfield).[9] Certainly this was the case at S. Winifred's where Emily Landor Lowe would go next. Inspection was becoming common and examinations formed part of this process. Universities were beginning to open their doors to women, even if they could not take degrees.

Ellen Bowyer Brown ran a different sort of ship, although she was not averse to claiming that the school stretched back 60 years.[10] At this point advertisements began to appear, very regularly, in the *Morning Post*, a London newspaper. The Lowes did not advertise for pupils but Ellen Bowyer Brown placed adverts nearly every month, sometimes twice a month from 1885 until at least January 1893. Despite this, the number of pupils there in 1891 was nineteen, only four more than Emily Landor Lowe had ten years earlier.[11] There was nothing like the expansion experienced at S. Anne's. The advertisements reveal an exclusive and expensive private school. Here is the first example: 'School for the daughters of Gentlemen; established 60 years. 5 resident governesses, one French, one German; visiting masters; specially good music.'

---

that Mayfield was exceptional. Rugeley Grammar School, for example, in 1812 charged £60 p.a. for boarders.

9. Throughout the nineteenth century education was a 'hot potato' and an increasing amount of public money was given to the churches who provided education to the poor. Accountability became an issue. The most famous illustration of this was Sir Robert Lowe's introduction in 1862 of testing the 'three Rs' to ensure that only successful schools were receiving grants.
10. Eliza began her teaching career in Bootle approximately 60 years earlier.
11. Nevertheless, the 1901 census records 29 pupils.

Chapter 9. Mayfield after Eliza and S. Winifred's

In February 1886 her advertisement extended its net: 'For the daughters of country gentlemen and others of good position. Terms (inclusive) 76-250 guineas.' A month later she included 'Officers in Her Majesty's service'.

In these advertisements the description of the education to be expected did not vary but in this advertisement from 11 June 1892 it was stated: 'Miss Bowyer Brown's Home School and System of Education, thoroughly modern teaching, but not on local examination lines; the school is best suited for girls of the upper classes'.

Miss Bowyer Brown made it clear that she was not interested in preparing girls for the universities. This was in contrast to the increasing number of girls' schools, both state-funded and private, which were pursuing an academic education on a par with that on offer in boys' schools. Much of this new brand of education was directed towards the middle classes but not entirely so. Upper-class girls, in the view of Miss Bowyer Brown and many others, would never have to earn their own living so exams were an unnecessary distraction. This approach, which took time to disappear, was vastly different to that taken in Edward Lowe's fledgling schools.

Mayfield House was demolished around 1924 to make way for houses. The avenue, named Mayfield Avenue, is still there today.

S. Winifred's Bangor and Emily Landor Lowe

On 3 May 1887 Emily Landor Lowe was in Garfield Terrace in Bangor setting up a new school, S. Winifred's. The Midland Division of Woodard under the Provost Edward Lowe had been approached by the Hon. Eleanor Douglas Pennant, a daughter of the local landowner, Lord Penrhyn, to extend its work into North Wales. This was attractive to Lowe as he had an ambitious plan to set up seven girls' schools within the division, schools which he envisaged as having not more than 100 pupils each and so requiring only a large house with extensions. Lowe thought of £4,000 being needed for each

Fig. 53 Emily Landor Lowe.

school but it seems that Eleanor Pennant provided most of the funds and it is she who is credited as the founder and inspirer in Nesta Roberts' book about the school.[12] Clearly Lowe had a major hand in the business of overseeing and running the school. K.E. Kirk says that the general direction of the school was in the hands of the warden of the girls' schools of the Division, Alice Mary Coleridge.[13] It must have been Edward Lowe or Alice Mary Coleridge who brought Emily Landor Lowe in as the first Headmistress.

Garfield Terrace was not Mayfield. The terrace is still there today and, although the buildings are well constructed with nice detailing, they are small and were occupied at the time largely by the lower middle classes.[14] Miss Pennant rented, at first, just three houses but, later, as numbers increased, two adjacent houses were added.

The school began with one pupil on 3 May 1887. Four days later another pupil arrived from S. Anne's, whose parents had been persuaded by the Lady Warden, Alice Mary Coleridge, to 'lend' her to the new school to keep the one pupil company. At half-term two new boarders arrived and each term numbers increased. The school was up and running. A former pupil remembered well 'the greeting of Miss Lowe, whom all girls of the time remember with loyal affection'.[15]

The census of 1891 shows 20 pupils with Emily Lowe as headmistress; assistant mistress is Evelyn Welchman, who had been a pupil at S. Anne's, and Lucy Cooper, music mistress. There were two student teachers who were aged nineteen and eighteen. There were four servants, one from Abbots Bromley and one from Colton (also in Staffordshire), one from Birmingham and one local servant from Caernarvonshire. Mostly pupils were aged fifteen to eighteen but there was one aged thirteen and one aged nine. Roughly half of the pupils were Welsh. The census lists numbers 4, 5, 6, 7 and 8 Garfield Terrace and in the margin has been written '(St Winifred's Girls School, church)'.[16]

Fig. 54 Garfield Terrace.

---

12. Nesta Roberts, *S. Winifred's, Llanfairfechan: The Story of Fifty Years 1887-1937* (Shrewsbury: Wilding & Son, 1937).
13. Kirk, *The Story of the Woodard Schools*, pp. 153-54.
14. In adjacent houses lived a printer, tax collector, bookseller and solicitor's clerk.
15. Roberts, *S. Winifred's, Llanfairfechan*, p. 14.
16. Brackets in the census record.

Chapter 9. Mayfield after Eliza and S. Winifred's

Whether or not Edward Lowe had difficulty persuading his niece to start up a fledging school in a row of terraced houses we will never know. However, it was certainly a new challenge and one that she seems to have both relished and in which she seems to have been successful. She was responsible for laying the traditions and for increasing numbers to a respectable 20 pupils by 1891. In 1890 the local paper reported a moving speech given by the Dean of Bangor on Speech Day thanking Miss Lowe and her teachers. They had begun in a modest way. He commented that it was difficult to move forward and attract pupils yet make a profit.[17] After she left, she continued to visit the school and to be present on prizegiving days. The same paper on 4 August 1900 reported:

> The Dean of Bangor, in proposing a vote of thanks to Miss Lowe, said that she was well known to a great many of them as having been connected for many years with S. Winifred's School since its establishment . . . it afforded him much pleasure to see Miss Lowe amongst them and he thought they owed her a debt of gratitude for the way she conducted the School for so many years. Archdeacon Price, in seconding, said he agreed that much gratitude was due to Miss Lowe as she began the work which had afterwards been carried on so successfully by others.

School Inspections

The *North Wales Chronicle* also reported at length the results of school inspections and these make interesting reading. On 27 July 1889, just two years after the school opened, Miss Lowe received a letter of approval for the standard of botany. In 1897 the same newspaper reported a very good standard in academic subjects, including: 'arithmetic, geography, English Literature and grammar, French, German, botany, divinity, Latin, theory of music and harmony and English history'. One report mentioned that the standard of divinity was high, except when it came to pupils being able to cite Biblical sources for their arguments.

Church Education as a Defence against Secularism

Speech Day afforded the clergy the opportunity to express their approval of church education. The clergy were clearly worried about creeping secularisation in their area and expressed this in strong and colourful language. The Reverend P. Constable Ellis, rector of Llanfairfechan,

---
17. *North Wales Chronicle and Advertiser for the Principality*, 2 August 1890.

'expressed his appreciation of these schools as the protest of Churchmen against the increasing secularisation of the age'.[18] On the same occasion Canon T. Williams and Reverend W. Edwards spoke of S. Winifred's 'helping to stem the torrent of secularism which threatened to overflow them in this parish'. There were seven clergymen present and this pattern of clergy attending speech days continued. As if to reassure the clergy, the Lord Bishop of Bangor spoke highly of their reverent demeanour and attendance at Cathedral services and holy communion. Reverend Ellis returned to his theme on 2 August 1890 when he declared: 'the setting aside of definite religious teaching in our schools was ruinous to the welfare of the nation . . . we wanted definite religious instruction in our schools, not a colourless milk and water type of thing'.[19]

This same concern was expressed by the Dean of Lichfield at a Speech Day in Abbots Bromley in 1882. Definite religious instruction was, of course, precisely what Woodard had argued for all along, as opposed to a vague religiosity that was not founded on dogma but on generalities and comfortable sentiments. The Dean said:

> Anyone who noticed the current of what was called public opinion must perceive that it ran counter to anything like exact and definite religious teaching. The present age was impatient of religious dogma, under the notion that it tended to restrain freedom of thought and to fetter the human intellect. And yet it was strange to find that dogma was freely admitted in every science but that which was the highest of all sciences – namely, religion.[20]

He went on to argue that unbelief was at the root of the matter: 'The true reason why definite religion was found fault with was because it treated as settled and certain what unbelief would fain regard as doubtful and false.'

Edward Lowe's schools for girls were finding a ready reception amongst the clergy but, in his lifetime, it was not easy to find the money to build the seven schools he had hoped for. It was not easy to recruit Welsh girls to S. Winifred's and perhaps the failure to include Welsh on the curriculum in this predominantly Welsh-speaking area proved a hindrance. Did it occur to Edward Lowe and Alice Mary Coleridge to bring in a Welsh teacher? Or to introduce Welsh poetry, even in translation? Lowe was keen to achieve high standards in the traditional academic subjects and to

---

18. *North Wales Chronicle and Advertiser for the Principality*, 27 July 1889.
19. Ibid., 2 August 1890.
20. *The Staffordshire Advertiser*, 29 July 1882.

follow what was being taught at S. Anne's. The cultural milieu favoured teaching in English. It was even the custom in some board schools to punish pupils found talking in Welsh. It is quite possible that girls were encouraged to study Welsh language and literature. Lowe's interest in Italian and Alice Mary Coleridge's love of literature might well have led them to investigate Welsh culture.

Chapter 10
Eliza's Letters

Six letters from Eliza have survived, a tiny proportion of those she must have written. Five were written in the 1840s when Eliza was based in Seaforth and one in 1862 when at Mayfield. The letters are wonderfully natural and informal, showing a fine sense of humour, a love of the outdoors and above all a love of friends and family. All her correspondents have appeared in the story so far. Four of the letters were to the Landor sisters, who had been pupils at her school, one was to her sister Emily Louisa and one to Sarah Landor, wife of Walter and mother of the three Landor girls.

The first letter was written c. 1840 to Lucy Landor:

> Most unprincipled abstractor of my woman's gear and at the same time my dearest Lucy Landor. Never fash your honest heart for one moment about the carrying off my worthless property. If however it would tranquillize your troubled mind to make restitution, I opine that Miss Dicken, my pupil from Stephen's Hill,[1] would graciously escort the stray goods on her return the week after next and to save you any useless plague, my Aunt proposes that you send the paquet to the house and she will transmit it. I had never missed the *things* in the least but the *persons* who flitted one by one from the stage were grievous losses. Oh! indeed it is not a contemptible world, the fault I find with it is that one has so little time and opportunity to enjoy what it has of good and fair. My mind is certainly constructed upon the plan of Mr Green's. I like to *live* amongst scenery and with people whom I like till I feel a wish to go away. (Do not publish this lest I never get another invi-

---

1. This was probably Frances Mary Dicken, whose father Thomas owned a large farm, called Stephen's Hill, close to Blithfield and the village of Abbots Bromley near Rugeley. Mention was made of a Mr J. Dicken by Cecilia Landor in a letter a year previously. See p. 99.

Chapter 10. Eliza's Letters   153

tation) but so it is & I felt dull almost to blue dismals when first you and Emily & then Mary, Harriett, and his Reverence vanished from the scene. Mary Smith is now with us & really seems so glad to be here and so pleased that it would be a base inhospitality of heart to write down a yawn or an impertinence that might possibly float up from the hidden naughtiness within me. We had a letter from Henry yesterday to tell us that Dr Anderson's sister is to be entrusted to our care. I hope she has a better opinion of the world than her brother for at seventeen she might prove a hearty and inconvenient despiser of every day folk. Our pictures too are arrived. I consider my Aunt's very like & my own a pleasing sort of young lady but not like me, which is a pity. It is far more humiliating to be drawn too well-looking than the contrary. It must be so satisfactory for a beauty to hear that the painter has not done justice to her inimitable charms. I am very angry, Lucy, that *you* made a wry face at your family on your return. You certainly shewed us a very agreable [*sic*] countenance & I should have liked the light of it to have been shed upon them. Reflecting however that women do generally their best to look well, I think perhaps, you couldn't help it, dear, & I forgive you and hope sincerely you are quite in your right looks now. I am not entirely free from reminiscences a vapeur, even yet. On Sunday I got an idea that the pews & congregation were slowly sailing past my pew & after struggling to dispel the idea I made a desperate effort and walked out of church to avoid going with the rest to Greenock. I got well the moment I was in the air but am yet subject to thick coming fancies of the same kind. I never will go on board again unless *pressed*. How I should like at this moment to be sitting on the Bridge at Donaquaich with you by my side & two *dear* Dhroskys in the avenue to take us whithersoever we would. It is a day to make that old Giant of the mountains rise up and shake his locks with pleasure. Oh Lucy – woman, we will go again some day. I can hear nothing of Mr Green nor why he did not come. Nothing less than an almost assassination on his way to Dalkeith that night can now be accepted as an excuse for I do not think we were altogether a far from contemptible *corps*, & that he might have been proud to enlist himself in our service.

Eliza has been in the west of Scotland on holiday with friends and family. Lucy left before Eliza and by mistake took something belonging to her. Lucy has written from home in Rugeley to Eliza, back now in Seaforth, asking what to do with Eliza's belongings. Lucy, as Chapter 6 showed, was a very serious young lady with a tendency to fret over what she perceived as her wrongdoings. So, rather than a conventional beginning to the letter Eliza teases Lucy, addressing her as 'most unprincipled abstractor' immediately softening it with 'my dearest Lucy Landor'. She makes a joke about it, trying to help Lucy not to worry about it.

Eliza takes every opportunity in this long letter to show Lucy how much she means to her personally. So, it comes as no surprise to read 'how I should like to . . . be sitting with you by my side and Oh Lucy – woman, we will go again some day'. At the same time she reprimands Lucy for frowning upon her return home. The sentence that follows is interesting: 'I should have liked the light of it [her agreeable countenance] to have been shed upon them.'

Here is the teacher who cares about her pupil's character. It may also be a nod to one of the forms of blessing of the *Book of Common Prayer* forms of blessing: 'Lord, let the light of thy countenance shine upon them.'

Nothing about this letter is predictable or trite. Phrases like 'the hidden naughtiness in me', 'base inhospitality of heart', 'almost to blue dismals', 'a far from contemptible corps' are vivid and unexpected. One gets the feeling that Eliza was animated by the process of writing the letter and enjoyed giving rein to her considerable powers of expression.

There is a French word, *paquet*, a reference to Russian carriages, Droskys, and possibly a reference to the sonnet by the Scottish poet Andrew Park, *Inverary*. In this poem Park refers to where 'Donaquaich's high-towering head is seen'. Ben Domhnaich is a mountain in Argyll overlooking Inverary. Eliza imagines the giant of the mountains rising up and shaking his locks with pleasure. Such cultural references are not overplayed but come quite naturally.

She clearly enjoyed being out of doors in beautiful scenery where she felt alive but blamed being on board for dizzy spells she experienced. She relished spending time with friends but also enjoyed time on her own.

Henry was probably Henry Landor, the cousin of the Landor girls who had written to tell them that their petition had fallen on deaf ears (see p. 104). Dr Anderson's sister may have come to Eliza's school on Henry's suggestion or recommendation, an example of how Eliza gained her pupils. The new pupil was seventeen years old. This illustrates that girls did not come at any particular age (nor did they stay for any particular length of time). Eliza hoped that the new pupil would not turn out to be a 'despiser of everyday folk'. Her school was for well-to-do families who were not short of money but Eliza did not want pupils to look down on the less fortunate.

Chapter 10. Eliza's Letters

The second letter, written c. 1847, was also addressed to Lucy at Rugeley. Eliza was in Burton with her brother George and his wife Cecilia, Lucy's youngest sister who had been a pupil at Eliza's school too (see Chapter 6). The occasion was the birth of a first child to Cecilia and George:

My dear Lucy,

True to my word, I sit down to report of Mamma & her little daughter, of the old collegian & the undergraduate, of Papa's progress in the art of dancing & of Aunt Lizzie's advances in the same. First of the Lady Mother. Dear Cecy is decidedly looking much better to-day. Her countenance has animation, her cheeks a little colour & her movements more strength; in fact I should say she is going on very satisfactorily. Aunt Lucy's darling has also conducted herself with much propriety & shown a very graceful mixture of complacency towards the Aunt who is left & of feeling towards the one departed. Certain it is my dear, that when I said in the true nursing dialect 'where's its Aunt Lucy?' the little cheeks wrinkled up in a miserable manner & tears came into the little blue eyes. A judicious change of subject restored tranquillity; but I registered the event for your peculiar satisfaction.

I grieve to say that the early morning lessons are laid aside. Perhaps the college Don does not consider me a worthy successor of the last instructress or she is taken up with imparting the mysteries of her art to the new nurse, be it as it may, she does not break my morning slumbers. I was particularly good this morning, downstairs no end of too early, with no companion but the teapot. At last came two letters one from Madde, one from E. Cardwell, & finally appeared the Master of the House, looking his approbation upon me & slightly conscious of his own inferiority. He did not show the decided hardihood of manner exhibited by myself the last two mornings of your stay. In due time we went to Church through pouring rain, & after an early dinner fell to nursing. Papa still carries the day in rolling and shaking & all sorts of *handi*craft; but he allowed that I surpassed him in a sort of soothing rocking movement performed by the *feet*. He tried to imitate it very ungracefully, snatching up his feet as if from hot irons, but not succeeding, fell again to tossing & shaking. Cecy looks on & smiles & then in a quiet way, does better than we all.

The new nurse is much approved & is pronounced by Mrs College to be very *handy* & to speak to the baby in the most feeling manner. I think, dear Lucy, I have now performed my promise.

Farther particulars when we meet, which if you please to order a fly to meet me at Oakley Gate a quarter before Five on Wednesday, will be, I hope, at no very distant period after my arrival. I shall hope to find Dear Mrs Landor pretty well & the rest of my friends flourishing.

    I am, dear Lucy,
     Affectionately yours,
     Eliza Lowe
     Sunday Night

Unlike the previous letter that ranged over many topics this one is concerned with just one: the new baby and how the household is adjusting. Yet there is still much humour, allusion and imagination in evidence. It also shows the same desire, as expressed in the first letter, to encourage and reassure Lucy of her affection and regard. Eliza takes pains to reassure Lucy that her visit was a success. She imagines that, while the baby regards her (Eliza) with complacency, she is reduced to tears on thinking about Lucy. Throughout the letter she refers to Cecilia in bookish terms. Cecilia was with Eliza at school for quite a number of years, perhaps to reflect this Eliza thinks of her in terms of being first a collegian, then an undergraduate, then a college don and finally Mrs College. Roles have been reversed and Cecilia has been giving Eliza instructions. Aunt Lizzie is Eliza herself. The art of dancing is Eliza's way of describing attempts by herself and George to nurse the baby. All very amusing and written no doubt to entertain Lucy. Mention of a letter from E. Cardwell is interesting. It is quite possible that this was Edward Cardwell, later Viscount Cardwell who was a highly respected politician in the mid-19th century. Cardwell was from a Liverpool merchant family, became MP for Liverpool in 1947, a year before this letter was written and was the son of Elizabeth Birley who was related to the Hornbys of Liverpool. Chapter 5 has illustrated something of these connections and Louisa Birley, a pupil of Eliza's in 1841 was a cousin of Edward Cardwell.

The third letter was to Fanny Landor, the second of the three sisters, written c. 1849:

My dear Fanny,
 Hearing that you have not joined yourself to any summer scheme as yet for change, it darted into my mind last night that you might not object to join me for ten days or a fortnight at the Ferry Inn, Windermere, whither I am going on Saturday next in company with Edward & Susan. My Aunt and Charlotte, if all

Chapter 10. Eliza's Letters   157

be well, will join us for a bit the week after. The terms of the Inn are reasonable, &, I fancy, very few pounds & pennies would give us all we desire. While *we boat*, you should have opportunity to sketch, & there are charming views quite within reach. We should be independent as regards the boating which Susan anticipates with as much joy as you do the contrary, & yet I hope, happy & sociable in our independence. Let me reckon then, dear F. upon your coming *here* on Friday next, & joining Edward & me on Saturday on our expedition. If not, come direct to me at the Ferry on Thursday week when Edward will have left me alone, and I shall be as quiet as any old lady in the land, trusting chiefly to such enjoyment of greenness and coolness as I may attain on my feet, or in a certain little carriage which we call 'the Tub', & which has the merit of being at the door at any minute you want it. There is a state carriage for great occasions.

I have not time to say more than that the chicks are better. Walter & Cecy have both had a sort of feverish influenza, & Oswald & Edward Mosley the same sort of thing. But they are now on the mend, &, I hope, in a day or two will be as well as ever. Best love to you all, not the less hearty for the hurry in which I send it,

Yours most affecty.,
Eliza Lowe.

If you come (& you must not say no) please to bring, if *spareable* for a little while 'The Fountain of Arethusa'.

Eliza was off on summer holidays again. This time to Windermere where she was gathering friends and family. On holiday with her were Susan Lowe, Charles' daughter, whom Eliza and her sisters had looked after perhaps from birth, and her brother Edward. Edward would have been 26 at the time and not yet married. In January of that year (1849) he had gone to Shoreham-by-Sea to start work with Woodard in his fledgling work of middle-class education. It was later that year, on 13 September 1849, that Woodard wrote to Eliza, explaining that his scheme would not be extended to girls (see p. 22). This means that Edward and Eliza had discussed Woodard's plans on holiday and perhaps, even at this early stage, the idea of bringing girls within the Woodard fold was formed in Edward's mind.

Susan would have been twelve years old and was looking forward to boating on the lake. Fanny clearly was not, despite or perhaps because of the sailing lessons she had had on Merseyside. It seems that boating on Windermere did not worry Eliza as it did on holiday in Argyll. As the head of the family Eliza seems to have wanted to keep everyone connected. Her reference to chicks was probably to Cecilia's brood of two children. Eliza mentions an expedition, going about on foot and in a carriage, sketching, all attractions that she hopes to enjoy with Fanny. Oswald and Edward Mosley were the younger children of Eliza's sister Maria Mosley, recently widowed. It is not clear but perhaps Eliza is taking a role in caring for them too, or it may be that they were staying with George and Cecy since all had caught the flu. The reference to *The Fountain of Arethusa* is interesting. This work, written by Robert Eyres Landor, brother of Walter Savage Landor and a cousin of Fanny and her sisters, had been published only a year earlier, in 1848. Eliza was clearly keen to get hold of a copy. It concerns a group of potholers who follow an underground river from Derbyshire until they emerge on the inner surface of the earth. This world is illuminated by its own sun and abounds with strange but edible plants. Scattered about are fine cities populated by spirits in corporeal form of the ancient Greeks and Romans. The bulk of the book consists of imaginary dialogues between the travellers and philosophers such as Aristotle and Cicero. An imaginative work and one best read by someone like Eliza who possessed a knowledge of the classics.

The fourth letter was written to her sister Emily Louisa Lowe from Rugeley where Eliza was staying with her aunt Mary Clarke. It is undated but written some time before 1849:

> My dear Em.
>
> Flattering myself that I may be considered a 'kindred spirit' I proceed to talk to you. In the first place – I severely reprimand you for being so long in writing when you promised to let us hear how you got home immediately. In the second place I proceed to forgive you this great neglect & condescend to inform you how we are going on here. Poor dear Aunt improves very slowly, so slowly that if it were not today for the absence of pain, I should scarcely call it improvement. She is so weak & languid. They are giving her besides a horrid medicine, which keeps up a perpetual nausea & makes her feel & appear worse than she really is, though there is no need of that, for I consider this attack a very serious one, and one from which she will be long recovering.
>
> You have not returned Fanny How's letter, which I want. I put in for a moments amusement dispatches from home, though there is little in them. I lead a solitary sort of life, the post man being the best friend I have in the world. Poor Aunt seldom talks and has never left her bed for five minutes since I came, except to have it made at night. Dear Good old Mary Landor is worth a world of moderns. She is quite a 'kindred spirit' and I desire

Chapter 10. Eliza's Letters

nothing more honourable than to descend into the vale of tears as usefully & christianly, and, if it may be, – in the same sort of brown bonnet & cockatoo cap, – why I shall not care. What good sense & refinement & religion that old body has! I should like with all my heart to make her Archbishop of Canterbury. She would settle the high & low Church parties admirably.

I want you to send me from Bladons, if you can procure them without difficulty a few patterns of Mousseline de laine or any other material that might make a morning dress, suitable for me, if something that might do either for morning or evening when alone & also patterns of something not expensive either in checks or Mousseline de laine for an Evening. I am only going to buy one & prices will determine me whether for morning or evening.

I have only time tonight to add my love & an improved account of dear Aunt C. She is much better than when I began to write & I trust will go on well, if she keeps better I shall perhaps not write to you again, I have so much to do &c.

Do not annoy yourself about the patterns, if you cannot get them easily. I beg my love to Mrs Clement & with best Compts. to yourself

I remain,

  Most affectly Yours

   (Signed) E. Lowe

Eliza has come to look after her aunt Mary Clarke in Rugeley. Her aunt was often with her in Seaforth but regarded Rugeley, where she had lived with her husband John, the headmaster of the grammar school, as her home. Eliza, ever concerned about others, is cross with her sister for not getting in touch to tell her she has arrived safely but, as with her letter to Lucy, soon goes into conciliatory mode. Emily was mentioned in letters from the Landor girls as 'spouting Shakespeare' (see Chapter 6) and was at the time a governess with the family of Clement Kynnersley, a barrister living at Uttoxeter Hall, Staffordshire, a grand Georgian mansion which is part of a school today. His wife Ellen Rose was born at Liverpool in 1813 and may well have attended Eliza's school in Bootle. The medicine which made her aunt nauseous would have been part of a series of remedies of the time which involved blood-letting, purging, starvation and bringing on vomiting. Dispatches from home may refer to goings-on at the school in Seaforth. The Walsham Hows of Shrewsbury were old friends of the Lowes. Perhaps Eliza wants to reply to the letter which Emily has not returned. Mary Landor lived next door to Mary Clarke and may have helped to relieve the monotony. She was the aunt of the Landor girls, Lucy, Frances and Cecilia. Mary Landor was known for her good works in the district but here Eliza shows her admiration for her grasp of events and good sense despite her age. Conversation had touched on conflicts amongst churchmen and Eliza tells Emily that, if Mary Landor was in charge of the Church, the problems would cease.

Emily must have had access to a supplier of high-class cloth. Mousseline de laine was a French woollen cloth popular at the time. The tone of the letter is slightly less effusive than the earlier letters. Perhaps relations with Emily were strained or perhaps Eliza was feeling the burden of living with her sick aunt, unable to communicate with her.

The fifth letter, or rather extracts from it, was from Eliza to Cecilia, written again from Aunt Mary Clarke's home in Rugeley:

> Mr Landor called yesterday, joined us at tea and sat an hour, which he made so pleasant an hour that I took shame to myself for having spoken of him in the morning as a silent man. . . . They [Edward Landor and his wife Ellen, née Harley] called here on Friday & both appeared to great advantage. I felt much more interested in her than before from the very frank & genuine expression of her dislike to strangers & of going about. [She said] 'Oh, I wish we were settled, Edward *even* in Australia' sounded very natural & I began to think I should perhaps like her, if I knew her. . . . [re. The Lowe family assembling at Seaforth] I have a great scheme revolving in my 'inner being' but I did not dare mention it when I was with you lest the doctor should look ferocious. I want you nevertheless to accustome your young minds to the idea of coming to us for a few days in the summer i.e. the doctor for a few days & the *Muthur* & child for as long a time as he will spare them in the sea air. Henry & in fact all the family,[2] if God permits, hope to assemble, it may never occur again, so do not throw buckets of cold water upon it.

She also mentions Fly (a small greyhound dog) as being there at the horse fair walking upon three legs.

This letter has been edited by William Noble Landor. The words in square brackets are his explanatory notes. Once again Eliza is contriving to bring the family together and has had some success ('all the family'). This time in Seaforth where in the holidays at least there will have been plenty of room. She anticipates that George (the doctor) will only be able to spare

---

2. Again, probably Henry Landor who seems to have become a firm family friend of the Lowes. At some point he worked in Rugeley as a clerk to the solicitor John Hickin, Cecilia's maternal grandfather.

Chapter 10. Eliza's Letters

a few days but hopes that Cecilia (the 'Muthur') and child will be able to stay longer. She adds the sea air as an attraction which will appeal to the doctor in him. Eliza is frank about both her opinions of people and the fact that she can be mistaken. She was not afraid to change her opinions when presented with new evidence.

The final letter was written from Mayfield in 1862 to Sarah Landor, the mother of the Landor girls. It concerned the marriage of Walter J. Landor, a much younger brother of the Landor girls:

20 Nov. 1862
Dear Friend

Though we have taken such a silent note of Walter's marriage, you will not, I am sure, think that an event of so much interest to you all as well as to the hero of the story himself, has been coldly regarded here. Very glad indeed were we all to hear that the marriage had taken place & very sincere good wishes did we wish & still do wish for the happiness of Walter & his wife in their married life & for the comfort of you all in this important addition to the family group. Cecilia has told us how pleasing & amiable the bride is. Pray give or send our hearty congratulations to Walter. If we knew the lady we should send the same to her, for I am sure she will have a very kind & devoted husband & true friends in his friends.

I should like to think that my dear & valued old friend had been able to enter into the full comfort of his son's happiness. I fear from all I hear that this cd. hardly be, but all wd. rejoice in the knowledge that had it been God's will, he would have been himself very happy in it. I often think of you both, my dear friends, with very tender recollections & I think of those better times & better things, which are one day to replace the feebleness & pain & anxiety of this season of care.

I pray we may all meet *then*. Our very kind love to all. I hope you & Lucy & Fanny are standing this early winter weather pretty well. We are all recovering from bad colds which in part must be our excuse for this long delayed letter.
      Always My dear Friend.
      Affectionately yours,
      E. Lowe.

This letter reflects Eliza's usual warmth and concern for others. She did not fail to mention Walter Landor senior who must have been suffering from dementia. A journey from Southgate to Rugeley in November would have been ruled out by the requirements of her school. Thoughts of Walter lead her to remind Sarah of their good times together and her faith that *then* better times will prevail. She was fond of underlining words. The language of this last letter is very measured. Unlike the other letters, it does not have one moment of levity or a phrase 'written as spoken'.

To summarise what these letters reveal of Eliza: she was a great encourager and not afraid to show deep affection. Lucy and her sisters must have felt that they were very special to Eliza. She had a great concern for her friends and family and entered into their problems and joys. She loved being out of doors and organised family holidays in beautiful places. When she heard that Fanny had no holiday planned she stepped in and told her she must join her. Getting the family together was important to her and she took on the responsibility of organising them all. She enjoyed writing letters and the challenge of crafting unusual and striking phrases. Her letters were intended to entertain and her sense of humour was never far from the surface. She was a cultured woman with a vivid imagination, possessed of great language skills but the teacher in her was evident more in her concern for the character of her former pupils than in a concern to inform them. What is striking is that there is so little of her own personal life and no hint of worries or troubling preoccupations. The only hint is her brief account of a fainting fit in church and of being 'subject to thick coming fancies of the same kind'. Her reprimand to Lucy about showing a wry face was sharp. It was important to Eliza to present a happy countenance to the world. It seems that she also possessed an innate sense of the joys of the world and the good in it. She admitted to a 'naughtiness' within her but did not lose sleep over her human shortcomings. Going to church was regular pattern in her life as with many of the Lowes. She had faith; a faith that enabled her to look beyond the cares of this life to 'better times and better things', which for Eliza included all meeting up again.

CHAPTER 11

Eliza Lowe and the Founding of S. Anne's School

This chapter sets out the connections between the founding of S. Anne's in Abbots Bromley by Edward Lowe in 1874 and the life (and death) of his sister Eliza. It finishes with tributes to her given by Lowe.

Eliza Lobbies Nathaniel Woodard

The first connection between the founding of S. Anne's and Eliza harks back to the 1849 summer holiday in Windermere mentioned in the previous chapter. Her brother Edward was 26 years old and had just started work with Nathaniel Woodard in the very early days of the Society of S. Mary and S. Nicolas in Shoreham-by-Sea. Like Woodard, Edward Lowe had studied at Magdalen Hall, Oxford, leaving in 1847 to become a teacher at the King's School in Ottery St Mary, Devon. He was soon ordained and became a curate in the parish. Concerned that farmers' sons were attending a school run by dissenters because of a lack of a Church of England school, he was advised to write to Woodard. Within a year Lowe was working for Woodard in Shoreham.

Edward travelled up to the Lake District with Eliza and other family members to stay at the Ferry Inn on the edge of Lake Windermere. He was not yet married. He must have talked to Eliza about the new venture and the ambitious plans that Woodard had for boarding schools for boys of the middle classes, beginning in Sussex but extending throughout the country. Eliza wrote to Woodard shortly after getting back from holiday. Her letter has not survived but clearly she and her brother had discussed the possibility of schools for girls run by the Society and she had written to Woodard on the matter. On 13 September Woodard replied to Eliza, telling her that he had no intention of extending the scheme to girls (see p. 22).

Given what we know about Woodard's views on educating girls in public schools it is likely that Edward Lowe did not pursue the topic at the time but it is possible that this holiday and discussions with Eliza planted in his mind at this very early stage the idea of public schools for girls alongside those for boys. But it would be a long time before the idea became a reality.

No Plans for the Society to Found Girls' Schools before 1872

There is no evidence of an intention to found girls' schools in the ensuing years while Lowe was headmaster of Hurstpierpoint and Woodard's closest colleague. Brian Heeney turned up nothing in his extensive research on the Woodard schools. William Gladstone (see Chapter 1) was a lifelong supporter of Woodard and his schools and Lowe wrote to him many times over his career. Surely Lowe would have canvassed his support for girls' schools, had he been planning them? The only mention of girls' education in Lowe's letters to Gladstone occurs well after the founding of S. Anne's, when Lowe was developing S. Winifred's in North Wales in 1886:

> You will, I think, hear with interest that in response to local invitations and substantial help, I am hoping in April on my return from a first visit to Rome, to open at Bangor a middle class boarding school for girls on a definite Church basis. My sister, Miss Alice Coleridge who successfully manages my girls' school at Abbots Bromley in Staffordshire will probably before long send Mrs. Gladstone a prospectus of the Bangor School.[1]

In 1860 Lowe wrote an account of the schools under the control of the Society for Sir John Coleridge (one of the inspectors for the Taunton Commission). A second and a third edition followed, until in 1878 as Provost of the Midland Division, he published a further account to bring the story up to date. The latter edition mentions S. Michael's and S. Anne's but the earlier editions give no hint of a plan to found girls' schools. When in 1878 S. Anne's was up and running, Lowe downplayed the seriousness of the development. The five years of the Midland Division, Lowe reported, have seen progress. He mentions that at last they have found a site for the Midlands Ardingly (a third-grade boys' school for poorer parents). However: 'The tedium of this delay has been partially relieved by the foundation of S. Anne's Girls' School, like the Middle School of S. Michael's, Bognor.'[2]

Therefore, it seems that there was no long-term plan to found schools for girls and when one was founded it was presented merely as a welcome distraction.[3]

---

1. The Gladstone Papers, MS 44499, British Library. Letter dated 18 November 1886.
2. Lowe, *S. Nicolas College and Its Schools*, p. 43.
3. Lowe probably felt he needed to reassure Woodard that the boys' schools were the

Chapter 11. Eliza Lowe and the founding of S. Anne's School

Woodard Approached to Found a Girls' School in the Midlands

In 1866 Sir Percival Heywood offered Woodard a site for S. Chad's, a middle school for boys in the village of Denstone in Staffordshire. Edward Lowe came to Denstone in August 1872 to be appointed Provost of the newly created Midland Division and discussions may already have taken place about establishing girls' schools. The first indication of movement in this direction was a letter to Woodard in 1867 from George Mackarness, vicar of Ilam on the border between Staffordshire and Derbyshire, suggesting that Woodard set up a girls' school in the Midland Division.[4] Woodard was not interested. However, there were those in the Midlands who were and Sir Percival's wife was keen to see a girls' school. General unease within the Church of England about the Forster Education Act of 1870, which heralded the development of board schools independent of church control (and the closure of the church school in Abbots Bromley) lent urgency to the matter of girls' education.

First Evidence of Lowe's Plan for S. Anne's

These were stirrings but the first hard evidence of Edward Lowe's plan to set up a girls' school is a letter that he wrote from The Crofts in Abbots Bromley, the retirement home for Eliza, Mary Manley and Charlotte Lowe. The letter was dated 1 August 1872. This evidence is found in the account of Marcia Alice Rice, *The Story of S. Mary's, Abbots Bromley*.[5] She was an Oxford scholar and very thorough in her approach. Unfortunately, the publisher required that the book be drastically shorter, and Rice cut the appendices which quoted her sources, including many begging letters

Fig. 55 The Crofts, Abbots Bromley.

---

main item on his agenda.
4. Mackarness became bishop of Argyll and the Isles in 1874. He was present at the inauguration of S. Anne's and was a keen supporter. See McPherson, *The Story of S. Anne's, Abbots Bromley, 1874-1924*, pp. 14 and 15.
5. Miss Rice was Headmistress of S. Anne's from 1900 to 1921 and of the School of S. Mary and S. Anne from 1921-31.

and early prospectuses. In the body of her text, however, she did record extracts from a printed letter from Edward Lowe addressed to the former pupils of his sister Eliza requesting subscriptions for the building of a chapel to be erected in memory of Miss Lowe in association with a boarding school for girls. Rice writes:

> Dr. Lowe made this an opportunity for issuing a printed letter to his sister's old pupils. No private grief of his own or of his family should interfere with duty to the Woodard schools. But, as he told those to whom he wrote: 'nor could even the duties which I owe to my office *have moved me to action* [my emphasis] in this direction, did I not recall with ineffaceable distinctness the words of sympathy and encouragement with which, in her last hours, my sister sought to cheer and animate me to the discharge of a work which she, who could then estimate things at their true value, knew nothing more glorious, for she said, "it was not only a great thing to be called to a great work, but it was still more blessed when it was for the good of great and glorious England"'.[6]

The letter continued: 'I speak before an estimate has been given, but I believe that £1,000 will erect a chapel suitable for the worship of ALMIGHTY GOD. An inscription in the chapel should perpetuate Miss Lowe's name, and the loving liberality by which it was erected.'

The words 'have moved me to action' are key. Lowe must have discussed with Eliza the idea of founding schools for girls in the Midland Division now that he was Provost. He knew that there was some support in the area but he had not yet decided to proceed. Eliza was the catalyst or the spur that he needed. Perhaps she felt she was passing the baton to him. Furthermore, Eliza wanted the schools to be sited in Abbots Bromley. This is made clear by a statement in Edward Lowe's will. Lowe made a bequest of half the income from his trust funds to the Provost of the Midland Division (the other half was to go to the Southern Division) for the express purpose of erecting buildings for the girls' schools in Abbots Bromley: 'He made this bequest in affectionate remembrance of his late sister Eliza Lowe with a view to giving effect to her general wishes for the interest of the parish by establishing useful institutions such as he knew were in her mind at the time of her death'.[7]

The siting of the schools in Abbots Bromley was therefore intended right from the start. Eliza, as has been mentioned, had hoped to retire to

---

6. Rice, *The Story of S. Mary's, Abbots Bromley*, p. 31.
7. Tim Tomlinson, private papers.

the village and perhaps envisaged being able to help her brother and to keep a watchful eye on proceedings. It is worth noting here her love of country and the belief, shared with those who supported her brother, that Church of England education was a divine calling and destined to be of great benefit to that country.

Finding a House

As has been mentioned above, copies of the letter were sent out to Eliza's former pupils on the day of Eliza's funeral, 15 August. Lowe could not have acted faster. Not only was there no estimate of the cost of a chapel at this point but Lowe did not yet have a house to put pupils in. The letter to Eliza's former pupils stated that the purchase of a house in Abbots Bromley for which money was available was under consideration. The house in question belonged to his brother John Manley Lowe and his wife Mary. They had bought it as a retirement home for the time when he had retired from his post as vicar of Abbots Bromley. It was a fine Georgian building with some land attached, but in need of repair.[8]

Fig. 56 An early postcard of S. Anne's.

On 23 August John Manley Lowe wrote to his brother-in-law, William Salt, who was also his solicitor, asking him for advice on the selling of his property for the building of a school for girls. He wrote:

> Now I have to consult you in confidence about the sale (if I consent to sell) of the large old house you looked over with Mary & me.
>
> We know, *privately*, that there is an intention to found a middle class school here & our large house has been looked at as suitable as the nucleus of one: certain other buildings being added. The negotiation is reduced therefore to one of cost.

---

8. An old postcard, origin unknown. An extension to the old house, visible on this image, was erected in the very early days of the school. According to McPherson, *The Story of S. Anne's, Abbots Bromley, 1874-1924*, p. 10, it was ivy-covered from the start. The names of the school and the village are misspelt.

> Now I am *most* anxious to have the school in Bromley and Mary is willing to give up her wishes as to having 'Bromley Hall' her own future residence but I do not think I can consent to sell at the price I bought especially as I believe property here to be surely if slowly improving in value. . . .
>
> What, if I sell, must I ask for the house & garden in addition? The promoters wish to buy all i.e. both house & land. Shall I say what do you propose to give me for the place as it now stands – half-repaired? Or shall I refer them to you. Only I want the school especially for reasons I cannot just now well enter into, so, if you treat(?) for the sale, do not go too high. If I could afford to give the place I would but as I cannot nor ought to give it I must put sentiment out of the question.
>
> Please reply to this at once as the negotiators (Sir Percival Heywood is one of them) are in earnest & apply in good faith.

So, eight days after Eliza's funeral negotiations were under way to buy the Georgian house and a quick reply was requested.

Mary Lowe also wrote to her brother William, a few days later on 26 August:

> My dear William
>
> I am writing too late for post but as I shall be busy tomorrow I will make sure of a few lines as John asked me to write. He left for Mayfield this morning but will be back again I hope at the end of the week. . . . With regard to the other house we both wish you to negotiate for us if you will kindly do so when the time comes – I do not think there is any chance of a lease being wished for, because if the school prosper they will certainly have to enlarge the house and also I think it not at all unlikely that a chapel will be built to the house in memory of our dear sister Eliza by her old pupils who are well able to do it if, (as I expect they will,) they take to the scheme which is not of *our* proposing.
>
> All this I tell in *strict* confidence. . . . It will be a good thing for us every way as it would provide a chaplain who would help John, & if the school prosper, the price of land & hence property would go up. I dare say you saw in the Times the account of the Denstone Meeting on the 8th – Lord Shrewsbury & many other influential men are taking up the cause & I think that there is not *a doubt* that the Staffordshire schools will thrive as they have down in Sussex & that the girls' school will do as well as one at Bognor in Sussex in connection with Lancing & Hurst.[9] . . .

---

9. Hurstpierpoint.

Chapter 11. Eliza Lowe and the founding of S. Anne's School

In every point of view we hope the plan will be carried out. In the highest point of view it seems most desirable for the village, & even in the lower & worldly view I believe to be very desirable for ourselves as well as for the place & this I think ought to be considered in putting a price on the house & land though I do not pretend to say that we can afford to be losers in the sale if it come to pass.

With love believe me
    Ever yr affet^e Sister
        Mary Lowe

I am writing to Edward Lowe & telling him that *you* will be our adviser in the matter of the house & that we shall make it over in writing to you to act for us.

Mary Lowe was less circumspect than her brother. The attraction to them was partly that help would be forthcoming in the form of a chaplain at the school who could be expected to help in the parish. Edward Lowe must have held out this possibility as an encouragement to them. On 8 August that year a luncheon was held at Denstone attended by Woodard to launch S. Chad's and to mark the appointment of Edward Lowe as Provost of the Midland Division. John and his wife Mary will have been there and were no doubt fired up by the possibility of a school in Abbots Bromley and the future of Woodard Schools in the Midlands. The luncheon, attended by four bishops and more than that number of peers, was a typical Woodard grand affair with 400 guests. Although Woodard's toast was to Lowe's efforts at S. Chad's only, it was announced that a 'middle class school for girls, like that at Bognor, is also contemplated' and that 'a subscription list has already been opened for each of these schools'.[10]

Edward Lowe Seeks Funds

A letter in the archives of the Guild of S. Mary and S. Anne, dated 13 September 1872, shows that Lowe had begun to seek financial support by the end of August or the beginning of September. The letter is from Bishop Selwyn, the bishop of nearby Lichfield. The approval of the diocesan bishop was part of the Woodard scheme and gaining his approval would have been one of the first steps taken. Bishop Selwyn told Lowe that his wife was keen to support him and had offered to be a subscriber at the rate of £10 a year for five years. The letter refers to Lowe's idea of siting the school in Abbots

---

10. *The Times*, 10 August 1872. The schools in question were S. Anne's and S. John's at Ellesmere.

Bromley (on which the bishop offered no opinion, stating that he was not familiar with the site). The matter of buying his brother's house was not yet settled but Lowe was not going to let this hold up the important task of raising funds. Very soon he was gathering together lady secretaries who would take on the task of raising funds from churchwomen in their area. Around this time also Lowe was writing a pamphlet setting out his vision for girls' schools in the Division. As a sign of his intent, according to Miss Rice, he had a simple banner made for his 'girls' school to be' which was carried in procession at the opening of S. Chad's College, Denstone in 1873.[11] It became known as the '1873 banner', and was carried at S. Anne's Commemoration for many years afterwards. This was a real act of faith as S. Anne's did not open until April 1874.

Was Eliza's School the Model?

The next question is how far the new school and those schools that would come later (Lowe would open three) took Eliza's school as a model. Edward Lowe and his sister-in-law Alice Mary Coleridge, who steered his schools (S. Anne's, S. Mary's and S. Winifred's), had lived for the past 25 years at Hurstpierpoint in Sussex, Woodard's middle school for boys. Their experience was that of a public school for boys. An interesting question is which model Lowe would adopt.

Buildings

In terms of the buildings, Woodard's public schools for boys were generally purpose-built on land donated by subscribers and always out in the country, well away from the temptations of city and town. They were built to a high architectural standard (if not always of comfort) and were built to last. Often, they were built on a ridge or rise and so they presented an imposing sight to those approaching. The costs were high and Woodard never flagged in his belief that money would be raised. The costs for S. Chad's at Denstone were estimated at upwards of £45,000 and for S. John's at Ellesmere £40,000. The amount of land involved was considerable. Denstone covered 46 acres, Ellesmere 60.

By contrast Lowe's girls' schools began life in existing houses and in the midst of town or village life. S. Winifred's began in rented terraced houses in the city of Bangor, not far from the cathedral. When the accommodation proved inadequate the school moved to a larger property, still within Bangor, to a college building which had become redundant. It was only much later that land was purchased outside Bangor and a fine chapel built;

---
11. Rice, *The Story of S. Mary's, Abbots Bromley*, pp. 15-16.

Chapter 11. Eliza Lowe and the founding of S. Anne's School

but still, much use was made of existing houses on the site. Enough money was raised to build S. Mary's but for the first years the school was run in rented property in the village of Abbots Bromley. In a letter in 1874 to subscribers to S. Anne's Lowe set out the costs expended for S. Anne's so far which amounted to £2,494. He estimated that a sum of £4,000 for each school would suffice.[12] He did not express any embarrassment about the disparity in cost between the boys' schools and those for girls. There was land associated with the house for S. Anne's with outbuildings and gardens but the area covered, a mere two acres, was tiny compared with Denstone and Ellesmere. The rent for S. Winifred's was paid in the early years by Lady Eleanor Pennant and only tiny gardens were available for the girls to play in.

Numbers

In terms of numbers of pupils, the boys' schools were intended to cater for up to 500 and the land available offered scope for expansion. Lowe's plan for the girls' schools envisaged up to 100 girls and this required only one house with enough room for any necessary extension. S. Anne's opened with eight girls in April 1874; by the end of the year there were 20 boarders and eight day girls. A tall house (Dandelion) opposite S. Anne's gates was rented later that year to accommodate the growing numbers. In 1878 Lowe reported that 54 girls were at S. Anne's, 50 girls at S. Mary's and three girls at the industrial school, making up the numbers to over the 100 for which he had planned. Lowe's scheme was similar to that of Eliza, catering for the numbers of girls able to be accommodated in a large family house with the option of adding accommodation such as Eliza did in Seaforth.

Life at School

It is likely that there was not much difference between daily life in Eliza's school and in S. Anne's. Eliza had offered the usual subjects alongside 'accomplishments' and Lowe did not depart greatly from this model. At the same time attention was paid to 'the homely duties of life'.[13] Accomplishments were also mentioned, although this was not a priority for Lowe (see below) and, of course, religious instruction was based on the Catechism and scripture as well as regular attendance in Church or chapel. The subjects were the standard ones with German as an option along with piano and singing. Dancing classes were arranged but no Italian. According to Miss Rice, he favoured the 'happy home school ruled over by his own

---
12. Lowe, *S. Nicolas College and Its Schools*, p. 46.
13. Ibid., p. 63.

sisters'.[14] Just as Eliza's birthday was celebrated by her girls so was that of Miss Rice at S. Anne's. At the same time Lowe emphasised the need for girls to be prepared for the world of work and this does not seem to have been the case for Eliza. In Lowe's account of 1878 he says of S. Anne's that the standard aimed at is one which would qualify girls to become governesses or schoolmistresses. The cheaper of his schools would 'qualify girls leaving school for some of those various remunerative occupations which are daily being opened more and more to women'.[15]

So far it is clear that Lowe largely followed Eliza's model and was modest in his expectations. Perhaps he would have preferred to have raised large sums of money in the style of Woodard, but this was unrealistic. His schools for girls were breaking new ground and were something of an experiment. Prevailing opinion was that public school education for girls was a waste of effort and expense. A modest start was necessary. There was also the fact that he was at the same time raising large sums for the lower school for boys at Ellesmere and looking to expand in other areas of the Midlands. However, in many respects Lowe was to adopt the Woodard model.

The Woodard Model

The Chapel

This was the case particularly in relation to the chapel. S. Anne's Chapel was to be beautiful and designed by Woodard's architect, Richard Carpenter, one of the finest church architects of the day. While not to be compared with the magnificence of Lancing, S. Anne's Chapel was a fine building and the architect was able to persuade Lowe to agree to expensive half-size bricks. It was the first purpose-built building for the girls' schools and, of course, reflected the importance Lowe placed on the religious life of his schools. For this he would have been glad to call on the wealthy pupils who had attended Eliza's school and who, according to Miss Rice, contributed sufficient money to build the choir for the chapel and the fine plaque to Eliza that was placed in the chancel. The photograph on the next page is a recent one and shows the carpet and chairs donated by the Guild. Much later S. Winifred's also gained a beautiful new chapel, designed by the distinguished architect Herbert North, which, following the sale of the school, was pulled down by developers the day before it was due to be declared a listed building.[16]

---

14. Rice, *The Story of S. Mary's, Abbots Bromley*, p. 24.
15. Quoted in Heeney, *Mission to the Middle Classes*, p.108.
16. S. Anne's chapel and the original Georgian house are listed buildings. The chapel, original house, Coleridge and Dandelion are Grade 11 listed buildings.

Fig. 57 S. Anne's Chapel.

Governance

In Lowe's mind the girls' schools would eventually sit alongside the boys' schools on equal terms, so he set the oversight of the school up to operate as far as possible in the same way as the boys' schools. The house and land were conveyed to trustees under a governing body of which he, the Provost, was head 'until such time as S. Nicolas College undertakes to give it a new constitution consistent with the terms of the trust'.[17] The governing body was made up of the same men who governed Denstone so that, once the girls' schools were fully incorporated into the Society, there would be no need for major changes.[18]

Another connection with the Woodard model was that from the start Lowe had in mind a three-tier system. So, alongside the main school was an 'Industrial School' and 'little S. Mary's'. The industrial school was for girls who would work in the school for certain hours and then receive some lessons in return. S. Mary's was originally for younger children from the village whose parents wanted a church education that the village school could no longer give.

---
17. Lowe, *S. Nicolas College and its schools*, p. 43.
18. It is unclear when this took place. Miss Rice became headmistress of S. Anne's in 1900. She states that the school must have been incorporated before this time, probably after 1897 when Provost Talbot came into post. See Rice, *The Story of S. Mary's, Abbots Bromley*, p.169.

The Curriculum

What is striking is the emphasis Edward Lowe placed on annual inspection by University of Cambridge examiners and the fact that girls could be prepared for the Cambridge local exams. This was very much the same as the Woodard model. Examiners were invited in as early as autumn 1874, according to Miss Rice. Nothing indicates more clearly than this that Lowe had high academic standards in mind for his girls' schools. He approved of university education for women, although the prospectus appealing for funds issued in 1872 for his Midland Division girls' schools did not mention university entrance, which was only on the verge of becoming a possibility (see Chapter 2). McPherson refers to the institution of cricket at S. Anne's in 1884 by some of the girls, a tradition that soon became entrenched. According to Rice the curate of the parish taught the girls cricket.[19] Apparently, Lowe was challenged about the playing of such an unladylike game: 'Is cricket really allowed after all in S. Anne's Schools? Do you remember our argument about it at B–?'[20]

Cricket continued so clearly Lowe did not disapprove of it.

To conclude: Lowe's school at S. Anne's was influenced in several ways by that of his sister Eliza but in other important ways it was to follow the model of the Woodard schools for boys, even in relation to cricket. The following section makes it clear that he had rigorous academic standards in mind and his curriculum would not depart to any great extent from that found in Woodard boys' schools.

LOWE'S VISION FOR GIRLS' EDUCATION EXPLAINED

A meeting was held in Leicester six months before S. Anne's opened.[21] At this meeting Lowe set out very clearly what education he had in mind for his schools:

> Dr. Lowe spoke particularly against training girls for accomplishments only, for which no scope remains after the younger days of life are over. Girls thus trained for accomplishments which attract for a time, are found as women in after life to deteriorate, their mental training neglected. . . . In these schools there will be no attempt at accomplishments as the end of education, although they will be provided for those who have the faculty of being proficients.

---

19. Rice, *The Story of S. Mary's, Abbots Bromley*, p. 101.
20. McPherson, *The Story of S. Anne's, Abbots Bromley, 1874-1924*, p. 40.
21. *Leicester Journal*, 3 October 1873. All the quotations that follow in this section are taken from this source.

Chapter 11. Eliza Lowe and the founding of S. Anne's School

Here Lowe clearly sets his schools against the fashion for ladylike accomplishments. In an early prospectus it was put rather coyly that pressure should not be put on girls to spend time on accomplishments for which they had no inclination. He argued that the church would benefit from girls receiving proper mental training. In Apostolic times, he said, women had great influence: 'deaconesses and elder women being appointed to be teachers of good things, as to correspond with the appointment of deacons and presbyters in the higher holy orders of the ministry. In the virtuous training of Christian women great results are to be expected to the Church.'

He foresees women and men being on a par in their service to the Church. Not quite women priests but his use of the word 'correspond' here in this speech and later in the same speech is revealing: 'It is now proposed to form a series of boarding schools for girls in the Midland Counties, in connection with the society of S. John, of Lichfield. These schools are to correspond with those successful schools already founded for boys in the South of England, and at Denstone.'

Further evidence that girls' schools are to be modelled on the boys' schools is the emphasis on what is to be taught: 'Girls will be well taught in all matters which strengthen their powers of accuracy, as in algebra, Euclid, agricultural book keeping, the use of the telegraph, &c., also in good reading, which is better than bad singing, plain sewing, cutting out, and domestic management.'[22]

This is 1873 when opportunities for educated women were few and far between. However, many middle-class women were married to farmers who would be glad of a good bookkeeper to hand and being adept at modern technology would prove valuable to any business endeavour. Lest any should worry about the effect such training would have on girls he added: 'This kind of training will speedily produce simplicity, honesty and sincerity of character, and under ladies' care will bring true refinement to bear upon others.'

Here Lowe shows his nineteenth century credentials (see Chapter 2). However, he might well argue in response that such virtues are not relevant solely to the domestic scene.

So far, I have argued in this chapter that the life and death of Eliza Lowe had a direct influence on Edward Lowe's decision to found girls' schools and also that aspects of the way she ran her school were a model for these schools. I now consider other aspects of her life (and the life of his other sisters) that may have influenced him.

---

22. Though the boys' schools of his day will not have learned sewing!

Edward Lowe's Debt to Eliza

Edward Lowe was the youngest of a very large family. All of his six sisters had to support themselves and so he knew from personal experience that women could not rely on being supported by men all their lives. Eliza ran a lucrative business for many years, supported by Mary Manley and Charlotte. Harriet and Emily Louisa worked as governesses and Maria was widowed young. Not only did his sisters have to support themselves but they did so with a measure of success. If certainty that women could run successful schools were needed, Lowe had a shining example in his sisters. Lowe's schools were to be for a different clientele and more modest in cost but Eliza's success would have convinced him that a woman could successfully run a school and attract pupils from respected families. By contrast he and his brothers had either had a university education or gone into the professions, as priests, doctors or lawyers. It is possible that he felt the unfairness of this and planned that the girls of his schools should have better opportunities.

His own family's financial difficulties meant that it was left to his oldest sister to carry the responsibility of raising her younger brothers and sisters. The fact that Eliza had had a good education was the family's passport to survival. It can be presumed that Eliza's sisters were educated in her school and then took their turn to help. Charles, who could have helped, was a liability. The younger brothers were aged fifteen, fourteen, twelve and four when their father Samuel died. George went to Repton School. John went to Cambridge and Edward to Oxford. George trained as a doctor as did William. All of this had to be arranged and paid for. Edward Lowe and his brothers owed a great deal to Eliza.

Edward Lowe's tributes to Eliza

The first public tribute to his sister was given at the laying of the foundation stone of S. Anne's Chapel in May 1875. This is how the *Staffordshire Advertiser* reported Edward Lowe's words at the service:

> The occasion was to himself (Canon Lowe) and many others of his family, and those included in the circle of his friendship and acquaintance, one of very deep and sacred interest, and they did most cordially thank the Bishop for the thoughtful and considerate way in which he had alluded to that venerated sister in whose memory the chapel in that place was to be erected. He, as the youngest member of his family of his own generation, had

more reason perhaps than any other member of that large circle of brothers and sisters to prize the memorial to her who was not only his sister and godmother, but his instructress from early years in that which he had lived to know was the most valuable and precious kind of knowledge that he could learn. It was indeed a joy to them to recall her long, unwearied and self-sacrificial labours in the cause of education – and to see that indeed her works had followed her, and that those whom she instructed were in their turn united to extend the blessings of Christian education to a yet larger body of their fellow-countrymen. (Applause) The chapel must be an important part of a Christian school, for worship was a large and essential part of education. They were thankful to be able in the early life of that school to begin with the Church.[23]

The second public tribute was paid two years later in 1877 at the dedication of the chapel choir for use by the pupils. It was a grand occasion and one where Lowe would hope to gain more donations; money was needed to build the nave and for the decoration and fitting out of the chapel. Transport there and back to Abbots Bromley was laid on from Rugeley and Uttoxeter railway stations. The village board schoolroom was hired in order that addresses could be given and lunch laid out. After lunch a service took place in the village church before all processed to the choir of the chapel for the dedication. The girls of S. Mary's (Lowe's day school for pupils of the village) followed the processional cross and then the girls of S. Anne's.

At the conclusion of lunch Canon Lowe stood up to give the first address.[24] He extended his warmest thanks to those former pupils of Eliza who had given so liberally to enable the choir of the chapel to be built. Their generosity was a testament to the character of the education they had received from his sister. The *Staffordshire Sentinel*, 30 June 1877, reported his words in this way:

> Silently, unknown – in a measure unappreciated, so far as the outer world was concerned – his sister passed a long and laborious life, but her labours were appreciated and valued by those who knew her. He would not dwell upon the many good qualities she possessed, the abundant intellectual powers with which she was endowed, the loyal services she never failed to render to the Church of which they present were members, but the outcome could not be otherwise than gratifying to those bearing her name.

---
23. *Staffordshire Advertiser*, 29 May 1875.
24. *Staffordshire Sentinel*, 30 June 1877.

This is a moving tribute. It is interesting that, of the 'many good qualities that she possessed', Lowe singled out her intellectual powers and service to her Church. This is appropriate of course to the founding of a school and one in close connection with the Church. Perhaps the greatest tribute he made to her lies in the last few words: 'to those bearing her name'. For a man, and a man of his stature and achievements, to be proud of his name because of what a sister has achieved is both remarkable and moving. He was still the youngest brother in awe of a gifted elder sister who had had such an influence for good upon him and so many others.

Finally, the wording of the plaque to Eliza stated that the choir was erected in memory of her: 'as a fruit of her training'.[25]

The gift of a chapel by her pupils would indeed be a fruit of her training but Edward Lowe may have been including himself when he wrote these words. Without her he perhaps would never have gone to Oxford, carried out a lifetime's work in the service of church education nor gone on to found S. Anne's, S. Mary's and S. Winifred's.

She was indeed 'that venerated sister.'

---

25. See Introduction.

Part Three
The Relevance Today

Chapter 12

Of More than Passing Interest?

I have told the story of Eliza Lowe and made a connection between her and the founding of S. Anne's in Abbots Bromley – my old school. It is a story that has lain dormant for a long time and it is ironic that it should be uncovered just at the time the school was closing. This chapter is by way of a postscript or a 'so what' chapter. Does her story matter and, if so, to whom?

To those of us who spent formative years at school in Abbots Bromley, to read about Eliza Lowe and her influence upon her brother, the Provost of the Midland Division of Woodard, is to add to our understanding and appreciation of our time at school. We all knew about what we called 'Commem' (Commemoration) and perhaps even could recall some of the names of the founders whose names were solemnly read out at the Commemoration service in the parish church following 'Jerusalem Heights', the procession of the whole school, in height order, from the chapel down the village to St Nicholas' Church.

We were too young to take much interest in past history. I spent seven years at the school, attending all the services I was supposed to attend, and never once noticed the large plaque to Eliza Lowe in the choir of the chapel. Nor was she mentioned in the list of founders and benefactors, let alone her sisters Mary Manley and Charlotte for whom, as I have shown, there are also memorial plaques in the chapel.

Yet in a real sense Eliza Lowe was the founder of our school. Without her and her formative influence upon her brother, it is doubtful that there would have been a S. Anne's, a S. Mary's and a S. Winifred's. It took enormous energy and commitment on the part of Edward Lowe to get the schools off the ground, make them succeed and grow into relatively large and successful institutions. Like Woodard, he did not do it on his own. Girls would eventually be admitted to Lancing, Denstone and the other Woodard Schools (from the 1970s onwards) but, without the girls' schools of the nineteenth century, many generations of girls would have missed out on the unique experience of being given the sort of opportunities that boys received. This is not the place to try to describe or evaluate what life was like at Abbots Bromley and S. Winifred's. Suffice it to say that for many old girls, myself included, school had a profound influence, whether good or (sometimes) not so good. When Abbots Bromley closed in 2019 there was shock and great sadness, expressed even by those who did not enjoy their time at school.

So, when the Guild of S. Mary and S. Anne meets and we say the Guild Office with its prayers of thanks in remembrance of the founders, we can remember Eliza Lowe and her sisters and make good the omission of her name in the list of those read out at Commem. It seems to me that the story matters to the former pupils and the Guild because it completes something that was missing in our history.

Similarly, it matters to those to whom the Woodard story matters. There have been several biographies of Nathaniel Woodard and several fine accounts of the different schools. However, there has never been a story of Eliza, nor a biography of Edward Lowe. So, my story is a small, but I think significant, contribution to Woodard history. Heeney points out the omission regarding Edward Lowe and suggests that a possible reason is that Lowe was a very private individual and did not give much away about himself. My story adds to what is known about Edward Lowe. It restates one matter. Woodard did not give his blessing to the founding of S. Anne's and did not use his great fundraising skills to help raise money. Yet it is sometimes stated that it was Woodard who founded the school.[1] It was all the work of Edward Lowe, with help from some leading lights in the Midland Division, such as Sir Percival Heywood and Reverend Henry Meynell. Many old girls will remember the names of the houses in S. Anne's: Lowe, Meynell, Heywood and, later, Rice. In S. Mary's the houses were named Alice Mary Coleridge (AMC), after the Lady Warden who did so much for both S. Anne's and S. Mary's, Selwyn, after the great Bishop Selwyn, and Keble S. Benet's (KSB). Apart from KSB and Rice all the names of the houses reflect individuals who had worked hard for the success of the school and had been involved from the beginning. It may therefore be significant that no house was named after Woodard.[2]

---

1. See Gibbs, *In Search of Nathaniel Woodard*, p. 66: 'It is one of the original schools founded by Woodard himself.' This statement formed part of the description of Abbots Bromley School for Girls sent out by the school.
2. Houses for S. Anne's were instituted in 1900 and in S. Mary's in 1909. Originally KSB was two houses, Keble and S Benet's. In recent times, when school numbers began to fall the houses were reorganised and renamed.

Chapter 12. Of More than Passing Interest?

The old girls of S. Winifred's may be pleased to read about the very early times of their school in Bangor, as may the parents' group who put great efforts into saving Abbots Bromley school, many in the village of Abbots Bromley for whom the closure of the school was a great loss, members of the school staff and family members of the Lowes and Landors. The story of Eva McLaren is not well known and the McLaren family of today have shown great interest. There are not many accounts of private girls' schools in the nineteenth century; most of them came and went, leaving no records, so my story is of value to historians of the period.

Relevance to the Broader Society

I believe that there are matters that are relevant to the broader society. I began this book with a brief outline of the way in which the Woodard community of schools attempts to carry out the vision of its founder today and I find this impressive. The idea of a family of schools which will help each other out, develop specialisms which can be shared, unite different classes and help to create citizens who are motivated to live out the Christian vision of love for God and neighbour is all to the good and sets an example that can inspire others.

Free Schools

Our education system in recent years has developed free schools and there is now a great variety of these schools in existence. Free schools are directly funded by the government but are set up and run by independent organisations and are not controlled by the local authority. These schools may or may not have a religious basis. There are now Sikh schools, Muslim schools and other religious schools maintained by the state, as well as others with no religious basis. Such schools must state their foundational vision and may then develop their school in accordance with this vision. What this means is that state-maintained schools no longer have to be neutral in relation to religion. They do not have to leave God at the door as Woodard feared all those years ago. Were Nathaniel Woodard alive today, he would be amazed and doubtless seize the opportunity with vigour. The Woodard community of schools today can and does take advantage of this situation, readily promoting its provision of a high-quality education in an actively Christian environment. One of the great advantages of these schools is regular worship and a fine choral tradition, often in beautiful chapels. Woodard and Lowe believed that worship was essential to a proper education and it is a point worth considering today. In 1944 the proponents of the Butler

Education Act understood this when it was put into legislation that religious education should comprise both worship in the assembly hall, coining the phrase 'collective worship', and religious instruction in the classroom.

What lies behind this recent move to allow schools to develop their own individual philosophy? It may be remembered that the Church of England Schools Review Group[3] found that Church of England schools were in great demand and as a result of this the number of maintained Church of England schools increased. Parents often say that church schools have something extra that they want for their children. Muslim parents like church schools because they feel that God is honoured there. The criticism is made that it is not God that parents want (and there may be truth in this) but rather the middle-class culture and contact with richer friends. Whatever the case church schools continue to thrive and attract pupils.

Is this not very strange in a society which has experienced an enormous decline in religious attendance and the established Church's loss of the moral high ground, a society which can report little serious debate on religious themes in the media, and in which secularism is the default position of most of our leaders even if they have personal religious faith? However, the fact that secular groups are still having to campaign[4] seems to imply that they are meeting resistance, that society is not quite ready to give up its adherence to religious beliefs and practices.

Religious Education in Schools

In 2004 Lutterworth published my book *Whatever Happened to Religious Education?* In this book I wrote about the problems facing religious education (RE) in the context of local authority schools and the different solutions that had been suggested. Outside faith settings, or, to use the official language, in schools not having a religious character, contemporary religious education is invariably defined by a separation of religious education from religious life. The problem of religious education is how to ground the subject when it is no longer grounded in religious life. What has happened is that with increasing religious and non-religious pluralisation in the UK and Europe, local authorities, whether they wish to or not, feel

---

3. The Archbishops' Council established the Church Schools Review Group, under the chairmanship of Lord Dearing CB, 'to review the achievements of Church of England schools and to make proposals for their future development'. The report of the review group was published as *The Way Ahead: Church of England Schools in the New Millennium* (London: Church House Publishing, 2001).
4. Humanists UK actively campaign on many issues to do with religion. See their website: www.humanism.org.uk.

obliged to include ever more religions and non-religious belief systems[5] alongside Christianity, still the major religious tradition of the country. The subject becomes unmanageable and finding a rationale problematic. The European Convention on Human Rights has added a legal issue to be addressed: that of the principle of non-discrimination on religious and philosophical grounds. A parent's religion or philosophical belief must be accorded equal respect with traditional religions and beliefs. This does not mean that every shade of belief and non-belief must be included, rather, that one may not rule out from a syllabus a religion or belief if sincerely held. To put it crudely 'any dream will do'.[6]

What Eliza and Woodard were able to do was to ground religious education within a particular form of religious life, in their case the Church of England, that has a system of beliefs and practices that has been developed and refined (and is still being refined) over time and so possesses authority. There is something to be learned and, yes, assessed. There is a way of life to be experienced, demonstrated and tested. A pupil learns that for this school and for these teachers there is a something solid about religion, even something worth rebelling against. This is important if pupils are to take religion seriously.

Now this can only take place in a school which has a declared religious foundation. However, there is no reason why an RE department in a local authority school which does not have a religious character should not work with its parents and governors and the local authority Standing Advisory Council for Religious Education (SACRE)[7] to develop something approximate to what a school with a religious foundation can do. It will not be the same but it may offer some of the benefits that an overtly religious school can provide. My friend and colleague Marius Felderhof developed a way of teaching RE in Birmingham based on what he called the 'treasury of faith', in which religions are 'mined' for what they tell us about how to live the good life and live before God, or 'the Eternal', as he puts it. In this way religions are presented as offering valuable resources for living, rather than problems and contradictions clothed in uncertainty. Another important principle of this syllabus is that it gives the opportunity for a religion to be studied on its own terms as opposed to from a disinterested and separate point of view.[8]

---

5. Humanists are often appointed by a local authority to the bodies responsible for religious education.
6. For an excellent discussion of the issue, see Liam Gearon, 'The Paradigms of Contemporary Religious Education', *Journal for the Study of Religion*, Vol. 27, no. 1 (January 2014), pp. 52-81.
7. Every local authority in England and Wales is required to set up a Standing Advisory Council for Religious Education to advise on RE and review the syllabus every five years.
8. See www.faithmakesadifference.co.uk. Also Marius Felderhof and Penny Thompson,

Much has changed since Edward Lowe founded my school. The Prayer Book is still there but there are other forms of worship authorised for use, new translations of the Bible and more emphasis on ecumenical relations, new liturgies, different styles of music and so on. All of these and more can be called upon in worship in schools with an Anglican foundation. Let pupils learn about Anglican divines and the early Doctors of the Church, Augustine and Aquinas, the poems of John Donne, George Herbert, the women of the Bible as well as the men. I think there is a place for learning prayers of the church like the General Thanksgiving, perhaps some psalms and attending regular services like compline. The main point is that schools should not be afraid of 'definite' religious teaching. This does not mean that nothing of the other religions is included on the syllabus. They bear witness to God too and interesting parallels (as well as differences) can be drawn. Nor does it require a form of teaching which excludes questions and debate. In fact, it is the security of starting from faith that allows for doubt and probing.

The Teacher as Friend

In Eliza's school friendliness was important and she gave a prize for what she called 'amiability'. Her letters show that she lived this out in her relations with her family, friends and former pupils. Lucy Landor knew that Eliza cared for her and liked spending time with her. She knew that it was important to Eliza how she lived her life, even many years after leaving school; Eliza was not afraid to rebuke her and also tease her when she took herself too seriously. Eliza was still her moral guardian, companion, confidante and friend. Perhaps we have all known teachers like this and Llywela Harris,[9] whom many Abbots Bromley old girls will remember, was certainly one. Is this sort of pupil-teacher relationship still possible today? The fact that every school must have its safeguarding rules and procedures to guard against the dangers should not mean that no relationship of trust and friendship is possible.

By requiring teachers to be neutral and distanced, have we lost something? Maybe not; the language of friendliness, care and guardianship has not disappeared altogether. At parents' meetings one can expect to hear a teacher say something along the lines of 'I was disappointed by her exam result' or 'I believe he can do better' or 'I enjoyed that last essay'. The relationship of teacher to pupil is one of nurture but also one which involves friendship and a degree of attachment. This was clear to Eliza.

---

eds, *Teaching Virtue: The Contribution of Religious Education* (London: Bloomsbury, 2014).

9. Every year at Guild executive meetings Llywela would bring news of teachers and old girls with whom she was in touch. The list was always very long!

Character Formation

Eliza, perhaps following Shirreff, was clear that character formation was central to education. It mattered what sort of person a pupil was and grew up to be. One aspect that was important to her was cheerfulness. For example, Eliza told Lucy off for her lack of cheerfulness when she returned home with a gloomy disposition. Cultivating this virtue was part of the early tradition of S. Anne's and S. Mary's. Alice Mary Coleridge, who was Lady Warden of both schools, wrote a letter to old girls for the first leaflet of the Guild in 1892. In it she wrote: 'one of our aims should be "Happiness of Heart". If we cannot be kohinoors (mountains of light), she wrote, we can be cheerful little brilliants, sound and pure.'[10]

Cheerfulness is catching and has to be cultivated. I remember a pupil I taught who always cheered me up. He was always cheerful, even though he had some difficulties learning and walked with a stick. He had a habit of saying to me after a lesson 'that was really interesting Miss!' It seems to me that Eliza and my pupil were onto something important here.

Can schools today cultivate virtues? How would this be achieved? We live, it may be argued, in a society of great moral uncertainty; and teachers in recent years have been careful not to impose particular moral standards on their pupils. However, the aim of education according to the Department of Education is to promote 'the spiritual, moral, cultural, mental and physical development of pupils at the school and of society, while preparing pupils at the school for the opportunities, responsibilities and experiences of later life'.[11] This means that schools must pay attention to the whole person, not just their academic development, and is also a recognition that, in so doing, a gift (or its opposite) is mediated to society. We are in this together.

Today there is considerable interest in this area of education. A major development in recent years has been the siting of the Jubilee Centre for Character and Virtues within the School of Education at Birmingham University. The centre, which is largely funded by the Templeton Foundation, is led by Professor James Arthur. It has carried out a large body of research and is staffed by 20 academics and support staff. The centre has an ambitious aim: 'Our vision for the Centre is . . . to shape the future attitudes and behaviours of the British people. We aim to enable British people to explore their character and virtues and, if and where required, transform them. It is as such that our prime goal is not theoretical, but practical.'

---

10. Undine Sykes, *The Story of the Guild of S. Mary and S. Anne* (London: published privately by the author, 1997) p. 29.
11. Education Act 2002.

The work focuses on schools but also on the wider community:

> The Jubilee Centre for Character and Virtues will address critical questions about character in Britain. The Centre will promote, build and strengthen character virtues in the contexts of the family, school, community, university, professions, voluntary organisations and the wider workplace. We believe that character is constituted by the virtues, such as courage, justice, honesty, compassion, self-discipline, gratitude, generosity and humility.[12]

Coincidentally, in Birmingham since 2007, and quite independent of the Jubilee Centre, a syllabus of religious education (referred to earlier) has pioneered a form of religious education based on virtues found in religions. A set of 24 dispositions forms the material of the syllabus drawn from the major religions represented in Birmingham. There is a remarkable similarity between the Jubilee Centre virtues and the dispositions of the City syllabus.[13]

So, there is today powerful support for the deliberate formation of character, both through education in schools and other fields and a measure of agreement as to what virtues should be taught. This was (as the present book has shown) self-evident to nineteenth-century educators. Emily Shirreff spent more than half of her book giving examples of how to do it. Is there anything to be learned from these educators? A comparison of the virtues advocated by the Jubilee Centre and Shirreff would reveal much in common and perhaps some interesting differences.

Women can no longer be expected to bear the weight of being the 'natural guardians of culture' and 'men's moral consciences'. Nor can they be expected to train and nurture the young as their sole, or even main, role in life. However, guardians of culture and bringing up the young to live well and with a clear conscience are necessary roles. It is perhaps more important now that attention is paid to these matters both in schools and in the home. Is there a danger that as women have taken a share in the world of work and public life that virtues traditionally associated with women and the home are relegated or given less importance? Is it, for example, still relevant to be refined as opposed to coarse, gentle as opposed to aggressive, ready to admit mistakes as opposed to not showing weakness, accepting of the faults of others as opposed to being ruthless, able to ask for help as opposed to independent action? Someone has to model concern for the sick and the less fortunate, show cheerfulness and perseverance and 'lend a helping hand'.

---

12. www.jubileecentre.ac.uk, accessed 23 June 2020.
13. www.faithmakesadifference.co.uk, accessed 23 June 2020.

Chapter 12. Of More than Passing Interest?

Learning for Its Own Sake

A final thought is this: the standard of academic learning reached by some girls in Eliza's school was impressive. I had not expected this. Similarly, the level of learning expected by Emily Shirreff looks to be equivalent to that at university level today. In the early to mid-nineteenth century girls did not have the opportunity to go on to further study at university. However, it seems that the opportunities to learn were there for some privileged girls and as the century went on more and more girls were studying at a high level. For most of the nineteenth century girls were not learning in order to pass exams but, nonetheless, or perhaps because of this, they developed their intellectual gifts to a high degree. In theory all girls (and boys) today have the opportunity to develop their academic gifts, whatever their background. Exams are not everything and life goes on after school. Love of learning for its own sake and for the sheer joy of it was important to Eliza. We should not lose sight of this.

I would like to finish with some words of St Paul that Miss Roch, my headmistress at Abbots Bromley, used to read at the end of every term, words which I like to think Eliza Lowe quoted at the end of term too:

> Rejoice in the Lord always; again I will say, rejoice. . . . Finally, brethren, whatever is true, whatever is honourable, whatever is just, whatever is pure, whatever is lovely, whatever is gracious, if there is any excellence, if there is anything worthy of praise, think about these things.
> *Philippians 4:4, 8.*

Bibliography

For a work like this today there are many sources of information, not least the internet. I have used Ordnance Survey maps freely provided by the National Library of Scotland. Ancestry.com may be accessed in most public libraries. Newspapers freely available on the website of the The National Library of Australia were sourced for details of the life of Charles Lowe. The British Newspaper Archive (BNA) also provided valuable information and all the references to newspaper reports in this country are from this source. I have used Wikipedia but information from this source needs to be checked. There are other websites that I have used such as British History. Family histories may be found on the internet and these have been useful. Some books long out of print have been digitised, such as those by Edward Lowe, Emily Shirreff, Maria Edgeworth and Anne Langton, and that has made research much easier than it might have been. However, not everything can be found on the internet and below I list my main sources beginning with Manuscript Sources.

Manuscript Sources

Tim Tomlinson, Private Papers. These papers belong to Rachel Gatfield a descendant of the Landor family. Much of this material was collected and transcribed by Walter Noble Landor, a noted antiquarian. Some of this material is stored in Staffordshire Record Office.
The Gladstone Papers, the British Library.
The Guild of S. Mary and S. Anne archives.
The Lucy Landor Reminiscences, Staffordshire Record Office.
The Rathbone Papers, University of Liverpool.
Women's Suffrage Collection, Manchester Central Library.
Women's Library Archives, London School of Economics.

Books and Articles

Brittain, Vera, *Testament of Youth* (London: Victor Gollancz, 1933)
Burstyn, Joan N., *Victorian Education and the Ideal of Womanhood* (London: Croom Helm, 1980)
Church Schools Review Group of the Church of England, *The Way Ahead: Church of England Schools in the New Millennium* (London: Church House Publishing, 2001)
Dumayne, Alan, *Southgate: A Glimpse into the Past* (London: Macdermott & Chant, 1987)
Dyhouse, Carol, *Girls Growing Up in Late Victorian and Edwardian England* (London: Routledge & Kegan Paul, 1981)
Edgeworth, Maria, and Richard Lovell Edgeworth, *Practical Education*, 2 Vols (London: J. Johnson, 1798)
Enfield, William, *An Essay towards the History of Leverpool* (London: Joseph Johnson, 1774)
Felderhof, Marius, and Penny Thompson, eds, *Teaching Virtue: The Contribution of Religious Education* (London: Bloomsbury, 2014)
Gearon, Liam, 'The Paradigms of Contemporary Religious Education', *Journal for the Study of Religion*, Vol. 27, no. 1 (January 2014), pp. 52-81

Bibliography

Gibbs, David, *In Search of Nathaniel Woodard: Victorian Founder of Schools* (Chichester: Phillimore & Co., 2011)

Heeney, Brian, *Mission to the Middle Classes: The Woodard Schools, 1848-1891* (London: SPCK, 1969)

Ker, Ian, *The Achievement of John Henry Newman* (Notre Dame, IN: University of Notre Dame, 1990)

———, *John Henry Newman: A Biography* (Oxford: Clarendon Press, 1988)

———, *Newman on Education*, Cardinal Newman Society, December 2008, www.newmansociety.org/newman-on-education

King, Peter, *Hurstpierpoint College 1849-1995: The School by the Downs* (Bognor Regis: Phillimore, 1997)

Kirk, Kenneth E., *The Story of the Woodard Schools* (London: Hodder & Stoughton, 1937)

Litzmann, Berthold, *Clara Schumann: An Artist's Life, Based on Material Found in Diaries and Letters*, trans. by G.E. Hadow, 2 Vols (Cambridge: Cambridge University Press, 2013)

Lowe, Edward C., *S. Nicolas College and Its Schools: A Record of Thirty Years' Work in the Effort to Endow the Church of England with a System of Self-Supporting Public Boarding Schools for the Upper, Middle and Lower Middle Classes*, Leopold Classic Library (first published in 1878)

McPherson, Violet M., *The Story of S. Anne's, Abbots Bromley, 1874-1924* (Shrewsbury: Wilding & Son, 1924)

Pederson, Joyce S., *The Reform of Girls' Secondary and Higher Education in Victorian England: A Study of Elites and Educational Change* (New York: Garland, 1987)

———, 'Schoolmistresses and Headmistresses: Elites and Education in Nineteenth Century England', *Journal of British Studies*, Vol. 15, no. 1 (Autumn 1975)

Philips, Ellen, ed., *Langton Records: Journals and Letters from Canada, 1837-1846* (Edinburgh: R. & R. Clark, 1904)

———, *Letters of Thomas Langton to Mrs. Thomas Hardy, 1814-1818* (Manchester: J.E. Cornish, 1900)

Purvis, June, *A History of Women's Education in England* (Milton Keynes: Open University Press, 1991)

Rice, Marcia A., *The Story of S. Mary's, Abbots Bromley* (Shrewsbury: Wilding & Son, 1947)

Roberts, Nesta, *S. Winifred's, Llanfairfechan: The Story of Fifty Years 1887-1937* (Shrewsbury: Wilding & Son, 1937)

Sharples, Joseph, *Liverpool: Pevsner City Guide* (Pevsner Architectural Guides: City Guides) (New Haven, CT: Yale University Press, 2004)

Shirreff, Emily, 'College Education for Women', *Contemporary Review*, Vol. 15 (1870)

———, *Intellectual Education and Its Influence on the Character and Happiness of Women* (London: J.W. Parker, 1858)

Syers, Robert, *The History of Everton* (Liverpool: G. & J. Robinson, 1830); see digitised version on the Everton local history website, www.evertonhistory.com, at: https://archive.org/details/historyofeverton00syeruoft

Sykes, Undine, *The Story of the Guild of S. Mary and S. Anne* (London: published privately by the author, 1997)

Tiffen, Herbert J., *A History of Liverpool Institute Schools 1825-1935* (The Liverpool Institute Old Boys' Association, 1935)

Toye, Ernest, *Rugeley: 150 Years of a Country Town* (Landor Local History Society, 2018)

Turner, Jocelyne V.C., *Down Memory Lane* (Platt Memorial Hall, 2016), available from http://plattmemorialhall.org/warmemorial/books/

Wells, Anna and Roch, Muriel, *S. Anne's Chapel, The School of S. Mary and S. Anne, Abbots Bromley, Staffordshire,* July 1998.

Williams, Barbara, *A Gentlewoman in Upper Canada: The Journals, Letters, and Art of Anne Langton* (Toronto: University of Toronto Press, 2008)

Credits and Permissions

Note: All of the images not present in this list are owned by the author.

Fig. 1   *Memorial plaque to Eliza Lowe, 1803-72.* I am grateful to Niki Gandy for this photograph and for those at figs 1a, 1b and 1c.
Fig. 1a *Memorial plaque in context.* See above.
Fig. 1b *Memorial plaque to Mary Manley Lowe.* See above.
Fig. 1c *Memorial plaque to Charlotte Lowe.* See above.
Fig. 2   *Lancing College Chapel.* I am grateful to Lancing College for supplying this photograph.
Fig. 3   *Liverpool Institute High School for Girls, Blackburne House, Liverpool.* The photograph is the property of Blackburne House Group to whom I am grateful for permission to reproduce it here.
Fig. 5   *Brighthelmston School.* I would like to thank Ingrid Guy, an old girl of Brighthelmston for giving me sight of an original postcard.
Fig. 9   *Samuel Lowe's signature.* Tim Tomlinson, private papers.
Fig. 10 *Map of Everton.* Reproduced with permission of the National Library of Scotland, published 1851.
Fig. 12 *Everton Village, c. 1820. W.G. Herdman.* Reproduced with permission of the Liverpool Record Office.
Fig. 13 *Everton Village, c. 1843. W.G. Herdman.* Reproduced with permission of the Liverpool Record Office.
Fig. 14 *The North Shore. W.G. Herdman.* Reproduced with permission of the Liverpool Record Office.
Fig. 16. *Location of the two schools in Bootle.* Reproduced with permission of the National Library of Scotland, published 1850.
Fig. 17 *Bathing machines.* Reproduced with permission of the Liverpool Record Office.
Fig. 18 *Seaforth House.* I am grateful to Allan Johnston for permission to reproduce this photograph here.
Fig. 19 *Map showing location of Eliza's school.* Reproduced with permission of the National Library of Scotland, published 1850.
Fig. 20 *Map showing Charles Lowe's properties.* Reproduced with permission of the National Library of Scotland, published 1850.
Fig. 24 *Blythe Hall.* I am grateful to John Knowles for permission to reproduce this photograph, taken in 2003.

Credits and Permissions

Fig. 26   *Miss Harriet Lowe*. The work of Anne Langton. Watercolour on ivory. Reference Code: F 1077-7-1-0-23. Archives of Ontario, I0028020. Reproduced here by permission.

Fig. 27   *Barrow House*. I am grateful to Derwentwater Independent Hostel for providing this photograph.

Fig. 29   *Sutton Oaks*. Photograph courtesy of the Macclesfield Express.

Fig. 31   *Cecilia Landor*. Tim Tomlinson, private papers.

Fig. 32   *Miss Fazakerley and her schooner*. I am grateful to Chris Kay and the Royal Mersey Yacht Club for permission to reproduce this painting by Henry Melling.

Fig. 34   *Map showing location of Skinner Langton's property in Southgate*. Reproduced with the permission of the National Library of Scotland, published 1868.

Fig. 35   *Mayfield House, Southgate*. I am indebted to Chris Horner of the Southgate Green Association for this photograph.

Fig. 36   *Map showing location of Mayfield House*. Reproduced with permission of the National Library of Scotland, published 1868.

Fig. 39   *Memorial to Eliza, Mary Manley and Charlotte in Christ Church Southgate*. I am grateful to Fr Chrichton Limbert, vicar, for this photograph.

Fig. 40   *Credenhill Court*. I am grateful to Philip Halling for permission to reproduce this photograph.

Fig. 41   *Thornton Lodge*. Now a bed and breakfast establishment: www.thorntonlodgenorthyorkshire.co.uk. I am grateful to the owner, Vanessa Kilvington, for permission to reproduce this photograph.

Fig. 47   *Electioneering in Inverness*. I am grateful to Michael McLaren QC for permission to reproduce this photograph.

Fig. 48   *Letter from Eva McLaren*. I am grateful to Manchester Libraries, Information and Archives for permission to reproduce this and the following image. M50/2/1/168.

Fig. 49   *Eva's signature*. See above.

Fig. 52   *Eliza Lowe's burial certificate*. Reproduced courtesy of the Staffordshire Record Office, ref. no D5191/4.

Fig. 53   *Emily Landor Lowe*. Image from Nesta Roberts, *S. Winifred's, Llanfairfechan: The Story of Fifty Years 1887-1937* (Shrewsbury: Wilding & Son, 1937).

Fig. 57   *S. Anne's Chapel*. I am grateful to the Guild for permission to reproduce this photograph.

Index

Abbots Bromley School, x, 1, 3, 4, 114, 182, 183
S. Anne's, xi, 1, 4, 22, 23, 24, 33, 46, 78, 86, 87, 98, Chapter 9 passim, Chapter 11 passim, 181, 182, 187
S. Mary's, 146, Chapter 11 passim, 181, 183, 187
S. Mary and S. Anne's, xi, 1, 6, 165
accomplishments, 29, 32, 36, 40, 44, 46, 100, 105, 116, 171, 174, 175
Anglo-Catholic, 14, 71, 119
amiability, 95, 140, 186
Barrow House, 84, 111
bathing machines, 58, 62, 63
Bennett, William S., 116-17, 127
Blackburne House, 26
Blythe Hall, 78, 79
Bodnant Garden, 138-39
Bootle, x, 3, 50, 57-60, 62, 74, 79, 81, 93-96, 159
Bowyer Brown, Ellen, 146-47
Bright, Priscilla, 32, 133
Brighthelmston, ix, 32, 33
Brittain, Vera, 45
Cambridge University, 19, 23, 32, 46, 117, 128
Catechism, 13, 17, 39, 171
Christ Church, Southgate, 114-16
churchgoing and chapel attendance at school, 17, 18, 109, 114-16, 171, 186
Clarke, Mary, 50, 51, 52, 70, 95, 96, 97, 98
Clarke, John, 50, 51, 52, 93, 94
Coleridge, Alice M., 50, 148, 150, 151, 164, 182, 187

cricket, 33, 174
Crofts, 86, 142, 143, 165
Dalglish, Lilias, 116, 122-23
Dante, 41, 95, 128, 130
Davies, Emily, 31, 34, 35, 128, 130
Denstone College, xi, 18, 165, 169, 170
Ecroyd, Edith, 116, 118
Ecroyd, Margaret, *see Tunstill*
Edgeworth, Maria, 44-45, 95, 96
education:
    character formation, 36, 39, 43, 44, 96, 154, 162, 175, 187-88
    curriculum, 11, 18, 21, 32, 34, 37, 39, 45, 60, 61, 150, 174
    friendliness, 186
    religious education, 12, 13, 16, 150, 184-86, 188
    role of the Church of England, 12-13, 15, 16, 17, 167, 184
    school Inspections, 146, 149, 174
    unity of, 16, 17, 21
    university education for women, 23, 24, 26-27, 32, 34, 46, 128, 131
    university examinations, 34, 35, 130-32, 146, 174
Ellesmere College, 17, 169, 170, 172
Everton, 3, 54-57, 59, 61
Favarger, Clementine, 74, 103, 104
Fawcett, Millicent, 32, 137
Felderhof, Marius C., 185
Forster Act, 13, 30, 88, 165
Free Schools, 183-84
Garfield Terrace, 147, 148
Gibbs, David, 1, 10, 15
Girton College, 39, 128, 130

Index

Gore's Directory, 53, 59, 65, 109
governesses, 30, 31, 34, 55, 75, 117, 120, 28, 172
Gladstone, William E., 14, 64, 65, 116, 164
Guild of S. Mary and S. Anne, x, 172, 182, 186, 187
Heeney, Brian, 12, 20, 23, 24, 164, 182
Herdman, William G., 56, 58, 63
Heywood, Sir Percival, 165, 168, 182
Hill, Octavia, 133
Holme, Vera, 139
Hornby, Anne Mary, 82, 86, 87
Jubilee Centre, 187, 188
Keble, John, 10, 20, 115, 182
Kirk, Kenneth E., 16, 148
Lancing:
    Chapel, 6, 14, 15, 16, 17
    College, 18
Landor:
    Cecilia, chapter 6, 145, 155, 156, 158, 160, 161
    Frances, chapter 6, 156
    Henry E., 154, 160
    Lucy, Chapter 6, 143, 152, 154, 186
    Robert E., 93, 104, 158
    Walter Savage, 93, 96
    William Noble, 93, 160
Langton:
    Anne, Chapter 5, 101, 105, 110
    Skinner Zachary, 84, 85, 110, 111
    Ellen, *see Philips*
Lowe:
    Charles, 65-73, 76, 99
    Charlotte, 5, 6, 52, 74, 86, 114, 115, 129, 142, 165
    Edward C., x, xi, 1, 3, 4, 6, 12, 17, 24, 27, 50, 54, 64-65, 70, 80, 87, 91, 92, 95, 98, 114, 142, 144, 147, 148, 149, 150, 157, Chapter 11, 182
    Emily L., 106, 141, 141, 145, 149
    Harriett, 80-81, 106, 144, 153
    John M., 69, 94, 142, 143, 167
    Mary M., 5, 6, 52, 60, 74, 86, 102, 115, 142, 165
    Susan/Susannah, 74, 142, 157
Mayfield, 3, 50, 84, 85, Chapter 7, 124, 125, 126, 127, 128, 135, 141-147
McLaren, née Müller, Eva, 132-140, 183
McLaren, Walter S.B., 133, 137, 138, 139
Mosley-Lowe, Maria, 144-145
Nightingale, Florence, 42, 132
Newman, St John H., 10, 11, 16, 19-21, 41, 43
Oxford Movement, 10, 17, 19
Pennant, Lady Eleanor D., 147, 148, 171
Philips, Ellen, née Langton, 82, 83, 84, 86, 88-89, 91
Quakers, 30, 32, 39, 109, 118
Rathbone, Alice, 27, 95, 124-32, 136
Rawson, William, 60, 64, 66, 74, 77
Rice, Marcia A., 165, 166, 170, 172, 174
riding, 60, 106, 116, 135
Roch, Muriel E., 6, 189
Salisbury, Lord, 13, 14
S. Anne's Chapel, 4-6, 86-87, 143, 166, 168, 173, 176, 177
S. Anne's Rewley, 144
Schumann, Clara, 117, 127
Schumann, Robert, 116, 127, 128
Selwyn, Bishop, 87, 169, 182
Shakespeare, 72, 98, 140
Sharp, Anne, 55
Shirreff, Emily, 39-44, 45, 106, 107, 108, 188, 189
S. Michael's School, 22, 23, 164
Southgate, 110-13, 122, 142
St Paul, 135, 189
Suffragette/Suffragist, 130, 137-39
teacher training, 19, 34, 39, 46
Tunstill, Margaret, 119-20
Wallis, Hannah, 32-34, 39
Woodard Community, x, 9-10, 183
Woodard, Nathaniel, 1, 6, 10-24, 163, 182